W9-BKO-455

IN THE MOUTH OF THE WOLF

IN THE MOUTH OF THE WOLF

(EN LA BOCA DEL LOBO)

A MURDER, A COVER-UP, AND THE TRUE COST OF SILENCING THE PRESS

KATHERINE CORCORAN

BLOOMSBURY PUBLISHING

NEW YORK · LONDON · OXFORD · NEW DELHI · SYDNEY

BLOOMSBURY PUBLISHING
Bloomsbury Publishing Inc.
1385 Broadway, New York, NY 10018, USA

BLOOMSBURY, BLOOMSBURY PUBLISHING, and the Diana logo are trademarks
of Bloomsbury Publishing Plc

First published in the United States 2022

This is a work of nonfiction. However, the author has changed the names of
certain individuals to protect their privacy and has reconstructed dialogue to
the best of her recollection.

LIBRARY OF CONGRESS CATALOGING-IN-PUBLICATION DATA IS AVAILABLE

ISBN: HB: 978-1-63557-503-3; EBOOK: 978-1-63557-504-0

2 4 6 8 10 9 7 5 3 1

Typeset by Westchester Publishing Services
Printed and bound in the U.S.A.

To find out more about our authors and books visit www.bloomsbury.com and
sign up for our newsletters.

Bloomsbury books may be purchased for business or promotional use. For information
on bulk purchases please contact Macmillan Corporate and Premium Sales Department
at specialmarkets@macmillan.com.

For my Katherines, Mom and Lisa

creer que un cielo en un infierno cabe,
dar la vida y el alma a un desengaño:
esto es amor, quien lo probó lo sabe.

—LOPE DE VEGA

(to believe that there is heaven within hell,
to give your life and soul to disillusion:
that is love, anyone who has tried it knows.)

CONTENTS

CHARACTERS

Regina Martínez (reporter; assassinated April 28, 2012)				
Fab Four	Family/ Colleagues	*Política* newspaper	*Proceso* magazine	Politicians
Rodrigo Soberanes (reporter/ protégé) Leopoldo "Polo" Hernández (reporter/ protégé) Juan Pablo "Eddie" Romo (videographer/ protégé) Lev García (colleague/ correspondent for *Reforma* newspaper)	Ángel Martínez (brother) Alonso Martínez (nephew) Norma Trujillo (reporter and friend) Andrés Timoteo (reporter and friend) Julio "Don Jules" Argumedo (photographer on one of her last stories)	Ángel Gutiérrez aka Don Yayo (founder and director) Yolanda Carlín (Don Yayo's wife) Alberto "El Gato" Morales (photographer boyfriend) Walter Ramírez (reporter) Lupita López (colleague and friend) Salvador Muñoz (assistant director) Yolanda Gutiérrez (Don Yayo's daughter)	Julio Scherer aka Don Julio (founder) Jorge Carrasco (reporter and current director) Rafael Rodríguez (retired director) Salvador Corro (retired assistant director)	Miguel Alemán Valdés (president of Mexico, 1946–52) Patricio Chirinos (Veracruz governor, 1992–98) Miguel Alemán Velasco (son; Veracruz governor 1998–2004) José Luis Soberanes (ombudsman, National Commission on Human Rights, 1999–2009) Alejandro Montano (secretary of public security under Governor Miguel Alemán Velasco, 2001–2004) Fidel Herrera (Veracruz governor, 2004–10) Reynaldo Escobar (second in command under Fidel Herrera, 2004–10; Veracruz state attorney general, 2010–11) Felipe Calderón (president, 2006–12) Javier Duarte (Veracruz governor, 2010–16) Gina Domínguez (spokesperson; media owner) Arturo Bermúdez (secretary of public security under Duarte, 2011–16) Amadeo Flores (attorney general under Duarte, 2011–14) Luis Ángel Bravo (attorney general under Duarte, 2014–16) Miguel Ángel Yunes Linares (Veracruz governor, 2016–18) Miguel Ángel Yunes Márquez (son, aka Chiqui Yunes; mayor of Boca del Río, 2008–11, 2014–17)

PREFACE

ON MY FIRST day as Associated Press bureau chief in Mexico City, I was awakened by a 6 A.M. phone call. The news agency had received a threat from a drug cartel. It came via cell phone text to one of our journalists, ordering us to publish a story about then-president Felipe Calderón protecting Joaquín "El Chapo" Guzmán, the world's most notorious drug lord (now serving a life sentence in the United States), or we would receive a "special visit." The message listed the address of the bureau. It was signed by the Zetas, El Chapo's rivals.

One of my responsibilities as bureau chief was the safety of more than a dozen correspondents and twenty freelancers around the region. At that moment, I was faced with protecting the entire Mexico team of a U.S.-based international news agency. The Zetas knew where we worked. In a flurry of messages among AP offices in New York, Buenos Aires, and London, I told my editors that we needed to take extreme actions, to the point of removing from the country anyone in danger. I wrote this at 6:47 A.M.:

"These guys don't fool around."

"Welcome to your first assignment as bureau chief," the Latin America editor told me.

I can't say I was surprised. In fact, I knew immediately what to do. I had already worked in Mexico for two and half years, and I knew the press there was under siege. It was the most dangerous country in the world to be a journalist, outside of a war zone. The forces that attacked the Mexican press usually left the international media alone. But this was an epidemic, and it was only a matter of time before it reached us.

By the time we received the threat, fifty-one journalists had been killed in Mexico since the Committee to Protect Journalists started keeping track in 1992. About half those killings had occurred since I arrived in Mexico in 2008. Ten were killed in 2010 alone, the year I got the early-morning phone call.

The same week, a Mexican news photographer was gunned down in Ciudad Juárez, across the border from El Paso, Texas. He was the second journalist killed at the local newspaper *El Diario de Juárez* in as many years. The first, assassinated in 2008, covered justice and organized crime and was far more in the crosshairs. But the photographer who was killed in 2010 was just twenty-one years old. An eighteen-year-old photo intern traveling with him was injured in the attack. What did anyone gain by attacking them? To the newspaper, its staff had become cannon fodder. That Sunday, the paper ran a headline and a front-page editorial addressed to the narcos: WHAT DO YOU WANT FROM US?

The *Diario de Juárez* front-page editorial was the first major public acknowledgment of just how bad things had gotten, especially for journalists at news organizations along the Mexican-U.S. border, where drug cartels were in fierce confrontations over shipping routes. Up to that point, editors refused to talk if their newsrooms were hit, under the illusion that silence would buy them safety. Now a newspaper flat-out identified drug cartels as the "de facto authorities."

WHAT DO YOU WANT FROM US? played around the world, as far as Japan and Russia, but particularly in the United States, where it garnered a *New York Times* editorial and networks calling my office looking for correspondents to interview. A week into my new job, I was thick into an issue that would dominate my time there.

Pedro Torres, editor of *El Diario de Juárez*, who wrote the headline, told me that his question, which everyone took literally as supplicating to the narcos, was in fact rhetorical. "We weren't speaking directly to [drug gangs]. It was an open message," Torres said in an interview. "We wanted to provoke a reaction that would call attention to what's happening in Juárez, and in the end, I think we met our objective."

Except that despite the global publicity, nothing changed. No one has ever been detained for the photographer's murder. One triggerman was sentenced to thirty years in the 2008 reporter killing, but whoever ordered the hit was never identified. Instead of pursuing the killers, Mexican officials had a way of blaming the victims, implying that if they were killed, they must have fallen into *malos pasos*, "bad ways."

Then one journalist killing changed the narrative.

On April 28, 2012, Regina Martínez, correspondent for the national investigative magazine *Proceso*, was discovered beaten to death in her bathroom in Xalapa, the capital city of the Gulf state of Veracruz. Her death made news around the world. In a state known for corruption, Regina was the author of many exclusives. And no one could argue that she was dirty. Nor could they argue that it was a cartel hit. Regina covered government.

Even so, people who knew her, or who worked with her, or who were family members, refused to speak publicly about the case, clearly out of fear. In effect, they were unwittingly helping those who wanted to obscure the facts. Within a year, authorities arrested an alleged suspect and declared the case closed.

It was closed for no one but the Veracruz government.

The case lingered in my mind as well, even as I managed one of the busiest news regions for the AP at the time. Perhaps it was because Regina and I were of the same generation and spent our entire adult lives as journalists. Perhaps because I talked to her on the phone once. Perhaps because her story revealed what was actually happening with these journalist killings. In the face of rampant corruption, which was crippling Mexico's new democracy, they were an attempt to shut down free speech.

And they worked.

As the attacks grew, the Veracruz media fell into lockstep, electing not to cover crime and publishing government press releases verbatim.

This was completely antithetical to my values and my career as a journalist, which began in the so-called post-Watergate era. When I graduated from college in the 1980s, journalism was considered a way to have an impact, to change the world, to make things better. It was also a great equalizer. You didn't have to have money or status to take the important role of relaying remarkable events to everyday readers or viewers.

In the United States, even if polls at times showed that the public hated us, ranking us just above politicians and car salespeople, we were part of the system, a vital institution for the preservation of democracy, protected by the First (not the Second or the Fifth) Amendment. Freedom of speech and transparency were fundamental to our system. One of my friends, a publisher of a small but aggressive newspaper, had this motto printed every day on his front page: IF YOU DON'T WANT IT PRINTED, DON'T LET IT HAPPEN.

My personal efforts to change the world and hold people accountable started humbly: In my first job at a small newspaper, I analyzed pedestrian accident statistics at an intersection and wrote a story that resulted in the installation of a Stop sign. I wrote about a public official who was using building materials from a Boys and Girls Club for personal home improvements; he resigned. Over the years, my targets grew in number and power. By the time I reached the Associated Press in Mexico, my team was involved in exposing extrajudicial killings by the Mexican Army and how the government, with great fanfare, arrested cartel assassins accused of dozens of murders and then quietly let them go.

Regina was the Mexican version of a Watergate baby. She started her career, also in the 1980s, around two seminal events: the 1985 Mexico City earthquake, which proved the federal government absolutely indifferent and impotent; and the 1988 presidential election of Carlos Salinas de Gortari, which was widely regarded as stolen. These events were key in breaking down the one-party system and ushering in free and fair elections. Regina was part of a small but emerging generation of journalists propelled by that same Watergate sense that the government had betrayed its people and that it was up to the press to expose exactly how.

But for her, it was a death sentence.

This is what ultimately grabbed me, along with the fact that it was happening right across the border from my own country. Yet, outside of studies by advocates and visits by UN representatives, which always resulted in no action, the murder of journalists in Mexico went unheeded by anyone with real power in the United States or the rest of the world.

My initial desire to dive into the Regina Martínez case was twofold: I wanted people to care about what was happening in Mexico, and I wanted to help Mexico. We, the American journalists, needed to show them how it's done, how to stand up to the bad guys, buttress the free press in Mexico so they could become more like us. As a reporter, I also wanted to solve the whodunnit, to shine a spotlight on those who had gotten away with murder. That's what journalists do.

My notion of American excellence turned out to be American naïveté. The realities of reporting in Mexico were far more complicated than anything I had encountered elsewhere. And my intention to find the culprits was compromised by these complexities.

By happenstance, I was able to get to know and gain the trust of some of Regina's closest confidants. But in a place where there is weak rule of law, and no particular value in telling the truth, it was still rough going. No question had a direct answer. Everyone was afraid—to the point where I started to absorb the paranoia.

A society without truth is a scary place to live.

When I first proposed an in-depth look at Regina's death to American editors in 2015, her story was a hard sell. They thought a journalist covering the troubles of journalists was self-serving. "No one cares about what happens to journalists except for other journalists" was one response I got. "Most Americans don't really care about Mexico" was another.

Then something truly extraordinary happened. In the course of investigating Regina Martínez's murder, my country started to look more like Mexico. Truth became optional; and information, a weapon used to control and manipulate. The independent press, the bedrock of our democracy, was called "the enemy of the people," corrupt purveyors of "fake news." The "good" press was one that supported the government, something I had never encountered in the United States in my thirty-plus-year career.

Suddenly, American journalists were prosecuted, chased, clubbed, and thrown over walls, and had their equipment was smashed. CNN and other newsrooms were evacuated under bomb threats. After decades of fighting for press safety around the globe, the Committee to Protect Journalists started tracking attacks in the United States.

This rattled me. I started out writing about Regina Martínez to help Mexico, but by the end of my time as AP bureau chief, one Mexican colleague jokingly (though, perhaps not so much) asked if we wanted them to come to the United States to train *us* in handling threats and attacks from *our* government.

I was watching the elements of what I saw in a weak emerging democracy, one plagued by violence and moral bankruptcy on the part of many leaders, occur in my own country. Suddenly, my impulse for telling the Regina Martínez story changed. As much as the whodunnit, I was motivated by the question that one beloved editor, the late Neil Westergaard, posted on his computer as a constant reminder: WHAT DOES IT MEAN?

For us in the United States, questions remain: What happens when this path of "fake news" and obfuscation we're on takes its natural course? To what end is the press ever controlled, discredited, attacked, and murdered? Who is really at risk? What's really at stake?

Nothing answers these questions better than the case of Regina Martínez.

PART I

CHAPTER I

Time

April 28, 2012

THE NEIGHBOR'S IRON gate stood ajar, something Isabel Nuñez failed to notice when she woke to her Saturday morning routine, during her household chores, or when she left at about 1 P.M. to go shopping.

It was on her way home when Yolanda Balderas stopped Isabel to ask her about the gate. Yolanda was a street vendor selling yogurt, as she always did on Saturdays, and stopped by the neighbor's house. Not only was the gate ajar, Yolanda said, but across the cleanly swept concrete patio with the giant palm, the front door was open as well. The neighbor was *never* that careless.

"I knocked on the gate," Yolanda told Isabel, "and I yelled her name, but there was no answer."

"When I get home, I'll give her a call," Isabel replied.

They had been neighbors for years in the Felipe Carrillo Puerto district of Xalapa, the capital of the Mexican Gulf Coast state of Veracruz. Their street, Calle Privada Rodríguez Clara, marked the bottom of a small urban canyon, probably carved out centuries before by mountain runoff that had now been trained into an open sewage canal. Boxy stucco homes lined the road. Most residents settled there thirty or forty years ago, before there was even pavement, and they had to jump the canal to cross the street. As their earnings increased, families expanded their humble bungalows over time in phases, giving the houses a look of skewed toy building blocks. The streets parallel to Calle Privada Rodríguez Clara ran high above the canyon on either side, reachable by concrete stairs built into the slopes. Rundown apartment buildings clinging to the canyon walls were nicknamed favelas, after the hillside slums of Río de Janeiro.

The area was once considered marginal, a landing place for misfits and squatters, but over time grew into a solidly middle-class barrio of small-business owners, government workers, and teachers. On the path of Mexican upward mobility, their children studied engineering at the University of Veracruz, just up the hill.

Vagrants and drug users still gathered down the street, at a rusted children's slide, to get high. The neighborhood had its share of petty crime. Isabel Nuñez knew that her neighbor was especially vigilant about security. She was a journalist, the Veracruz correspondent for the national investigative magazine *Proceso*. The neighbor told Isabel at one point that there were a lot of people who didn't like what she wrote, who wanted to "erase" her, though she never named names.

The two had a cordial relationship. Sometimes the neighbor gave Isabel magazines. Sometimes Isabel watched the house when the neighbor was traveling for work. They also had their differences. The neighbor complained about the kids playing soccer in the street and about Isabel's son playing his music too loud. The neighbor told her family and friends that Isabel was nosy. She didn't like how Isabel always kept tabs on her from a second-story window, which directly overlooked the neighbor's patio.

In fact, when Isabel was getting ready for bed the night before, she noticed from that same window that the gate was open, and called her neighbor to let her know; the neighbor didn't answer. Or, maybe she did and thanked Isabel and said she would close it; then, maybe, Isabel went to bed. Or, maybe Isabel stayed up after the call and saw her neighbor come out and close the gate but not lock it, as if she were expecting someone. There were several versions of what Isabel Nuñez saw and did on the night of April 27, 2012, depending on which court documents or which person you consulted.

What is certain is that when Isabel arrived home the following afternoon, she knew something wasn't right. She called the neighbor's landline: no answer. She tried her cell: no answer. Now she was worried. She decided to wait a little longer for her neighbor to appear. At about 5 P.M., she finally called 066, the Mexican equivalent of 911.

A woman answered.

"My neighbor's a journalist," Isabel told the dispatcher, "and I noticed since this morning that her door is partly opened. But when I called the house and her cell phone, I couldn't reach her. Could you send an officer please?"

The call went out to Patrol 1401 as a possible robbery at 208 Calle Privada Rodríguez Clara. Four state police officers in blue uniforms showed up twenty-five minutes later. Two of them entered the neighbor's house, walking past the slightly open metal gate and pushing aside the metal door. Then one came back out and asked Isabel if she would accompany them inside. She agreed.

The front door of the tiny bungalow opened onto the living room, which was set up as an office and, to Isabel, appeared disheveled. From there they passed to the kitchen, on the left, and then walked straight into the single bedroom, where the dresser drawers were open and their contents dumped on the bed. Isabel's eyes followed the floor to a pair of legs jutting out from the bathroom. It was the neighbor, lying on her back, arms outstretched, on the marble-patterned linoleum.

Her head lay against the stone finish of the tub, her face to one side, a bloody cleaning rag around her neck. There was a bloodstain on her brown vest and another on her orange blouse, the same clothing Isabel saw her wearing the day before, when they briefly greeted each other as Isabel took out the trash. The neighbor's jeans, unbuttoned, with the zipper halfway down, had dust and blood spots at the knees.

"Is this Regina Martínez?" the officer asked.

"Yes," Isabel said, and ran from the house in distress.

The officer leaned down to feel the dead woman's wrist for a pulse, knowing he wouldn't find one. Then he called for backup.

★

I AM STANDING in front of the same iron gate, which is locked now. There's a taxi crammed into the patio. The bungalow looks abandoned, except for a light on near the front door and men's clothing drying on a line strung outside. There is no bell, so I try knocking on the gate. My knuckles make no sound, and no one answers.

I ring the bell at Isabel Nuñez's house. I figure enough time has passed—eight years. I am wrong.

A second-floor window with metal mullions slides open. I look up at the lavender stucco façade to see a small middle-aged woman with a round face and dyed-brown hair.

"What do you want?" she says crossly.

I think of one of my earlier times in Mexico, when I went to study Spanish and stayed with a family in an ample house surrounded by a garden and a big wall. Whenever anyone rang the bell, they never answered the door, but rather, hollered, ¿Quien? "Who?" from inside the house. It was a way to screen unwanted visitors.

The street I am standing on is of patchy pavement and hard mud. The late-afternoon sky is gray this work-holiday Monday, the day I decide to approach Isabel, thinking the street will be quiet and I won't call too much attention to myself. The water in the nearby canal whooshes from the recent rain.

"I'm working on a project about this area, and I'd like to talk to you," I say vaguely. I don't want to yell the subject of my inquiry up to the second story. I am trying to be discreet.

"About what?" Again, cross. "Why me?"

I tell her I prefer not to shout the details and ask if she could come down and talk.

She stares back. I have no choice.

"It's about your neighbor."

"What neighbor?"

I nod my head toward the iron gate where I am standing, which abuts Isabel's home. From the corner of my eye, I see a young dark-haired man with a similar round face watching from the second-floor balcony.

"I don't talk about that," she says.

I tell her it's a project about her neighbor's life and her work as a valiant reporter.

"No," she insists. "It was a terrible hit for us."

"I can imagine," I say. If she were standing next to me, that would have been my entrée to ask how. But from twelve feet below, it is impossible.

"We don't talk about it," she repeats sternly. "That chapter is closed."

CHAPTER 2

If Not You, Then Who?

April 28, 2012

R ODRIGO SOBERANES PICKED up his cell phone to six missed calls. He had left his phone to shower and dress for a Saturday night out. He and his new wife, Brenda, were attending the annual festival in her hometown, nearby. It was a quiet spring evening, somewhere around seven or eight o'clock, in the modern, two-story town house the newlyweds rented in the Playa Dorado subdivision, south of the Port of Veracruz. They liked that it was big, two stories with three bedrooms and tall windows shedding lots of light. Like most of Mexico's new construction, it was boxy, with flat concrete walls painted industrial white. And it was only a half-mile walk from the beach—important for Brenda, who was born in the port and forever tethered to the sea. On windy days, the bone-colored tile floors became dusted with sand.

Rodrigo returned a call to one of the two friends who seemed desperate to reach him. "What's going on?" he asked.

"You need to answer your phone, *güey*," the friend said, using the Mexican slang for "dude." "Polo needs to talk to you."

Rodrigo dialed Polo Hernández.

"Where are you?" Polo asked.

"At my house."

"Sit down."

Rodrigo, in the second-floor hallway, perched himself on the top stair, resting his free hand on the round, white metal railing. "What? Tell me."

"They killed Regina."

Brenda, still getting ready in the nearby bedroom, suddenly heard Rodrigo shouting.

No mames! No mames, güey! he yelled into the phone. "Don't fuck with me."

"I wouldn't make up something like that!" Polo insisted. He said they found her at home not two hours earlier, after a concerned neighbor called the police. She hadn't been seen since the night before.

"But what happened?"

"I don't know anything more," Polo said. "I've got to hang up."

Rodrigo, still shouting, punched the staircase wall repeatedly with his fist. His thoughts came fast and stung like BBs: *It can't be true. She can't be gone. Did she try to defend herself?* It was no surprise to him that it took them a whole day to discover her. Regina always sequestered herself on weekends.

He started to cry, noticing for the first time that his hand was throbbing from having punched the concrete. He wished he could rewind his life back, just a few hours.

Brenda ran to his side. In the few years they had been together, she had never seen Rodrigo fall apart. But she understood. Regina had been his teacher, his mentor, a journalist of extraordinary rectitude.

In Mexican parlance, Regina was *brava*, tough. Her role as a journalist (and his) was to be a watchdog, to give voice to the laborers, the campesinos, the indigenous, the opposition—the people in Mexico who the official media never covered. This ferocity came from a pint of a person just under five feet and weighing one hundred pounds, with the sharp, long facial features signaling her Totonac roots, large wire-rimmed glasses, and brown hair. Favoring jeans and platform sandals, Regina raced from interview to interview, always with strong coffee in a paper cup and a bright floral *chamula*, a giant handbag woven by the indigenous women in Chiapas, which held all her reporting tools and the latest copy of *Proceso*. She was strong-willed and unapologetically opinionated in a way that was off-putting to many, but that had earned her a circle of fans. Years after this day, her colleagues—especially the men—would chuckle affectionately when remembering how she fought her editors and ordered around the rookie reporters, kicking their stories back to them seven or eight times to be rewritten.

¡Pinche chaparrita! "Damn shorty."

Her fact-based independent reporting would have been considered normal news coverage in the United States or other Western countries. In Veracruz, though, it made not only the political class nervous, but her colleagues as well. Other reporters didn't like how Regina threatened a long-held system of obedience and self-censorship, and she didn't care much for them. But to hungry young reporters like Rodrigo Soberanes, Regina Martínez was a high beam on a dark road.

Rodrigo was tall, freckled, and handsome, a *güero* ("whitey") with light features and eyes. His family on his mother's side emigrated from England and France, but the currency of light skin in Mexico didn't count for his grandfather, who worked much of his life as a laborer in the United States. Rodrigo's roots on his father's side were equally humble. His great-grandfather was killed in the Mexican Revolution, but his grandfather, despite his beginnings, managed to reach the rank of general in the military and later served as a senator for the ruling party from the central state of Querétaro. This changed everything for Rodrigo's father, who grew up in Mexico City and studied chemical engineering at the university.

By the time Rodrigo was born, the family had moved to the southern state of Chiapas, where his father set up a cashew orchard, among other farming ventures, just across the border from Guatemala. Rodrigo grew up running among the short, top-heavy trees colored with red, orange, and yellow "apples" that produced what's known in Mexico as *nueces de la India*, "nuts of India." There he saw another side of Mexico: rural, indigenous, poor. He knew what it was like to feel dirt on his hands, and he never lost his love for working the harvest, even as an adult.

When Rodrigo was still young, the family moved again, to Xalapa, where his engineer-farmer father wanted to get an advanced degree at the university. There Rodrigo learned to follow his own lead. Not enamored of the formalities of school, he was kicked out of his private high school in Xalapa, but finished his secondary education in the neighboring town.

He wanted to be a journalist from the time he entered the University of Veracruz in Xalapa, and he was thrilled to encounter someone like Regina on his first job, someone who corralled him into her flock of "children," the cub reporters she meticulously trained. His parents were not as excited about his chosen profession. They never discouraged him from doing what he wanted, but they did ask him if he could avoid certain topics for security reasons. They also had official connections who could look out for him—like Rodrigo's uncle José Luis Soberanes, a prominent Mexican attorney and head of the country's National Human Rights Commission.

For Regina, there were no sacred cows—not even Rodrigo's uncle, whom she skewered at times for being weak on human rights even as she schooled his nephew. But Rodrigo admired her just the same, his *pinche chaparrita*.

When they learned of Regina's death, Rodrigo and Brenda canceled their plans instantly and decided to make the ninety-minute drive north to Xalapa, where the murdered woman's friends were already gathering and planning a response. Before they left, another call came, this time from Miguel Valera of the governor's press office. He began asking Rodrigo questions about Regina and how she lived.

"Did she have a boyfriend?"

Rodrigo said no and hung up. He found the call strange. Why was the governor's office probing him when he himself barely knew what happened?

On the drive north, Brenda tried to console her husband. He had never felt this kind of pain, as if someone had scorched the inside of his chest. For days, he would wake up thinking he dreamed Regina's killing.

They drove quickly along the well-traveled highway that connected the Port of Veracruz with its state capital in the interior foothills, hugging the coast and then aiming westward toward the mountain range, past the mango orchards and empty fruit stands; past the highway litter lodged in the brittle shoulder grass; past the abandoned swimming pool; past Comedor Karen, the roadside restaurant with the giant painting of Jesus on the side; past the vendors selling dried fruit and popcorn in the middle of traffic to cars lined up at the tollbooth. The closer they got to Xalapa, the more real the killing became.

★

ANOTHER OF REGINA'S friends, Lev García, had gone to the nearby state of Tlaxcala for the weekend. Thanks to the great sources he had as the Veracruz correspondent for the national newspaper *Reforma*, he was one of the first reporters to get a call when Regina's body was found. Her identity was confirmed, but he couldn't go see for himself. He called an old friend and coworker, news photographer Julio Argumedo, and asked him to go by Regina's place to see what was going on. "Don Jules," as Argumedo was known to his friends, rushed to the modest bungalow, only to be held back by caution tape and an anthill of authorities, including soldiers from the Mexican Army.

As the media stories started to appear online, word spread to other Xalapa journalists, then to the state, then the country and even the world. In just a few more hours, the story would appear on the wire of the Associated Press.

One hundred thirty miles away, in Córdoba, a colonial city at the foot of the Sierra Madre, Leopoldo "Polo" Hernández was trying to numb his pain with water glasses full of whiskey. It wasn't working. Despite having several, he didn't even feel drunk, just destroyed, as if he had been split open by lightning. As with Rodrigo Soberanes, Regina was Polo's mentor and guide. They ate lunch together in the same restaurant almost every day.

Polo had planned a weekend of partying. He traveled from Xalapa, where he was a reporter for the state-owned news service Notimex, to his hometown to attend a friend's wedding. He was dressed up, helping to shuttle relatives of the groom between the hotel and the reception, when his cell phone rang with the readout "Lev García."

Carnal! Polo answered in a festive voice, which in translation means "flesh" but is Mexican slang for "brother."

Carnal. The voice on the other end was hesitant. "Are you sitting down?"

"I'm in the car. Of course I'm sitting down."

"They killed Regina."

Another call buzzed on Polo's cell phone. It was Andrés Timoteo, the Veracruz correspondent for the national newspaper *La Jornada*. He, too, was one of Regina's closest friends—and biggest rivals, always working to scoop the state's best reporter.

"They say they killed Regina. Is it true?" Andrés asked.

"Yes," Polo said.

Andrés was also in Córdoba for the weekend. Polo suggested they meet at the bus station in the morning and head to Xalapa together. Andrés declined. After he hung up, he packed a few things and headed for a bus to the Veracruz airport—and a flight to Mexico City. Whatever happened to Regina, he feared he was next.

Polo dialed the governor's press office to see what they knew. Miguel Valera answered: "We've heard the same, but we can't confirm anything."

"Fuck you!" Polo said and hung up.

Then he rang the personal cell phone of the governor's communications director, Gina Domínguez, who answered immediately.

"Motherfuckers!" he yelled into the phone. "What the fuck happened?"

"We have no details," Gina said, then paused for a second. "It sounds like you think *we* did this."

"Well," Polo answered, "if not you, then who?"

CHAPTER 3

"We're Living in Madness"

April 29, 2012

T HE NEXT DAY, after Polo Hernández returned home from the wedding to find his mother waiting up and begging him not to go back to Xalapa; and as Lev García sat at his computer, covering the aftermath, his tears soaking his beard, I was taking a flight from Mexico City to Columbus, Ohio, where I would be attending a seminar at Ohio State University on using social media. I handed the reins of the bureau over to someone else for a week. Still, I checked the news on my phone, as I did every minute of every day and every time I was about to put it in airplane mode—and I read this on the AP wire:

> A correspondent for the Mexican news magazine Proceso has been found dead inside her home in Veracruz state. Authorities believe the journalist, who often wrote about drug trafficking, was murdered. Regina Martínez's body was found by police inside the bathroom of her home in the state capital, Xalapa, and there were signs of heavy blows to her face and body, the state's attorney general's office said in a statement. Authorities said initial evidence suggested she died of asphyxiation.

Mexico was seeing an epidemic of journalist killings, more than a half dozen each *year*. The reporters targeted were anything but high-profile—nothing like Jamal Khashoggi or Anna Politkovskaya, each of whom made real trouble for a very powerful world leader, and world headlines, before they were killed. All the victims were local, some as small as bloggers or citizen reporters who posted news stories on Facebook pages. This made them easy to dismiss by both the government and the public.

The Mexican press was historically weak at best, corrupt at worst. The country was only two presidential terms into its new democracy, after being ruled for *seventy-one years* by the Institutional Revolutionary Party, or PRI, its initials in Spanish. The PRI's sole political ideology for seven decades was to stay in power. The press in Mexico was considered mostly a paid voice of the government rather than an independent watchdog. While they didn't control the press outright, PRI governments had various ways to keep the press in line, with money, perquisites, and, if that didn't work, threats. With few exceptions, the media over the decades learned to self-censor and follow the rules, what Mexican historian and essayist Daniel Cosío Villegas called, "A free press that does not make use of its freedom." Many journalists, in turn, charged sources for positive stories and used their contacts other ways for personal gain.

This allowed the state governors and justice officials who had the job of investigating journalist deaths to accuse the journalists of having gotten crossways with the criminal or corrupt bosses who paid them under the table to do their bidding; they brought on their own fate, government officials asserted. It was a very effective strategy. Even my own colleagues, other foreign correspondents, would dismiss these assassinations, saying those killed were not real journalists. But no one actually knew, because the cases were never investigated.

Not so with Regina's killing.

Correspondents for the major national media in Mexico were rarely assassinated. Though they were often harassed for their stories, they also carried a measure of protection working for large newspapers or for a journalistic institution like *Proceso*. According to the unwritten rules in place up to that point, killing a high-profile correspondent would cause too much noise, draw too much attention to groups who liked to operate with stealth. With Regina, an invisible line had been crossed. Every reporter in Mexico City and elsewhere in the country read the killing the same way: If they hit Regina, no one was safe.

The case was different in another way: It would be difficult for authorities to paint Regina as corrupt or associated with criminals. Everyone, including me, knew she was beyond reproach.

I had tried to hire her once.

★

I STARTED COVERING Mexico in 2006, as a correspondent for a California newspaper, making periodic trips there for stories. I had fallen in love with the country a decade earlier, when I did a Spanish immersion there.

To the foreigner, Mexico charms, cajoles, and seduces. There are so many Mexicos: so many climates, cultures, foods, and languages; contiguous, concentric, stacked; native and colonial; current and past; invisible yet present. In his famous essay comparing Mexico and the United States, Mexican Nobel laureate Octavio Paz describes every Mexican as carrying the continuity of two thousand years of civilization, "the ruins of Tenochtitlan, the Aztec city that was built in the likeness of Tula, the Toltec city that was built in the likeness of Teotihuacan, the first great city on the American continent," he wrote. ". . . It is not something known, but something lived."

Mexico was so antithetical to the American emphasis on getting ahead and a lifestyle that made me feel I was under constant stress. Among the middle and working class there was zero sense of entitlement. To an outsider, Mexicans lived in the moment. They seemed to wake every day looking not for ways to get ahead, but rather, for the necessities to survive, which made them infinitely more gracious. They handled misfortune with a dark sense of humor that was funny until they turned it on you. Nothing was off-limits.

I had no idea, like most Americans, that a country so culturally rich and radically diverse stood just down the road from the serapes and cheap tequila of the border towns and the high-rise hotel zones of the Americanized resorts. When I found out, I couldn't stay away.

For linear-thinking gringos, there's a complexity to the culture that was difficult for me to process—maddening, even. It was as if the country had a way of taking most of the norms I had brought from "El Norte" and tossing them into the air. In Mexico, yes meant no, *ahorita* (now) meant "perhaps never," and if you had a problem, the last thing you did was call the police or the government. That would only bring you more trouble. People kept their heads down.

This was in part due to events throughout Mexico's history, like the savage treatment of native Mexicans under the three hundred years of Conquest, forcing them to live double lives. In the vast Maya territory on the Yucatán Peninsula, for example, the people were devout Catholics loyal to the Spanish Crown by day, while maintaining their religious traditions and the native language under cover of the night. If they were caught, they were beaten or even tortured. The modern rule of the PRI mimicked the Conquest with its iron fist and its corruption. People learned to go along to get along, but never to trust authority. In Mexico, you said what people wanted to hear, not what you knew.

Mexicans had become over the decades (or centuries, perhaps) ingenious at solving their own problems. Some were clever, some criminal. Some struck us gringos as absurd. But that reaction was all about us, not the Mexicans.

One time, I was meeting a new source, who showed up on a nag of a Harley-Davidson, saying he would take me to the spot where we had agreed to do the interview. Though he offered me a helmet, I thought immediately about what would happen if we had an accident on that rattletrap of a bike. I was between jobs and without health insurance. Even if I were not injured, a spill could kill my laptop, which held my entire life. I told him I would follow in a taxi. He laughed. "That's the difference between you and me," he said. "Mexicans don't worry about what could go wrong, because we know it will. We *know* we're fucked."

Covering the country was magical. The big stories were migration and the surprisingly tight presidential race between Felipe Calderón and Andrés Manuel López Obrador, who everyone had thought would run away with a victory then, in 2006. A foreign reporter could roam freely. All you needed in the pre–Google Maps world was a *Guia Roji* (Mexico's remarkably detailed street guide) and a taxi driver *de confianza* (trustworthy).

Ever since the 1985 kidnapping, torture, and murder of U.S. Drug Enforcement Administration agent Enrique "Kiki" Camarena in Mexico—when the U.S. government nearly shut down the border and used its full power to take down several top drug lords—the conventional wisdom was that the cartels didn't attack U.S. officials inside Mexico. The same went for U.S. journalists, who were not susceptible to the political or criminal pressures endured by the Mexican press. Going after us would *really* create unwanted attention and possibly activate the gringo posse, which always got its man. When Alfredo Corchado, Mexico correspondent for the *Dallas Morning News*, faced a cartel threat in 2007, the international news media publicly rallied around him, and the U.S. embassy in Mexico issued a press release demanding his safety.

A lot had changed by 2010, when the AP received a threat. The following week, after the threat, and after the Mexican news photographer was killed in Ciudad Juárez, the Committee to Protect Journalists issued a report on journalist assassinations in Mexico and held a conference. The group was pressuring President Felipe Calderón to increase protections for the press. I covered the conference and, in the process, met a newspaper editor named Patricia Mercado, director of *El Imagen* in the central state of Zacatecas. Mercado had been educated in the United States, was a Knight Fellow at Stanford University, and before deciding to return to her home state, was the director of *El Economista*, a respected national business journal.

When I interviewed her for my story, she told me she had no problem following directions from drug gangs on what to report. She had published an article handed to her by organized crime to keep her staff from being attacked. "If it's a question of life or death, I have no trouble making a decision. The lives of my reporters are most important," she said.

Her quote stunned me, not because she took orders from narcos, but because I was starting to realize that, when I thought about what I would have done in her situation, I had no answer. In my case, when we received a threat, we had the strength of an international news agency. The vice president of global security was on a plane to Mexico City the same day to lead an investigation and put in mitigating measures.

The American way of fighting back—of exposing the bad guys, of believing that publishing what you know is power—didn't hold up in a place with shaky rule of law.

Patricia Mercado had no backup.

The AP changed the way we covered the country. Journalists had to travel in teams. We had GPS tracking and regular phone check-ins for people reporting in sensitive areas. Reporters negotiating unknown territory were instructed to map out stopping points, where they would investigate whether it was safe to advance. Sometimes they followed army or police convoys for protection, though we also had to consider that such caravans were targets for cartel potshots.

There were close calls. A photographer covering a hurricane in rural northeastern Mexico accidentally ran across uniformed Zetas, who simply told him to scram; he did so gladly. In 2012, we sent a reporter to the border state of Coahuila after Mexican marines killed Zetas leader Heriberto Lazcano there. Wandering around the tiny town of Progreso with a local freelancer, the AP reporter came upon some workers in a boathouse at a local reservoir. They told her the drug lord had owned a ranch nearby and moved freely in that area. While the reporter was outside, calling me with this information, the men said to the freelancer, "You can go, but we're keeping the girl." The freelancer, thinking on his feet, told the workers, "You don't want her. She has a chip," meaning a GPS locator. Then he walked outside while the reporter was still on the phone with me and said, "We need to get out of here, now!"

The most difficult moment in my job came in 2014, when one of our teams was investigating what we suspected was an extrajudicial execution of twenty-two people by the Mexican Army. The government issued a three-sentence press release about a supposed shootout with drug cartel gunmen. A gang opened fire on army units in México state, south of Mexico City, provoking a fierce gun battle. Twenty-two gunmen died, while only one soldier was wounded. Everyone who read those three lines thought the same thing: How could twenty-two people die in a confrontation, and government forces walk away with barely a scrape? It sounded like a massacre. The AP broke the story that it was.

A reporter and photographer set out for the scene, a large warehouse in a rural area in the heart of cartel territory. There were signs of stray gunfire, but none of the pockmarks or damage a building would have sustained in a battle with high-powered weapons that killed twenty-two people. Instead, they saw a cinderblock wall periodically dotted with two bullet holes close together, chest high, and bloodstains, as if people had been lined up and shot. A surviving witness later confirmed that most of the twenty-two indeed were shot after they surrendered to soldiers.

While reporting this story in the remote town of San Pedro Limón, our team came across four young men in civilian clothing with ammunition belts and semiautomatic rifles guarding a white SUV, presumably members of the drug gang that controlled the area. We in the Mexico City office and the team in the field were in telephone contact, per the security protocol. But just as our reporter and photographer said the armed men were fixing on them, they lost phone service. We tried dozens of times to call them back, without success.

For the first time in my job, I considered calling the Federal Police for help getting our team out of there. It was drastic, not to mention risky. We investigated and covered the Federal Police; we didn't rely on them. Sometimes they were working for the cartels. Sometimes they were just blatant criminals. Once, during a massive protest in Mexico City, a band of Federal Police officers pushed one of our photographers to the ground amid the chaos and flat-out robbed him of his camera equipment, cutting the pack right off his back.

But I was out of ideas in that moment. My boss, who had reported in many war zones, told me to give it another twenty minutes.

In my five years as bureau chief, my biggest fear was that someone would get hurt or worse on my watch. Sometimes I woke in the middle of the night, moon-eyed, thinking about a correspondent who was out in a volatile part of the country and wondering whether I had made the right decision to let them go. Still, this the was the longest twenty minutes of my career.

Just as the time was up, the photo editor got a call that the team was okay. They returned safely, and the story they told brought international attention to human rights abuses by the army. Soldiers were arrested, and two survivors of the extrajudicial mass murder, who had been jailed to be kept quiet, were freed.

After five years, my job as bureau chief came to an end.

I was relieved to hand security matters over to someone else, but I couldn't seem to put one perplexing notion behind me: Mexico, a country that was not at war, that had a democratically elected government, and that was arguably the most strategic partner to the United States, was one of the most dangerous countries on earth for journalists. The situation has only grown worse over time, with Mexico more recently ranking number one—tied with Afghanistan—in murdered journalists. Dictatorships and oligarchies are enemies of the free press, but democracies? Wasn't a free press crucial to any democratic system? How can free speech be guaranteed, as it is in the Mexican Constitution, and be lethal at the same time?

Like everything else in Mexico, the answer came with layers and contradictions. While the press was clearly a target, it was also a participant. The narcos were tapping into a system of co-opting the media that was decades in the making, but this time with much deadlier consequences. There were countless rumors of top editors who were paid to carry cartel news in their newspapers or who benefited financially. The director of a local news agency in the western state of Michoacán, someone who the AP used regularly, appeared on a leaked video with drug lord Servando "La Tuta" Gómez, who was counting out bills for the journalist as the two discussed how the cartel could get better media coverage. When journalists like him got caught, they said they had no choice but to participate and take the money. The old *plata o plomo*, take the money or take a bullet.

One Veracruz television anchor told me that he was contacted several times in 2009 by cartel representatives offering money for coverage. At first, he heard from the journalists who worked on behalf of the cartels. He turned off his phone to avoid getting more calls, until he was visited by the local cartel boss himself, Braulio Orellano Domínguez, aka El Gonzo.

El Gonzo suggested the anchor start answering his phone. "Think of your family," he said.

"I'm not the station owner, I'm not the director," the anchor protested. "There's nothing I can do."

"Then tell your bosses," El Gonzo said.

Even after El Gonzo was murdered in a shootout a short time later, the threats didn't stop. The anchor received an order from the Zetas to show footage on his program of a banner they had hung to warn their rivals. After he did so, the cartel decided it wasn't enough and ordered him to read the banner aloud on air, which he did. Later, they ordered him to stop reporting on a major news story: the disappearance of Francisco Serrano Aramoni, head of maritime customs for the Port of Veracruz, who, according to security camera footage, was detained on his way home from work by Veracruz transit police. He had been sent to clean up corruption at the port by the president himself, but presumably was taken out by the Zetas, who wanted to maintain control. More than a decade later, he remains missing. I knew this story because we had tried to investigate it at the Associated Press, but in the end, people were too afraid to talk.

The station was preparing an update on the case. The anchor went to his editors: "If this story runs, I'm not coming to work." The station killed the story.

When I tried to check out the veracity of this anchor, I asked a trusted colleague in Veracruz what he knew about him. The reporter scoffed. "That guy's paid by the governor," he said. "He takes expensive diving trips every year, paid for by the governor."

This is how reporting was in Mexico when you attempted to verify information. Journalists trashed other journalists. No one trusted anyone. This distrust kept the Mexican press corps successfully divided in the face of a real enemy. In the Colombian drug war of the 1990s, the media combatted threats and intimidation by banding together. Normally competing publications would agree to print the same investigative story on the same day, without a byline, so that no single medium or writer could be targeted by the cartel. The story would go everywhere at the same time.

The Colombian model continually came up as a remedy suggested for Mexican media trying to report on corruption and drug trafficking—and was dismissed almost as quickly. Alejandro Junco de la Vega, the founder of Grupo Reforma, with two of Mexico's most professional and aggressive newspapers, *Reforma* and *El Norte*, once told me he could never agree to a consortium of Mexican journalists publishing the same story. "I wouldn't know who I'm working with," he said. "I wouldn't know who *they* are working for."

Junco, in turn, was criticized by other journalists for abandoning Mexico. Though he still ran major newspapers in Mexico City, Guadalajara, and Monterrey, he and his family lived in San Antonio, Texas, for security reasons.

In such a dubious environment, I had to carefully vet any Mexican reporter we hired to collaborate on AP stories. This is what led me to Regina Martínez.

In September 2011, I needed someone to cover a particularly grotesque cartel mass murder in Veracruz. Just south of the gritty Veracruz port is an upscale city called Boca del Río, or "Mouth of the River," where the Jamapa River dumps into the Gulf of Mexico. While Veracruz resembles a crumbling seaside Havana, Boca del Río is Miami, modern and gleaming, with the white façades of chic restaurants and shopping malls. In the middle of the city, next to the convention center, is a circular expressway surrounding a three-story sculpture called *Los Voladores*, a tall pole with men flying in circles around it, tethered to the pole by their ankles. The sculpture depicts a pre-Colombian ceremony of the Totonac, indigenous to Veracruz, which legend says was performed to call on the gods to end a drought. It stands at the center of a proud modern city.

Just as Mexico's state prosecutors were set to meet in the convention center there, two white cargo trucks stopped in the middle of the expressway in broad daylight, dumped thirty-five bodies at the base of *Los Voladores*, and drove away. The criminals were getting bolder by the day and seemed to be in a contest to see who could inflict the most terror.

The freelancer we normally hired in Veracruz told us he couldn't get any information on the body dumping, even as we read ample details online from the local papers. After a while, we could only conclude that he was too scared to cover the crime, and the AP was caught flat-footed on a huge story. It would take almost a day for one of our corre-spondents from Mexico City to get there, but we needed someone on the ground at that moment to get us an accurate picture, given that the "officials," the state government, kept changing the details of what had happened.

"How about Regina Martínez?" said our desk supervisor, who spent many years in Mexico as a reporter and editor and who had worked with Martínez during her stint as an AP contributor from Veracruz. "I don't know what happened to her," he said. "I think she got another job, but she was really good."

Regina's name remained at the bottom of our freelancer list, which I inherited as bureau chief; I had noticed it. But the names at the bottom of list represented the people we no longer called, mostly because they were no longer available, some because they had proven to be prob-lematic. In that moment, I was desperate, and willing to try anything. I knew nothing about Regina Martínez, but if the desk supervisor said she was good, that was all the recommendation I needed. I dialed the number, and Regina answered right away.

"Regina? This is Kathy Corcoran. I'm the AP bureau chief in Mexico," I said. "I see you have worked for us in the past, and I wonder if you could help us out on the bodies dumped in Boca del Río."

"I don't know," she hesitated, "I'm really busy." She told me she was in the middle of covering this act of narco terrorism for *Proceso*, but in true reporter form—or, perhaps Regina form—she hesitated to say no. Reporters have a tendency to want to help if it's a big, breaking story. "Let me think about it," she said. "Call me back."

I phoned her again a while later.

"I'm really sorry," she said, "but I just don't have time."

We found a way to report on the crime, and that weekend, Regina had the cover story in *Proceso* along with a colleague, Jorge Carrasco, another person who would become central to her story.

That was the extent of my interaction with Regina. Until I was taking off on my flight to Columbus. Reading about her murder was for me a *parteaguas*, literally, "a parting of the waters," a watershed moment. Her death brought the faceless, distant assassinations closer. I made a mental note to do more when I returned, to give the story an in-depth treatment.

I remember reading, in early reports right after Regina's death, that she had been drinking and dancing with friends the night she was killed and that an argument broke out early in the morning. Oddly, that made sense to me. In places like Xalapa, everyone knew everyone from at least grade school. The narcos and *malandros* (thugs, bad guys) were people you grew up with, family members, even. Sometimes they showed up at your parties. Sometimes their rivals showed up, too, and people ended up dead. We wrote a lot of those stories.

I even found myself with a vivid image of Regina in her living room, partying with friends until 4 A.M., the time they estimated she was killed, because I had done just that several times with my Mexican colleagues in Mexico City. It was always casual, around a table with some beer, cigarettes, and tequila. Just as you thought about calling a taxi, the arrival of a new guest jolted the dying evening back to life. Eleven P.M. became 1 A.M., then 3 A.M., then 5. At some point, someone always got up and started dancing.

I could recognize almost immediately the journalists at the parties. We shared the same reporting sensibilities. But the Latin American journalists were more renegade, bohemian, cynical—with reason. Some grew up under authoritarian rule; or, if not, they lived real memories of dictators and tyranny their parents or grandparents escaped. Francisco Franco ruled Spain until the 1975; Pinochet, Chile until 1990; and Fujimori, Peru until 2000. These reporters knew terrorist bombings in theaters and martial law.

Many had originally studied to be lawyers or poets, some the children of socialists and old-school Communists who had lost their livelihoods or were driven into exile. Though these journalists now lived in democracies, they took nothing for granted, especially not the free press—and they found it naïve that we Americans did.

They also lived modestly. Decent pay for a journalist in Mexico City was about $1,000 a month, but the average in Xalapa was $350 a month, with some salaries as low as $65 a month. Most journalists there worked at a minimum of two media outlets to make a living wage. (This was part of what made them vulnerable to corruption.)

In Regina's case, I imagined an impromptu party in a one-story stucco bungalow with a garden in front—not unlike her real home when I finally went there. The one in my mind was painted yellow against a green hillside. I conjured a very specific picture in my brain from the small details of the early stories: a tattered couch covered by a throw and a rustic wooden coffee table heavy with beer bottles and stuffed ashtrays.

I pictured Regina with her short hair wearing a *huipil*, the traditional Mexican cotton blouse with embroidered yoke that was popular among female journalists. They were cheap, colorful, and roomy, great for working in the humid subtropics because the breeze could sail right through the fabric.

I had already dived into the case in my head. (I would later learn that my imagination got only two things right: the short hair and the bungalow.)

There was another news story around the time of Regina's death that failed to enter my head then, perhaps because I had unwittingly bought the version the authorities were seeding in the local media. But it had buzz, I later discovered, especially among Regina's friends and colleagues at *Proceso*. Three weeks before Regina was killed, the magazine's writer Jenaro Villamil published a story about two Veracruz politicians, Alejandro Montano and Reynaldo Escobar, who were both running for seats in the Cámara de Diputados, Mexico's lower house of the national Congreso de la Unión. The story, citing leaked documents, said Montano had accumulated a large amount of wealth for a public servant. Escobar, meanwhile, as the number two man to ex-governor

Fidel Herrera had overseen the takeover of the state by a cartel known as La Compañía, according to testimony from protected witnesses.

When the story came out, three thousand copies of *Proceso* disappeared from Xalapa's newsstands.

On my last day in Ohio, I got a phone call from the AP: Three more journalists, all photographers, were murdered in Veracruz less than a week after Regina's death. This time, they were found hacked in pieces in green garbage bags that were fished from a sewage canal in Boca del Río. They had been reported missing the day before.

This was one of several moments in covering violence in Mexico when the act seemed so extreme that I couldn't really process it. Four journalists were killed in a week—that happened nowhere, not in war zones, not in dictatorships. It was beyond explanation for us, the people assigned to explain events to the rest of the world.

The editor in charge wanted to send a team to Veracruz.

"Go for it," I said.

Regina's story was overtaken by something bigger and more horrific.

The international media—the Associated Press, the *New York Times*, CBS, the *Guardian*—descended on Veracruz as local journalists left the state. No one knew how many fled. Rumors said dozens. *Proceso* reported twenty or so. Most newspaper editors refused to take our phone calls or talk about what happened.

"We're living in madness," one editor told the AP. He wouldn't give his name for fear of his life.

CHAPTER 4

A Heaven inside Hell

I N THE FAMOUS mariachi song "Guadalajara," the crooners proclaim Mexico's third-largest city and its state, Jalisco, to have the "most Mexican soul" in all the country. Indeed, everything Americans have seen in a standard Mexican restaurant is derivative of Jalisco, the birthplace of mariachi music, tequila, and the *charro* image of the Mexican cowboy in tight chaps and a wide sombrero.

There could be a strong argument, however, that the soul of Mexico is really Veracruz. Four hundred miles long and an average of only sixty miles wide, Veracruz cuts through every slice of Mexico, its full breadth of ecosystems, terrain, culture, and history. It is the site of the first Spanish settlement in Mexico. Hernán Cortés landed near what is now the Port of Veracruz and named the point La Villa Rica de Vera Cruz, "the rich village of the true cross." It was also the place where the last Spaniards were kicked out during the War of Independence, some three hundred years later. Nearly every major invasion of Mexico throughout its history, including by the French and the United States, started in Veracruz.

The port is low and hot, with Afro-Caribbean influences, a strong coffee culture, salt-corroded buildings, and bear-hugging humidity. The local specialty drink, known as a *café lechero*, is ordered and poured with great theatrics. A waiter serves a tall clear glass with espresso at the bottom, and the patron then clinks the glass with a spoon to summon another waiter with a giant kettle of steaming milk, which he pours from three feet above the glass, raising and lowering the height of the spout to create an aerated layer of foam. A busy morning in the Veracruz cafés can sound like an American wedding reception with the constant clinking of spoons against glass.

People from the port are known as the original *jarochos* (though the term now refers to anyone from the state), stereotyped as emotional, loud, and festive, but with tempers as steamy as the weather. (One TV comedian added the term *odio jarocho*, "jarocho hate," to the national lexicon; it means "to hate something or someone beyond words.")

The state is also home to the highest volcanic peak in North America, Pico de Orizaba, snowcapped at more than eighteen thousand feet above sea level. In between lie Alpine-like villages reminiscent of Switzerland, sugarcane fields, citrus orchards, coffee bean hillsides, cloud forests, jungles, and dunes. It was the first destination for most of the slaves headed for sale and work in "New Spain" and the site of the first free black colony in the Americas, liberated eleven years before the Pilgrims landed and named Yanga, for Gaspar Yanga, the slave who fought the Spaniards for thirty years to obtain the land. It is a state where Mesoamerican cultures and traditions have survived, isolated in the highlands, and where the Totonac, indigenous people whose civilization dates back at least two thousand years, still occupy the central north.

Veracruz is also home to such Mexican originals as the vanilla plant, the Alamo's Santa Anna, and the actor Salma Hayek. Much more than the mariachi song "Guadalajara," Americans know "La Bamba," recorded by Ritchie Valens in 1958 and, later, in 1987, a No. 1 *Billboard* hit for Los Lobos. But they probably don't know that it's the rock-and-roll version of a Veracruz folk song, originally sung in the high-pitched, jarana-plucking sound known as *son jarocho* (the Veracruz Sound).

Veracruz was always an important state to the Institutional Revolutionary Party, or PRI, not only for its eight million inhabitants and huge bloc of voters, but also as it became a top producer of Mexico's oil and gas. One other geographical coincidence made it especially attractive.

Its four-hundred-mile-long coastline stretch puts Veracruz smack-dab on one of the most lucrative smuggling routes in the hemisphere. The quickest shot between the Guatemalan and U.S. borders runs through Veracruz.

The PRI ran the state like a banana republic, making it the seat of one of the most corrupt governments in Mexico. There were always Mafias, caciques (local bosses), and contraband. But with the rise in cocaine trafficking in Mexico in the 1980s and '90s, its significance grew.

There was violence in Veracruz in the way that Mexico was traditionally violent: land disputes and political rivalries. *Porros* (thugs) and pistoleros helped the PRI keep people in line, and the government cracked down on alleged leftist guerrilla groups and violently removed the indigenous and campesinos when the state wanted their valuable rural land. But organized crime operations were historically discreet.

Most Veracruzanos can identify the exact moment when this changed: March 3, 2007, in an incident known as the Shootout at Villarín. Efraín Teodoro Torres, known as Zeta-14, had come to race and bet on the horses at a private hippodrome known as Villarín, near the Veracruz airport. Torres, who defected from the Mexican Army in 1998 to join the Gulf Cartel, was a founder and leader of the cartel's corps of assassins, the Zetas, and he controlled drug trafficking in Veracruz and the Gulf region. The parking lot filled with Hummers and luxury SUVs as the men came to play the quarter horses, placing bets in the millions of dollars. At one point, shooting broke out. Torres was injured as he tried to flee; he later died in the hospital. Some say it was a dispute over a race that ended in a photo finish. Others say the killing was ordered by a rival capo with the Sinaloa Cartel who wanted Torres's territory. In all, two men were murdered, at least two injured, and five detained, including a member of the Federal Police. Narco shootouts began popping up around the state.

Still, it was a shock when the violence arrived in the capital, Xalapa. Bad things were not supposed to happen in Xalapa, a university town and state capital where cobblestone streets and bright façades of rose, periwinkle, and burnt orange were carved into the foothills of the Sierra Madre Oriental. Xalapa was government suits and Guatemalan patchwork pants, politicos and patchouli, bureaucrats and a film school named for the Spanish surrealist Luis Buñuel. Walking the street on a hot summer night, you could pass families gathered in their living rooms with the doors and windows open, or hear a classical flute piece and look up to see the flutist playing from a balcony. It was the place where people came to protest the injustices happening in other parts of the state, where students came to study and never left, smitten to the point of ignoring the warning signs that the arcadian city was changing.

Parque Juárez, named for the great Mexican liberator and president Benito Juárez, preens at the center of town. If American parks are wide open, designed for running and playing, Mexican parks are for strolling and socializing. The stone walkways in Parque Juárez, which are too hard for play (though they are now ceded to skaters), bisect large sections of lush green plants set off by thick hedges and ornate wrought-iron fencing. Not only does it resemble a botanical garden, but Parque Juárez has plaques identifying all the flora, guarumo trees bearing figlike fruit, jacaranda, magnolia, and *Carpinus caroliniana*, a hardwood tree known as the American hornbeam. It preserves elements of another era, one with organ grinders, cotton candy, women with parasols, and men in tailcoats— maybe from the year 1847, when Gen. Ulysses S. Grant, while fighting the Mexican-American War in Veracruz, called Xalapa "decidedly the most beautiful place I ever saw in my life."

At one end of the park is the Veracruz statehouse, a block-long neoclassical building whose color changed periodically from pink to avocado to orange. At the other end, the park, carved into a hillside, juts out like a terrace over the city streets below. From that hillside balcony on a clear day, you could take in a gorgeous span of blue broken only by the snowcap of Pico de Orizaba in one direction, and Cofre de Perote (Naupa-Tecutépetl, or "Four-sided Mountain," in Nahuatl, the Aztec language) in another and be converted right there in the brilliant sunshine—because only God, or perhaps Quetzalcoatl, could have created such a view.

The worst started in early 2011, just after Governor Javier Duarte took office. Suddenly, ordinary citizens in quiet neighborhoods could find themselves flat on their kitchen floor at night while the sound of semiautomatic gunfire rang outside, and then walk out in the morning to find their cars riddled with bullet holes. A residential shootout in January that year left fourteen dead: two Mexican soldiers and twelve gang members. In July, two people were gunned down in their car at the Plaza Las Américas shopping mall. The Duarte administration gave little information about these incidents, or simply lied by claiming far-reduced numbers of casualties. The information coming from Duarte was so obviously false that I banned reporters from quoting him on a key breaking story in Veracruz.

In Duarte's first year in office, 2011, four journalists were killed in Veracruz. (The number in all six years under his predecessor, Fidel Herrera, was three.) The situation surprised us at the AP, as Veracruz was normally a very quiet state. About halfway through the year, we found out why this had changed.

In June of that year, Miguel Ángel López Velasco, a thirty-year veteran editor and columnist for *Notiver*, the largest newspaper in the port, was gunned down in his home. A legend in the local press corps for his deep sources, López was known for columns that carried insider details of the organized crime forces at work in Veracruz. He was old school, having spent decades in the political backrooms and seedy bars of the port, and he could touch topics no one else dared to.

With the pen name "Milo Vela," López wrote a column in *Notiver* called "Va de nuez," a Mexican idiom that basically means "repeat" or "again." In one of his more astonishing pieces, he detailed the 2009 kidnapping operation that disappeared customs official Francisco Serrano Aramoni.

When he was killed, there were rumors that Milo Vela was about to come out with another blockbuster column on organized crime. On the morning of his death, he returned home from work at three o'clock after putting the paper to bed, as was often his custom. Two hours later, a black pickup pulled up to his modern two-story home. Three or four men got out, according to neighbors, and broke through the heavy wooden front door with a battering ram. They sprayed Milo Vela and his wife with thirty-three bullets and hunted down his twenty-one-year-old son, a photojournalist, shooting him execution style in the nape of the neck. The first reporters to arrive saw blood everywhere, along with dozens of .45-caliber bullet casings, the kind used in police- and military-issued semiautomatic pistols. Milo Vela's face had been destroyed.

A month later, Yolanda Ordaz de la Cruz went missing while on her way to her daughter's high school graduation. Ordaz was a reporter and editor for *Notiver* who worked closely with Milo Vela. Her decapitated body was found two days later behind the offices of the newspaper *Imagen del Golfo* in Boca del Río—the location taken as a threat to the press in general.

The day after she was found, a video appeared on YouTube of about two dozen men in balaclavas with automatic rifles announcing their arrival in Veracruz to rid the state of the scourge of the Zetas cartel. They praised Milo Vela and Yolanda Ordaz as "amigos" who were killed by the Zetas, they said, for reporting information that could lead to their capture. They also expressed their "respect and admiration" for Governor Javier Duarte for fighting the Zetas. They signed off as Los Mata Zetas, or "Zeta killers," of the Jalisco New Generation Cartel, at the time an arm of the Sinaloa Cartel, run by Joaquín "El Chapo" Guzmán.

The cause of the violence became clear. Veracruz had become the center of a vicious turf war between two very powerful cartels.

State Attorney General Reynaldo Escobar called a press conference to say that Yolanda Ordaz's death had nothing to do with her work as a journalist and that the line of investigation was into her ties with drug traffickers. In his comments, he implied that most of the journalist assassinations had involved reporters with drug ties. *Notiver*, the newspaper where both Ordaz and Milo Vela worked, publicly demanded Escobar's resignation the next day, calling him irresponsible for smearing Ordaz's name and inept at handling the crime wave during his six months as top prosecutor. Regina wrote the story about *Notiver*'s demand for *Proceso*.

It was no secret that Escobar wasn't a fan of the press or of free speech. A month after Ordaz's killing, he jailed two people for tweeting information about threats of shootouts at banks and schools, which caused traffic jams and a stampede by parents running to pull their children out of class. (Between the explosion in crime and the lack of reliable information from the co-opted press, citizens had taken to social media to warn others of problems and areas they should avoid.) But the tweeters' information happened to be false, and Escobar put them in state prison, charging them with terrorism. They were released a month later, after protests and outrage worldwide.

The atmosphere for journalists had only grown worse when, on Friday, April 27, 2012, Regina ran into her longtime friend and colleague Lupita López in Parque Juárez after a press conference at the statehouse. Strange things were happening to Regina, she confided to close friends: odd phone calls, interruptions in her Internet service.

But the conversation was light when the two women decided to catch up. Both were fixtures in the local media, sharing a long history and reputation as the most fearless and independent women in a profession that remained mostly male. They had met roughly twenty-five years earlier, when both decided to work for a new newspaper, *Política*, founded by a PRI operative who wanted to create a new, independent kind of media. Along with the local newspaper, both women were correspondents for national media, Lupita for the Mexico City–based leftist daily *La Jornada*, and Regina for *Proceso*. In all that time, they competed for the front page but also became a support system for each other, two women asking tough questions of the powerful in a *machista* world.

Lupita, in her fifties, always dressed professionally in a blouse and slacks or a skirt, with her brown hair in a bob. Her voice was soft and her face flat and calm, though her eyes darted constantly, vigilant after so many years of negotiating a hostile environment that included threats, veiled and overt, and government spies. She eagerly told me in a whisper that the restaurants, cafés, and hotel rooms surrounding Parque Juárez were rumored to be bugged.

Even in casual conversation, Lupita, who was used to Regina's strong opinions, avoided talking about books or music or anything she liked, knowing her tastes could be macheted by the woman whose favorite word was *imbécil*. But she noticed that Regina had softened lately, even as the reporting environment had become more complicated. She laughed more and seemed more relaxed. The two had crossed paths just a few days prior to the press conference, in a state representative's office, where Lupita found Regina bantering with the secretaries over the quality of the office cookies. "These are so bad, I'm going to have to bring my own," Regina said. The office assistant joked that she would buy better ones, if only to shut Regina up.

As the two women were walking out of the statehouse following the press conference, Regina spotted Mariela San Martín, a seamstress she and Lupita had both used for years. Regina and Lupita had become great shopping mates as well over time, but on their many outings to department stores, the tiny Regina always complained that she couldn't find clothes that fit. "That's because they're for adults," Lupita would quip, "not Barbies."

Mariela San Martín worked for the secretary of government, the state's number two official, in information. She was one of the legions of people sent out by the state government to report on who attended press conferences, protests, and opposition events. She had worked in that position for at least twenty years under several administrations, including those of Miguel Alemán Velasco and Fidel Herrera, two governors especially intent on watching their enemies.

The journalists called people like Mariela San Martín informants, or *orejas*, "ears," in Spanish. When I finally got to Xalapa, the reporters pointed them out in the crowds at events and protests. If Regina and fellow reporters saw Mariela coming, they joked that it was time to talk about the weather.

Mariela ran her sewing business on the side, making clothes for lots of women in state government: legislators, governors' wives, even. She attached herself to the female press corps, a lucrative, if small, client base. Not only did she make clothes, but she sold lotions and perfumes and was constantly acquiring new products for the women to try. "*Pinche Mariela*," Regina complained to Lupita once. "I ask her for one thing, and she brings me all this stuff."

Some found San Martín's constant presence annoying, suspicious even. But when questioned why she would patronize the business of a spy, Regina said she didn't mind helping a woman who was trying to earn extra to do better by her children. Mariela came from a humble background, but her two daughters had completed college; one was a lawyer, and the other, an engineer. Regina admired that.

No one thought much about Mariela's role in government until later. She had entered Regina's house to measure for curtains. She had also worked in the office of Reynaldo Escobar.

Regina called out to Mariela after the press conference. "Wait up!"

"What's going on?" Mariela answered. "What do you want me for?"

"Listen, I would like you to make me two vests and three blouses."

"Okay."

"We're going right now to buy fabric. Can you come?"

Mariela agreed, and the three women headed for a nearby fabric shop called Moda Nova. Regina went through bolts and bolts of material, showing off various options for Mariela and Lupita's opinion. Lupita had always encouraged her to pick brighter colors over her usual blacks and browns, and that day, to her surprise, Regina complied. For some vests, she chose a dark gray with popping silvery pinstripes and a bright denim blue. For the blouses, she chose a blue-and-white check pattern to match the blue vest and two types of white embroidered Spanish cotton.

As they headed back to the government palace, Regina stopped to buy coffee at her favorite spot, Café Colón, and then, after browsing some racks outside on the street, a book. They walked under the neocolonial arches of the government palace, and Regina looked up and waved. "I'm waving to the cameras," she said, as they laughed about being under constant surveillance. They ran into another group of reporters and stopped to chat casually about the news of the day. Regina was about to go grocery shopping and said she was in the mood for a salad.

Then the three women parted, Lupita and Mariela to their offices and Regina boarding a taxi to the Comercial Mexicana, a giant grocery and department store, to do her shopping for the week. Lost in the wide aisles behind an enormous cart, she threw pancetta, Italian greens, carrots, cherry tomatoes, avocado, and blackberries for her salad into her basket. She picked up rice, soup, and pasta and, browsing the clothing racks, chose two men's logo T-shirts. She saved her grocery slip as always and checked when she got home for missing items or overcharges.

Then she disappeared, as she did every weekend, behind the white iron gate into her modest one-bedroom bungalow just a fifteen-minute walk from Parque Juárez.

Her bungalow, her refuge, was a paradise for hoarders of the written word. A wooden desk was the centerpiece of the living room, with her personal archives of magazines and newspapers stacked everywhere, even in the kitchen. A paint-curdling mold, pervasive in Mexico's humid climate, scrawled billowy designs in the plaster. Stacks of government reports decorated her shelves. Other shelves were stuffed with cassette tapes and music CDs: Elvis, Jimi Hendrix, John Lee Hooker, and John Mayall mixed with the Mexican ballads of Chavela Vargas and the pop songs of Luis Miguel. There were hundreds of books, an eclectic collection ranging from Latin American classics by Carlos Fuentes, Gabriel García Márquez, and Mempo Giardinelli to Joseph Conrad's *Heart of Darkness*, plays by Tennessee Williams, a biography of John Lennon, and the Popol Vuh, the sacred text of the ancient Maya. A flat-screen TV peered down from the top of a bookcase onto her desk, which was cluttered with computer equipment, recorders, and several telephones.

With the exception of Lupita, most close friends had never been invited inside her home. Papers and books filled every free space, including the chairs, so she couldn't offer anyone a place to sit.

Weekends were for work. She would take the uninterrupted time to write her longer pieces for the magazine, tapping at her computer keyboard late into the night along with the drone of television news, a cigarette, and a supercharged cup of Veracruz coffee as her staples. She declined all social invitations, saying she was too tired or had too much work.

This was one such weekend. She was finishing a project, though being so competitive and protective of her stories, she didn't let on to anyone what it was.

Months earlier, she told her *Proceso* editor, Salvador Corro, that she had something on former governor Fidel Herrera and corruption. They were speaking by telephone, and could not talk candidly. (All reporters' telephone calls were assumed to be listened in on by the Mexican government.) She had just started working on it and had few details. As with many of Regina's investigations, Corro figured he would not know what the story was until it landed on his desk.

On that Friday afternoon in late April, the news cycle had been particularly busy. Mexico was in the middle of a presidential campaign, with the PRI attempting to regain executive power for the first time in twelve years. As usual, Veracruz was strategic for the campaign in terms of money and votes.

That Friday alone, Regina filed reports on marines arresting nine local police officers for links to organized crime and on a former leader in the local Democratic Revolutionary Party who was found dead in his home. After constant calls to the phone company, her Internet still was not fixed, and she was forced to send her stories from the government offices of her sources or from a public café, where she filed her last story that day at around 7 P.M.

As Regina settled in at home for the evening, she cooked beans and a Mexican stew known as a *guisado*. At around 9 P.M., she called a source to cancel an upcoming interview. Other than her neighbor Isabel Nuñez's story about the gate, it was the last verifiable record that Regina was still alive.

CHAPTER 5

"Mr. Governor, We Don't Believe You"

April 28–May 3, 2012

B Y TEN O'CLOCK at night, Rodrigo and Brenda had arrived at the home of fellow journalist Norma Trujillo, which became the impromptu situation room for Regina's closest friends. Javier Hernández and Lupita López, Regina's longtime colleagues from the newspaper *Política*, were there as well. They sank into the navy-blue cushions of the living room sofas to decide what to do, speaking in whispers as if they didn't want to be overheard. They were the only ones in the house.

Everyone knew the atmosphere had become more poisonous. The normal type of harassment that independent reporters suffered had become more unpredictable and sinister. They had been surveilled, chased; their homes broken into; their files and equipment stolen.

But until that night, the murdered journalists in Veracruz had been crime reporters, ambulance chasers. In Mexico, crime news made big money. The country's most lucrative newspapers were police tabloids, one aptly named *El Gráfico* (the Graphic), which thrived on front-page photographs of bloody corpses and car accidents. The newsrooms traditionally had crime reporters on staff who had sources inside the police departments and the netherworld. But the popularity of crime news spawned a fleet of freelancers, who sped around on motorbikes fueled by tips and police scanner chatter to get images they could sell to the tabloids. Often, there were two on the bike, the driver plus a photographer perched on the back like a paparazzo, with his lens trained on the scene. They were young, all male, sleeping in the day and working in the middle of the night, when everything went down, adrenaline speeding at the same pace as their motorbikes along the dark, empty streets. They often arrived at a crime scene before police did, snapping the bloody mess before any roadblocks or caution tape could keep them out. Pay was meager, maybe 50 pesos a photo at best (about $3.50 at the time), which was why they worked all night, trying to snap as many crime scenes as possible.

When the macabre incidents of warring cartels played out in various regions of Mexico, the work of these crime reporters became exponentially more lucrative—and dangerous. The images they collected had a shock value the tabloids had never seen: a severed head left on the hood of a car, a row of bodies hanging from a bridge. The cartels committed the gruesome acts to send messages, so of course they wanted to control the messengers. These were the first inklings of "narco journalism," organized crime infiltrating newsrooms.

The legions of young freelancers earning a few bucks a shot suddenly found themselves wedged between some of the most lethal forces in the country. You could get crossways with a drug cartel for covering the wrong crime. "A cartel calls the newsroom and tells you not to publish a story. Then a second cartel, enemy of the first, calls the newsroom and tells you *to* publish the story. Then a third cartel calls and tells you to publish the story, run a photo, and put it on the front page," journalist Javier Valdéz told me one time when we caught up in Mexico City, where he was promoting his book *Narcoperiodismo*, about the phenomenon of drug cartels in newsrooms. "The reporter has to operate in this dispute and go with one side or the other. The reporter can't decide for himself . . . It's do what you're told or be killed, or go into exile, or leave journalism."

Valdéz was internationally recognized, the cofounder of *Ríodoce*, a weekly newspaper in El Chapo's home state of Sinaloa, which was run entirely by the international drug cartel that bore the same name. Valdéz and his cofounder, Ismael Bojórquez, had the only publication that regularly covered drug trafficking and the cartels. Even after all that he had published and accomplished, his job remained as precarious as ever. "I have to learn on every story how far I can go, what information I can't publish," he told me in the same conversation, ". . . and I know if I cross the line, they're going to kill me."

Six months after our conversation, Javier Valdéz was pulled from his car near the *Ríodoce* offices in the capital city of Culiacán and shot dead on the street.

★

REGINA DIDN'T COVER drug cartels; she investigated politicians. And the details of her murder—being beaten and strangled to death—didn't fit the cartel pattern. This was something different, a whole new territory for which her bereft colleagues had no bearings.

The group of her friends who had gathered at Norma Trujillo's home started going down the list of people who Regina may have disturbed most:

"Fidel Herrera?" The governor before Duarte sparred many times with Regina. Her investigations included state funds that couldn't be accounted for during his term and Herrera's possible ties to organized crime.

"Miguel Ángel Yunes?" Yunes was the number two under former governor Patricio Chirinos and rival to Herrera. Regina had written about charges of political and human right abuses against him.

"Alejandro Montano?" Regina had written that the congressman and former public security secretary was accused of protecting drug traffickers.

There were so many targets of Regina's stories, past and present, including the Mexican Army. Her murderer could have been anyone.

What the group didn't know was that at the same moment they were trying to figure out who did it, the official answer was already being planted online. Just six hours after Regina's body was found, when the investigation was just beginning, two comments appeared at the bottom of the story about her death posted on the *Proceso* website. The first comment, by "Laura," asked why police arrived so quickly to a call about a door being left open when it often took them hours to respond to the shootouts that were becoming commonplace in Xalapa. She implied that police knew about the crime before they even got the call.

"My condolences to her family," Laura wrote. "We are all fucked."

A commenter named "Dann" responded to Laura with what would become the official line: "Lamentably," he wrote, "the death of the journalist had nothing to do with her work."

The group stayed up most of the night, no one able to sleep. No one knew how to contact her family. They put their grief into planning a protest march for the following afternoon and drafting an open letter. It was addressed to the president of Mexico, Felipe Calderón, the president of the Congreso de la Unión, the governor, the state congress, the federal attorney general, and the state prosecutor, and it demanded justice for Regina and *resultados*—"results."

"We are indignant. This is the fifth journalist killing since 2010 in Veracruz," their letter read. At the top were the signatures of Norma, Lupita, and Rodrigo, followed by twenty-eight others, including Andrés Timoteo, Regina's colleague who had fled to Mexico City the minute he heard of the murder.

When the dawn cast its gray into the living room, Norma went into the kitchen, searched in the refrigerator for breakfast fixings, and scrambled some eggs for her guests.

"We have to go to the morgue," she said to the group.

"Why?" Rodrigo asked.

"Because Regina is alone."

The weight of reality fell on him once again.

Another of Regina's colleagues had already showed up at the morgue hours earlier, so "Regina wouldn't be alone." Walter Ramírez, a fellow reporter in the early days of *Política*, went with his wife, Marisa Sánchez, after they heard the news. Sánchez, a devout Catholic, wanted to pray over her friend, according to the story Walter Ramírez later told me, and the two were there when investigators arrived with Regina's body. The investigators asked who Ramírez was and what he was doing there. When they found out he knew Regina, they requested his help in the investigation. They told him that night, just hours after finding her, that the killing appeared to be a crime of passion.

Ramírez started repeating the official version to everyone.

Just one day before her death, Regina had told a friend that Ramírez had asked her to loan him some money. He had suffered various bouts of unemployment, including at that moment. He told Regina he needed the money because his mother had cancer. Regina told him she didn't have it, though she wondered aloud to her friend whether she should reconsider.

★

AT 8:30 THAT morning, Alonso Martínez was ready to leave home for his soccer game. The twenty-year-old engineering student played soccer in a local league with his father every Sunday at 9 A.M. Alonso was enjoying the last moments in his room while waiting for his father to finish getting ready when he heard the phone ring.

"Are you ready? Come on," his dad called out.

When Alonso came out of his room, he discovered that they weren't going to the soccer pitch. They were headed to the morgue. His father, Regina's younger brother Ángel, had just received a call from one of his siblings, who saw the report of Regina's death on the news.

"I have an extremely delicate issue for you to check out," Ángel's brother said, "and when you hear this, I want you to stay calm. I just received some information that Regina suffered an attack. Her body is at the morgue. That's all I know. Can you see what you can find out and let me know?" Ángel and Regina were the only family members living in Xalapa. Most of the rest were in another state.

Ángel hung up and asked Alonso to call the morgue from a pay phone. This was the way Mexicans dealt with sensitive information, because everyone assumed their phones were tapped: Call from an anonymous number, never from your personal cell phone, especially not to authorities. Alonso dialed 066 and asked to be transferred to the morgue, where an attendant confirmed that his aunt Regina was indeed there. It was his first realization of a loss that the young college student was never going to get over.

Ángel grabbed Alonso and hailed a cab, which dropped them at the wide walkway leading to the Veracruz state forensics crime lab, a white sheet cake of a building with dozens of square windows built on a hillside above one of Xalapa's main expressways on the outskirts of town. Plain white coroner's vans were parked all around the building, which was heavily guarded by Mexican Army troops. Reporters mingled outside with their cameras on tripods along the concrete berms under the shade of a large tree. Ángel and Alonso ignored them as they made their way to the two-story glass entryway.

Alonso recognized some of Regina's colleagues: Norma Trujillo, Rodrigo Soberanes, a photographer named Rubén Espinosa, and Alberto Morales, another photographer, who Regina had once dated.

Norma Trujillo was trying to find out what would happen to the body if the family didn't show and whether Regina's friends could claim it, when she saw Ángel walk in. Then she witnessed something odd: Walter Ramírez rushed to Ángel and Alonso and commandeered them away from the others.

★

SEVENTY MILES AWAY, at the Veracruz International Airport, a commercial flight from Mexico City landed with *Proceso*'s founder and retired director, Julio Scherer, on board. Scherer was arguably the father of modern Mexican journalism. As a man who famously stood up to the censorship efforts of several Mexican presidents, Scherer was credited with steering the profession in general from its sycophantic, pro-government roots to an independent and critical watchdog. He was Regina's idol. As much as she hated socializing, she had made the trip to Mexico City every November for the *Proceso* anniversary party just so she could pay her respects to Don Julio, as Scherer was

known, and have her photo snapped alongside him. Don Julio, now
eighty-six years old, had shown up early that morning at the Mexico
City airport for the flight to Veracruz. He was dressed in a blue sport
coat and a tie (church clothes), even though he was headed to the
steamy subtropics. Today, it was Don Julio who was going to pay his
respects to Regina.

Julio Scherer's was a riches-to-rags story. Born in 1926, he grew up in
a stately home in Mexico City's upscale San Ángel district, until his
father lost the family fortune due to a "breach of trust"—the way Julio
described it without going into detail. The family's giant home, along
with its art, antiques, and other valuables, had to be sold. Julio's journalism trajectory started in college, when he became a copy boy at *Excélsior*, a conservative national newspaper founded during the revolution in
1917 by Rafael Alducin. From the 1940s, he worked his way up the
ranks. Then in 1968, he was named director in a split and somewhat
contentious vote by the employee cooperative that ran the newspaper.

Newspapers and radio were private enterprises. And many post-
Revolution presidents liked presenting a veneer of support for free
speech. But the ruling party, with its usual carrot and stick, let editors
know where the lines were. It wasn't difficult in many cases, as media
owners agreed with the government's nationalistic policies of political
stability, anticommunism, and growth. Others opted to obey them in
exchange for lucrative rewards: cheap paper, low-interest loans,
government advertising, and paid news stories, not to mention offers
of money, houses, and expensive gifts to reporters.

Julio set out to shake up the journalistic status quo at *Excélsior*, rejecting
the old guard and hiring more aggressive talent. His goals, he said, were
to make the journalism more professional, the finances more transparent, and the newspaper policies more oriented toward the reader.
But it wasn't quite the radical change he envisioned. To maintain support
for his new editorial stance, he was forced to tolerate many of the traditional corrupt systems inside the newsroom.

The front page was no longer for sale, but he couldn't manage to
do away with other common ethical breaches, such as so-called *igualas*,

the commissions reporters charged sources to place their stories. Journalists could earn from two to ten times their salaries in commissions. Though Don Julio assembled a team of talented reporters, they still practiced such indiscretions. As Mexican historian Arno Burkholder wrote of Julio Scherer in his book on *Excélsior*, "He was obligated to admit a painful yet inevitable reality: He preferred a skilled reporter, even though immoral, to a weak one who was honorable."

But by all accounts, Don Julio had succeeded in taking *Excélsior* from a faithful supporter of the Mexican government, which mostly meant the president, to one that opened its pages to the full gamut of criticism and news. It was produced by some of the top writers and journalistic voices of the time, including novelist and playwright Jorge Ibargüengoitia and future Nobel laureate Octavio Paz. (Coincidentally, the late 1960s was also a time when growth in private advertising reduced the media's reliance on the government dole.) One study, by the University of London, ranked *Excélsior* among the best newspapers in the Americas and among those that rivaled the major press in Europe. Some called it "*Le Monde* of Mexico."

The newspaper suffered for veering outside the lines, with attacks from presidents, boycotts from advertisers, and even a bomb left outside the building. By 1976, it had come under constant attack from people discrediting its reports and from officials who refused to take journalists' calls. At one point, Don Julio received a message from a PRI operative—a man who was forced to resign his university director position because of *Excélsior*'s critical articles—who said that if Don Julio fired one of his outspoken columnists, his problems would go away. Don Julio refused.

The newspaper's editors decided to print a manifesto decrying a campaign that had cast them as "enemies of the country" (and that predated Donald Trump's similar casting of the U.S. media by more than forty years). They wrote that the attacks came from "those who suppose that the function of the press is to serve the powerful and flatter them and hide the national reality from Mexicans."

Then, in the early hours of the morning—three o'clock, to be exact—of July 8, 1976, a date that many Mexican journalists know by heart, an angry mob from the cooperative that ran *Excélsior* took over the newspaper, killed the manifesto, and called an immediate general meeting to vote Don Julio out of power. By workday's end, Julio Scherer and his editors were told they had fifteen minutes to leave the building. Don Julio put the blame squarely on the shoulders of Mexican president Luis Echeverría, who he refused to believe wasn't behind the mob.

The international press certainly took this angle, even as the rest of the Mexico City press remained silent about Don Julio's ouster. Articles appeared in the *New York Times*, the *Washington Post*, and *Le Monde* saying *Excélsior* was a shadow of its former self after a coup orchestrated by the government. Some named Echeverría directly as "the man who killed *Excélsior.*" Don Julio told him as much to his face in a heated standoff.

The president returned fire: From the beginning of his regime, he said, he had supported *Excélsior*, given the newspaper absolute freedom, and helped during an advertiser boycott. "How did *Excélsior* repay me? With attacks on my government day after day. With the accusations now from foreign correspondents!" Echeverría said.

Without a job, Don Julio set November 6, 1976, as the first edition of *Proceso*, a new independent magazine he was creating, thanks to some one thousand investors and an art auction to benefit his new venture. In the months leading up to the magazine's inauguration, the government put on the pressure. A top government official got word to the group that waiting until the new president, José López Portillo, was inaugurated on December 1, 1976, would only be prudent for a nation in transition while also facing a financial crisis. As an added threat, he said, "Fifteen missing journalists would not alter the tranquility of the country at all."

Don Julio's response: "We're going on November sixth."

A strange "architect" showed up at the rented offices of the new magazine, always with workers and projects that no one had requested. The government agency that controlled the sale of newsprint denied Don Julio's new media company, *Comunicación e Información, S. A.*, a request for printing paper, forcing him to buy it on the black market. Finally, Don Julio received a court summons to respond to accusations of fraud and other crimes outlined by *Excélsior* in a criminal complaint. He was told to appear in court just days before November sixth. His appearance was a media circus, with the international press again reporting it as a political attack on freedom of expression in Mexico.

But he succeeded. The first edition of *Proceso* hit the streets on the day he had promised, less than a month before Echeverría was to leave office. The magazine devoted nearly all its pages to skewering him and his presidential term.

From that moment, Julio Scherer became a legend and a mentor to so many, a journalistic gangster of sorts who understood the power and corruption of the PRI and could go head-to-head with anyone.

Don Julio had seen or experienced a lot of intimidation. But in the thirty-six-year history of the magazine, he had not lost a single correspondent—until now. With the murder of Regina Martínez, the man with journalistic *huevos* of steel—who had interviewed Chinese premier Zhou Enlai and Cuba's Fidel Castro—the man who wouldn't be cowed by presidents set on silencing him landed in Veracruz terribly shaken, unable to grasp what exactly had just happened.

There was no divining what power had decided to commit such an audacious act.

★

SCHERER WAS MET at the airport by *Proceso*'s director, Rafael Rodrí-guez; Regina's editor, Salvador Corro; photographer Gérman Canseco; and staff writer Jorge Carrasco. They, too, were mostly silent from shock and anger.

Rodríguez turned to Jorge Carrasco at one point: "What do you think?"

Jorge had been spending a good deal of time recently in Veracruz, as well as covering stories from Mexico City with help from Regina on the ground. He told Rafael that Regina had been working under a lot of hostility. The magazine disappeared a few times from Veracruz newsstands when *Proceso* wrote critically of the government. And offi-cials were blocking her from getting information.

With that kind of environment, there was no doubt among them: Her killing wasn't a random hit.

A state helicopter awaited to fly them a short eighteen minutes from Veracruz to Xalapa. They arrived to a cloying display of Governor Duarte's largesse, like an old-school pol showing them who was in charge. Duarte offered each of them a room at the Camino Real Hotel and use of the state plane. They refused all of it, except a meeting room where they could draft their response.

It was noon by the time the *Proceso* group reached the governor's official residence, Casa Veracruz, a Mediterranean-style stucco estate where peacocks roamed the manicured lawns behind a high security wall. When they entered the reception area, they noticed on the coffee table a neat display of editions of *Proceso*, including a special publication on the Zetas drug cartel. It looked anything but coincidental, if that was the intention. Rather, the visitors viewed it as a prop, part of the staging of a play that was about to be performed.

They were quickly greeted by Javier Duarte, a portly man with a nasally tenor voice that he once proudly noted resembled that of Spanish dictator Francisco Franco. He was dressed in a carefully pressed white guayabera: a loose, Cuban-style tropical shirt with ribbing down the front, the uniform of Veracruz politicians. As Duarte took his place at the head of a large wooden conference table, he sat so carefully and stiffly that his visitors imagined he was afraid of wrinkling his shirt.

At one end of the room was a red velvet curtain with the flags of Mexico and Veracruz in front. On the wall to Duarte's left was a large map of Veracruz, a long, thin, curved state resembling a tumorous serrano chile. Attorney General Felipe Amadeo Flores Espinosa sat below the map, along with a phalanx of state officials who filled most of the sixteen chairs. To Duarte's right was the team from *Proceso*.

The governor opened with a predictable lamenting of how painful the assassination of Regina Martínez was for them and a promise to pursue the case to the fullest extent of the law, throwing "outstanding journalist" and "your prestigious media" into the mix. He announced that the federal attorney general's office and the National Human Rights Commission would join the case, along with *Proceso*, saying he would create an interinstitutional commission to investigate the crime with full transparency. Then his deputies listed every action they had taken in the eighteen hours since Regina's body had been found.

Julio Scherer found Duarte's words to be "abusively boring." He decided to interrupt. "What we've just heard is nothing more than superficial," Scherer said. "There's not a single explanation of the deep troubles in which the assassination of our reporter occurred."

A silence fell over the room. Scherer continued: "The death of Regina Martínez is a product of the decomposition of this state and the country. And we want to know what's beneath the surface. To sum it up, Mr. Governor, we don't believe you."

No one spoke for several seconds.

Rafael Rodríguez, the magazine's director, broke the silence. "There's a hostile environment against our magazine in this state," he said, mentioning the disappearance of issues of *Proceso* from newsstands.

Duarte looked stunned. He was not accustomed to being spoken to in this way by the editors in his state. The meeting ended shortly thereafter.

Before leaving town, Regina's editor, Salvador Corro, ran into Lev García, who had worked for him and *Proceso* before coming to Xalapa as the *Reforma* correspondent. Lev avoided the morgue and the funeral home, covering only what he had to for *Reforma*. He didn't like writing about personal tragedies, interviewing family members about their losses or covering funerals, even under normal circumstances, and he especially wanted to stay away now. But he liked and trusted Corro, and the two stopped to compare notes and try to make sense of what had happened.

"What was Regina working on?" Salvador asked Lev.

"I don't know." No one seemed to know.

★

BY 12:45 P.M., Regina's brother Ángel was in the investigator's office taking an oath promising to tell the truth under threat of perjury. Ángel Martínez knew how the justice system worked. Investigators solved crimes by arresting someone and putting them away. It didn't matter who, and they would be looking for the easiest person on which to pin the crime, someone close to Regina, someone like him. Under questioning, he told them as little as possible. He didn't want them to know his real relationship with his sister; nor did he want them to know anything about Alonso, who was probably the closest of all the family to his aunt Regina. Ángel told his son not to say anything to anyone.

The investigator asked if Regina had a boyfriend. Ángel mentioned her ex-boyfriend Alberto Morales, nicknamed El Gato, or "the Cat." Ángel had seen Morales in Regina's house years earlier, when he came by for lunch one day. But he didn't know when they broke up. He said in the testimony that Regina had said that she and El Gato had problems, that Alberto had started seeing someone else while still dating her. Ángel didn't share that Regina had told him that Alberto was informing on her to the state government.

"He's the only person I know that she dated," Ángel said. "She was very reserved in her personal life."

What about her friends?

"She had friends, but she invited very few of them to her house. She had a strong character and was very centered on her work. She loved her work."

Did they have a lot of parties?

Ángel didn't know.

Did she drink a lot?

She didn't drink hard liquor, just beer, and only with meals, Ángel replied. He had never seen her drunk in his life.

Did she have any trouble with her neighbors?

If she had, it would be with Isabel Nuñez, Ángel said.

What did she have in the house?

He said she had many cameras, and he listed all the equipment he remembered seeing: a black laptop, an Acer maybe; several cell phones, including a Nextel; and a plasma TV. He said she used three cell phones on average.

Did she like women?

"My sister didn't prefer women. She wasn't a lesbian," Ángel said. "All her relations were with men." But he repeated that he had known only about Alberto and no others.

The investigator let him go, not asking anything about Regina's work.

It took hours for the coroner to release the body to the place where people were already gathering for a vigil. According to Mexican custom, the vigil would last all night, with a burial on Monday morning. At around 7 P.M., the hearse finally arrived at the coroner's office to take her away. By then, twenty-four hours after Regina had been found, the news was everywhere. The drivers knew who they were transporting. They passed a crowd of reporters waiting outside. Normally, the teams would enter the morgue and go to the steel slab to pick up the body, which would be lying with its clothes folded neatly to the side. This time, the attendants were blocked from entering the morgue. Regina's body had been left on a gurney in the hallway near the door, with her clothing carelessly wadded on top of her. Some items were missing. As the morgue workers lifted her body into the casket, her belongings fell to the floor. Then the forensic examiners realized they had forgotten to take photographs. They lifted her back out, quickly took photographs of the body and the pile of clothes that had fallen on the floor, while a morgue worker went back inside to search for a pair of brown tennis shoes with laces. The drivers had never before been blocked from entering the morgue or seen a body treated with such lack of care and procedure.

"That was strange," one said to the other when they returned to the hearse.

Over the coming weeks, the hearse drivers noticed something else. There was talk early on that Regina was killed by someone she knew, perhaps in a lover's quarrel. Norma Trujillo heard Walter Ramírez say, when among the group of reporters, "It was her macho," a boyfriend. (Walter denied in an interview with me that he ever said that.) Official leaks to the local government-friendly press in June said that investigators were using a bite mark on Regina's neck to identify the killer. The hearse drivers had picked up dozens if not hundreds of bodies, including victims of crimes of passion killed in a burst of emotion. They didn't see a love bite. They saw a jaw that was severely broken and dried blood from her nose and mouth that had spilled over her right shoulder. Bruises covered her body, including her arms and her legs. Her face was still frozen in a look of terror. It appeared to the drivers that Regina had been tortured. "We knew what everybody knew," one said. "This crime wasn't what authorities were saying it was."

★

THE OAK CASKET lay with a spray of roses, lilies, and chrysanthemums on top, vases stuffed with tuberose and flickering red church candles alongside. A kneeler was placed at one end in the long, narrow room lined on both sides with white floral arrangements, including the standing wreaths that are customary at Mexican funerals. Each giant flower wreath carries a sash bearing the name of the person sending condolences. One generous display of roses, yellow pompons, lilies, and carnations bore the name of the governor, Javier Duarte de Ochoa. Rodrigo Soberanes cursed it as he walked by. When he saw it later, he noticed that someone had torn the governor's name off the flowers.

As the overnight homage was getting under way, Julio Scherer was back in Mexico City after an eighteen-hour day, preparing for bed. He felt feverish and couldn't sleep. When he finally dozed off, he had a nightmare. Four men were trying to kidnap him. As he tried to fight them off in his sleep, he hurled himself out of bed and woke up facedown on the floor. From the impact, he was sure he had broken something. He quizzed himself on his family members' names, his address, and the date and decided his mind was okay, though he struggled to count from one to one hundred. When he finally stood up, he felt dizzy. He got to the mirror and noticed that everything was intact except for a large welt emerging over his left eye.

Earlier that day in Xalapa, about one hundred people with protest banners gathered near the central Plaza Lerdo, which was already hosting another demonstration. Polo Hernández was there. Rodrigo Soberanes carried a handmade sign reading, BASTA DE REPRESIÓN (ENOUGH WITH THE REPRESSION). Another of Regina's protégés, Juan Pablo "Eddie" Romo, carried a sign with the image of a typewriter. It read, WE WILL NEVER FORGET YOU, MAESTRA [TEACHER].

After the march, Lupita López decided to head to her office, and Norma Trujillo to her home. Because the main plaza was blocked by the other, unrelated protest, they had to take a back street behind the cathedral. As they were walking, they realized they were being followed by a man with an earpiece like that of a security person. They became nervous and ducked into a bakery to lose him.

Polo remained as agitated as he was the night before, when he first received the phone call. But he also kept working, filing a story on Regina's death from the wedding and now covering the march. As he returned home to finish his story, his friend Mar Zamudio decided to go with him. She and another friend figured he could use some company. They stopped to buy a six-pack of beer and met him at his apartment on a residential street uphill from the town lake. They had met many times before at Polo's, climbing the narrow stairs to his tiny dwelling, a square pink afterthought of a structure plopped onto the roof of a three-story building. The interior wasn't much, but the apartment opened onto a wide and roomy terrace double the size, with a view of Mexico's mesmerizing rooftops, water tanks, clotheslines, tension wires, satellite dishes, washing machines, and barking dogs so chaotically displayed, they resembled a Rauschenberg painting.

The terrace was the site of many classic journalist drinking fests, usually small gatherings, where he and Mar would strum *son jarocho*, the plaintive native folk music of Veracruz, on their jaranas, a Mexican guitar-like instrument adapted from the Spanish vihuela. It was also a place where they could discuss their most sensitives stories and topics without fear of being overheard.

There was no celebrating or music this night. Polo grew more furious with each emerging detail, the brutal manner in which Regina was killed. He wondered who was behind this and rehashed everything he could remember about Regina in the recent months, every potential signal or event that could have foreshadowed this attack. Mar simply listened.

After about an hour, the group noticed a police helicopter flying low overhead. They thought nothing of it at first. Police helicopters routinely chased criminals through the streets at night. It buzzed the terrace and then flew away to the nearby baseball stadium, then returned. Back and forth, back and forth, just forty feet above the building. It hovered so closely that, at one point, Polo could see the pilot's face. They felt weird and under surveillance, so they decided to go inside. Polo was still writing his story on the march. The helicopter continued buzzing in place for a time, until it finally lifted and whooshed away. Mar called her boyfriend to come get her, because she was too afraid to leave Polo's apartment by herself. They didn't know what that was, only how it felt. Intimidating. Harassing. Was it planned? They would never know. That was how things happened in Veracruz. Events could easily be dismissed as coincidental or taken as a surreptitious warning, a normal beam of light hitting a prism of fear. It left the targets to wrestle with their own paranoia and questions of what was real.

After a while, Mar's boyfriend showed up, and everyone but Polo left.

As he tried to process the helicopter incident, he decided that it had to be a message. "They"—whoever *they* were—had gotten Regina, and they were looking for him, too. He had been harassed before, had had state police parked outside his apartment, but this was a whole new level. When he told friends the next day what happened, they laughed at his paranoia. That was their defense mechanism, and it unwittingly added to his insecurity and doubt.

A while later, Polo ran into Miguel Valera, from the governor's communications office. "I know you all are mad at me," he said to Valera, "but you didn't need to send the black helicopter."

"You're not important enough for us to send a helicopter," Valera said with a sneer.

★

THE MARTÍNEZ FAMILY went into lockdown. Ángel sent Alonso out of the state for his protection and security. Ángel declared that only he and another brother would attend the funeral—no one else, not even Regina's elderly parents. The family had no idea that her work had put her in such danger. Now they felt they were in danger, too, and they didn't want to be photographed by the press or do anything to help authorities identify who they were.

Bosques del Recuerdo, the private cemetery where Regina was buried, is a grassy manicured field dotted with neat headstones on a hilltop at the edge of town, the place where officials and the wealthy of the city rested. The state of Veracruz was paying for Regina's funeral, as it often did in cases that were, in Mexican parlance, "raising dust," and state officials, not the family, chose the burial site. The working man's public cemetery is Palo Verde, a choppy expanse of terrain toward the center of town.

Polo and Rodrigo arrived together in the same car, following the hearse up the cobblestone road to a flat hill overlooking the city. When they came to a stop near the burial plot, Rodrigo and Polo helped remove the casket. Rodrigo was startled by how light it was. She was so tiny. *Pinche* Regis.

About fifty people showed up for the burial: friends, colleagues, and some of her sources. Rodrigo noticed Regina's ex-boyfriend Alberto Morales in the crowd. He looked terribly shaken. Things between him and Regina had ended badly. *See what you did?* Rodrigo thought. *See what happened?*

Ángel ordered that no photographs be taken at the burial, but one photographer snapped Polo and Rodrigo carrying the casket. It was an image of his mentor Polo wished never had to exist. After setting the casket down, he moved off to the side.

Norma called him back. "Say goodbye to Regina," she said.

They each threw a handful of dirt on the casket, along with the other mourners. The ceremony was quick under the overcast sky. All around, the Mylar balloons and colorful pinwheels decorating the well-kept graves danced and whirred in the breeze.

Ángel had very few words: "She was very brave," he said. "She never gave in. And the only thing we can do now is let go."

There was a heartfelt round of applause, and it was over. Esperanza Morales, a journalist friend of Regina's who drove from the port to attend, noticed that the pinwheels on the other graves were spinning backward. In Veracruz lore, it meant the deceased was protesting, that the person had been stolen before her time.

★

THAT SAME DAY, Julio Scherer arrived to address a distraught staff in the newsroom of *Proceso*, housed in a low-slung white building on a short street in one of Mexico City's tidy middle-class neighborhoods. After updating the reporters, editors, and photographers on the meeting with Duarte and the news that *Proceso* would both be a party to the criminal investigation and continue its journalistic work on the case, Don Julio had a message for everyone gathered. They had taken a big hit, but there was one way to fight back: more journalism.

"Our therapy for our hyper-emotional state right now is work, as deeply, responsibly, and scrupulously as possible," he said.

Vicente Leñero, a well-known Mexican writer, *Proceso* cofounder, and another of Regina's idols, reinforced the notion of duty in the face of their own tragedy: "We journalists are not the protagonists of the story," he said. "We are its rapporteurs, plain and simple."

★

THE DAY AFTER the funeral, May 1, 2012, Labor Day, was a federal holiday in Mexico. For the third day in a row, crowds took to the streets of central Xalapa to protest Regina's killing—this time, the peasant and farmers groups she had covered so regularly, wearing all-white clothing and black awareness ribbons, carrying wide protest banners and bull-horns along the same route as the official Labor Day Parade.

Rodrigo Soberanes watched in anger over these two days as jour-nalists who had disparaged Regina, who had accepted bribes and written soft stories, now gave testimonies about her courage and valor and what a good friend she had been. Suddenly, everyone knew Regina. It was more than he could handle. He needed to get out. His uncle José Luis Soberanes, the former human rights ombudsman, urged him to come to Mexico City. José Luis was worried about his nephew's safety, and the best way they could talk frankly about what had happened would be in person. Rodrigo's phone was certain to be tapped, his uncle said.

José Luis made an appointment for Rodrigo to talk with a personal friend of his, who had worked in communications at the National Human Rights Commission and who was now serving in the same capacity for the federal attorney general's office. Perhaps he would have information about the case that could help Rodrigo evaluate the overall danger. The two met in the main justice department headquarters, a sleek high-rise on the Paseo de la Reforma, Mexico City's central promenade designed after the grand boulevards of Europe. Rodrigo expected a speculative conversation, like all the others he had had about the case. He wasn't prepared for what his uncle's friend was about to tell him.

"We're considering the Regina Martínez killing a political assassination," he told Rodrigo. "You could be in danger, too, so I suggest you stay here in Mexico City for a while."

CHAPTER 6

The Fab Four

May 2012

AFTER REGINA'S DEATH, Polo Hernández walked around in dark sunglasses for a time, to hide the tears that would spontaneously well in his eyes. He was a wiry man with a long face and a goatee, and when he first met Regina, in the early 2000s, he was already a true journalistic curmudgeon in the making. Even as a young man, he was cynical, with a quick wit he used to slice the nefarious characters he covered.

The son of a lawyer and a homemaker, Polo was born and raised in Córdoba, a colonial town in central Veracruz, where the snowcapped Pico de Orizaba hung like a masterpiece in the background and where much of the state's sugarcane and coffee were milled. While migration to Mexico City and the United States had significantly impacted the country's traditionally tight family culture, the bonds remained strong in Córdoba at the time Polo was coming up in the late 1980s and '90s. Everyone knew everyone, if they weren't already related, and everyone tended to stay close to home.

Polo grew up with people who would one day become his journalistic adversaries; none more than the future governor Javier Duarte, who went to the same school but was in a class with Polo's elder brother. The Duarte family owned a bakery, where Javier worked as a young teen hauling sacks of flour, helping the family survive after his father was killed in the 1985 Mexico City earthquake. The kids teased young Javier for being fat and ugly, giving him the nickname "Caremo," short for *Cara de moco*—or "Booger Face."

As the child of a family in Mexico's professional class, Polo Hernández went to the Universidad Popular Autónoma del Estado de Puebla, in the neighboring state, to study law. He went there for his parents and could not have cared less about practicing law. He wanted to be a writer. After he finished his undergraduate studies, he enrolled in the University of Veracruz in Xalapa for a master's in literature. He figured the easiest way to make money while in school was to get a job at the local newspaper. So, in 2003, he climbed the two flights of concrete stairs of the 1970s-era shopping complex in downtown Xalapa to the offices of *Política* and applied to be a news reporter. At the end of his first week, a diminutive woman walked into the newsroom and asked, "Which one is the new guy?"

Everyone pointed to Polo, a scraggly sight with a ponytail and Guatemalan patchwork pants.

Let's see what this guy has for a brain, Regina thought, and invited Polo to help her with a story. With his eager *yes*, she told him to show up at 7 A.M. on Saturday downstairs from the newspaper. Polo arrived early and waited alone. After a while, he called Regina.

"Where are you? I'm here already," he said.

"I'm on my way," she answered and arrived a short time later with wet hair, apologizing for being late. The fact that Polo had shown up to an assignment before her was the first step in welding their friendship.

The story they were covering was in Coatepec, a neighboring town where you can smell the coffee roasting as soon as you hit the outskirts. It was about farmers who were being forced to abandon their coffee plantations to plant sugarcane to survive, because the price of coffee had tanked. Sugarcane was dirtier, more difficult labor, and it wrought terrible havoc on the land. Among other things, it meant ripping out the shade trees planted to protect the coffee plants. The growers wanted to make money, but the fieldworkers were protesting the back-breaking work.

Polo immediately started scribbling in his notebook:

> Abandoning the benefits of coffee because of the terrible economic conditions of the producers . . . The environmental risk high . . . fields to sugarcane will deforest area, provoking climate changes, water and temperature cycles.

Regina wanted to see Polo's temperament, how he acted under the pressure of reporting a story. Polo loved the work, slogging through the hillside coffee plantations with his camera and notebook. She noticed that he didn't seem to be afraid of anything. Later that week, Polo, ponytail and all, appeared on camera with Regina to talk about the protests for *Política*'s weekly cable-access TV news show.

Until then, the dress code for journalists had been formal. Polo wore tennis shoes and had his shirttail out, but this never mattered to Regina. She always went to bat for him. This included the times he got fired from *Política* for his acerbic ways. Polo called Ricardo Gutiérrez, the newspaper owner's son and head of TV, an idiot. He refused to ask a question of Governor Fidel Herrera that he was under orders to ask. "Don't send me to ask your stupid questions," he told Gutiérrez. "Ask it yourself."

Regina, even with her own sharp tongue, had to teach her young charge office decorum. "Even if he is an imbecile," she said, "you can't say that *to the owner's son!*"

Polo also refused to cover an event sponsored by the newspaper for the society ladies of Xalapa. "I cover politics," he protested. "Send a society reporter."

Finally, Ricardo Gutiérrez had enough and told Polo to leave his camera and telephone and *Adios!*

Adios! Polo responded as he defiantly walked out the door.

Regina went into heavy negotiation mode. "Look, you don't ever have to get along with Polo again," she pledged to Ricardo. "You won't even have to deal with him. From now on, he'll be under my orders, but, please, let him come back."

Polo was surprised to hear from Regina a few days later. He had his job back.

By 2004, Regina had a loyal crew of seven novices on her team, just like Polo, a band of long-haired hippies with cameras roaming the halls of the congress among men in suits. It was something no one had ever seen before. The rest of the newsroom rejected this ragtag crew. With the Mexican penchant for nicknames, the other journalists dubbed them "Maldita Vecindad" (Bad Neighborhood), after a 1980s Mexican rock group. Or they were simply known as Regina's children. None of them realized, at least initially, that with them, she was in fact building her own circle of protection: colleagues she could trust.

Regina was the *maestra*, "the teacher," though she was subtle about it. Her lessons were in history and context over lunch at Los Alcatraces, just down the street from Parque Juárez, one of her favorite places to eat. The conversations were always about the news, what was happening. Regina never ordered her reporters or told them what to ask. Instead, she shared the vast amounts of background she had gathered in some twenty years of reporting. It allowed them to see what they were covering on a deeper level. She would put an issue on the restaurant table and ask, "What do you think?" The conversation took off from there. In the end, her "children" showed up to their interviews with better questions.

She was not so subtle when it came to editing their copy. Rodrigo said Polo got chewed out the worst for his stories, which Regina edited while muttering, *Pinche Polo!* Polo remembers it differently. He said Regina was hard on everyone. When they finished their stories, they had to print them out and leave copies with her. Then they had to wait until she was done with her own stories for their edits, sometimes sitting for hours when they wanted to go home. The pages came back looking like "graveyards," as Polo put it, with crosses everywhere.

Of all her "children," Polo was one of the three who became the most loyal, creating a bond that carried the two well beyond their years at *Política* and until her death. Another was Juan Pablo Romo, who grew up with Polo in Córdoba and followed him to study at UPAEP in Puebla. After Polo finished his law degree and headed to Xalapa to study literature, the younger Pablo followed suit. With one degree in communications, he decided to study fine arts and photography.

Pablo was small and wiry, like Polo, but with wild curly black hair, thick eyebrows, and dark Mediterranean looks thanks to his familial roots in Spain and Italy. Everyone called him "Eddie," a nickname he earned in childhood due to his strong resemblance to Eddie Munster in the dubbed reruns of *The Munsters* that aired on Mexican TV.

Eddie, despite his equally scraggly, hippie look, exuded a spirit entirely opposite to Polo's. He was easygoing, with a wide smile that won over just about everyone. A self-professed, self-effacing peacenik, he didn't thrive on butting heads with the power structure like the other of Regina's charges. He wasn't particularly enamored with journalism, but he needed some money. He saw the protests and political spats of the day as nothing more than a giant telenovela. He had a comical way of expressing it, casting himself as the reluctant "fraidy cat" in Regina's forays into the lion's den—like the time she asked him to swing by the office of the young legislator Miguel Ángel Yunes Márquez to pick up "something" for her. What he thought would be a piece of paper turned out to be a box of hundreds of documents holding evidence of alleged misspending by the governor's office. Eddie told the story years later, laughing yet wide-eyed, as if she had sent him unwittingly to pick up a load of dynamite.

In a way, she had.

Over time, the excitement of the telenovela hooked Eddie as well. He became a convert at Regina's knee, where she hammered him on integrity and ethics. The first time a source offered Eddie a bribe for favorable coverage, he rushed back to the newsroom to tell Regina.

"Write about it," she said. "Put it in the story."

"What?" Eddie protested, terrified of causing problems with the source for exposing an attempted bribe.

"Write it!" Regina ordered.

He pleaded, negotiated, and finally agreed, but he told her it would not be the first sentence in the story.

"That's fine, but put it in the story," she said.

He buried the bribe and survived without causing himself any trouble.

There were other incidents, which Eddie remembered without much humor. There was the time Regina introduced him around congress as the new reporter. Then-state representative Alejandro Montano approached Regina and greeted her with a hug. Eddie felt gooseflesh as he watched this encounter, unable to explain his negative reaction. Later, Regina told him, "Montano is bad news. Don't ever get mixed up with him."

Regina's other close protégé was Rodrigo Soberanes, the only one who showed up at the offices of *Política* with a longtime desire to be a journalist. Rodrigo had just graduated from the University of Veracruz, where he studied communications.

About the time Regina was assembling her team, Lev García showed up in Xalapa as the Veracruz correspondent for *Reforma*, a new Mexico City national newspaper claiming independent journalism, though its roots were in the conservative northern region of Mexico. It intentionally paid its journalists a professional wage and forbade them from collaborating with other organizations on the side, news or otherwise, to prevent the kind of corruption that traditionally seeped into the reporting ranks. It was the first Mexican newspaper to teach reporters ethics.

Regina and Lev first met at an anniversary party for *Proceso* when Lev also worked as a correspondent there. When she told him she came to the event to meet Julio Scherer, he responded, "I'm here to get drunk."

Stocky yet fit, with tight curly hair and a trimmed beard, Lev was a classic rogue. He dressed in Harley-Davidson T-shirts, rode motorcycles, and never had trouble attracting women. He grew up middle class in Mexico City, where many Communist and leftist families gave their children Russian names like "Lenin" or "Vladimir" or "Lev." But García was named not for the Bolshevik revolutionary Lev Kamanev, but rather for Lev Tolstoy, better known to the rest of the world as Leo. Lev's mother, a leftist but not a Communist, loved Russian literature.

During his young life, Lev was surrounded by two sisters, a brother, a stepdad who coached one of Mexico's professional baseball teams, and myriad rescue dogs.

When Lev graduated in communications from the Universidad Autónoma Metropolitana in Mexico City in 1995, the Zapatista war was at its height. Lev the idealist wanted to help. He loved his country and decided that joining a revolution would be the best way to save it from itself. Many Mexicans, particularly young people like him, were looking for their own way to partake in the demolition of the PRI. For Lev, it was to run off to Chiapas, Mexico's poorest state, where he imagined he could provide food, clothing, and other services to the front line. When he arrived, he learned the harsh lesson that all "white" Mexicans of European descent learn when deep in the Mayan region bordering Guatemala: To the indigenous who made up the Zapatistas, he was the oppressor. They called him *kaxlan,* or "outsider," a slur for "white" in the native Tzeltal language. His job was driving a bus to transport the Zapatista insurgents, and by the time he left, his nickname had changed to the more flattering "Zotz," or "Bat," a mystical creature in Mayan culture.

Seeing a revolution up front taught Lev another lesson, one that Salman Rushdie called "the tendency of revolutions to go wrong, to devour their children, to become the thing they had been created to destroy." The Zapatistas were not going to bring the kind of change Lev thought Mexico needed. He returned to Mexico City deciding that journalism would be his contribution to forging the new democracy.

Lev worked in several states and learned from the top reporters of the time. One mentor, Martín Morita, *Proceso*'s regional editor for the southern states, had worked many times with Regina. He helped Lev get his job with *Proceso.* Then, when Lev left *Proceso* for Veracruz and *Reforma,* Morita sent him with these instructions: "I want you to be the best reporter, the best drunk, and the best womanizer the state has ever seen. But whatever you do, you son of a bitch, don't mess in any way with Regina."

When Lev arrived in Xalapa in March 2003, his first stop was a visit to Regina. Her reputation as a daring reporter had already started to

spread. Lev and Regina recognized each other as the same kind of journalist. As Lev put it, "We were on the same train."

They met in the cantina of the Hotel Mexico, which faces the central
Plaza Lerdo and the cathedral, about a block from *Política*'s offices. Sitting
at one of the spare tables overshadowed by the large wooden bar, Regina
lit into Lev almost immediately for working for *Reforma*.

"Traitor," she said. "How could you leave *Proceso* for a right-wing
publication that doesn't even cover social issues?"

She was serious, he thought. But he found her generous and friendly
as she continued speaking: She offered him certain contacts and gave
him a lay of the land. "Look, this place has always been complicated
for anyone trying to be a journalist," she said. Of all the states where
Lev had worked as a reporter, "this one will be the most backward,"
Regina warned him. "I've gotten a lot of pressure in the last few years.
If you want to be a critical reporter, you're going to get doors slammed
in your face."

Lev sat silently as she spoke, absorbing, taking long drafts of his beer.
Hers—as he would notice over the many times they drank together—
remained nearly untouched. What she said that day would prove true
over the more than fifteen years he stayed and covered Veracruz.

Lev found Regina to be very acute in matters of politics and the state
legislature, as she was one of the rare human beings who found congress
interesting to cover. "Legislative power defines a state," she told him.
"It gives a society its moorings."

Lev didn't see her much that first year as he went to work building
his own sources and mapping out the state's underbelly. He was fascinated by organized crime, one of the reasons he wanted to come to
Veracruz as a journalist. It was the premier state for that. He considered organized crime one of the most efficient business models in the
world, and he never tired of studying it. Before long, he could recite
Veracruz's history and identify its important players, both out front and
behind the scenes, just as he could quote famous writers, from Ibargüengoitia to Kerouac, from his college days. He always carried a book or
two in his backpack, which he would readily pull out when he had the

slightest bit of downtime. He thought writing the truth could change his country. He thought he could make a difference.

Lev's renegade tendencies served him well as a reporter. He joined a motorcycle group in Xalapa and discovered it was filled with lawyers and government types who became his best sources. He also bought and ran two bars in town, one called El Conspirador—an appropriate name, he thought, for a bar where journalists went to drink. It occupied a squat white building on a small avenue of drinking and eating establishments just below Parque Juárez, called Allende Street, named for Ignacio Allende, one of the four original leaders, or conspirators, who started the war for Mexican independence from Spain in 1810. All four were eventually captured and executed. Outside, there was a sign with a large drawing of Ignacio Allende in his signature *chapeau de bras* military hat, surrounded by the Victoria beer logo.

The place looked small from the street but was cavernous inside, with a simple bar, wooden tables, and bare walls. A nook in the back known as "the Editing Room" was decorated with old typewriters, framed newspaper front pages, covers of *Proceso*, and a giant poster of Pancho Villa. Lev did interviews for his articles with a telephone in the crook of his neck, to free his hands for pouring beers from the tap and collecting payment. He said the bar, mixed with journalism, was what had turned his hair prematurely gray.

Lev entertained all the journalists and activists in town on weekends, except for Regina. As he put it, Regina didn't exist on weekends. She liked to stay home. Her disciples honored her strict personal boundaries and never saw her on those days, with the exception of Eddie Romo. Long after they both had left *Política*, Eddie rented a house a few doors from Regina's, and she would sometimes invite him and his girlfriend for a beer or a cup of coffee on the weekends when she saw them passing by. She'd tell them to move the stacks of folders and magazines on the chairs so they could sit down. If the weather was hot, they would pull chairs onto the patio and sit outside.

She talked about work or gossip from the political world, but in a much more relaxed, weekend kind of way, and they would laugh at the absurdity they were living. She always had something going at her desk in the living room, with two computers and the TV news droning overhead. (Eddie went into Regina's kitchen only once, to get coffee. His girlfriend used the bathroom once and commented how nice it was, with decorative stones in the tile work.) Eddie would laugh to himself that she couldn't let it go, even in her downtime, and thought, *Geez, it's not that important. Who cares about these people?*

During the week, Eddie would stop and let out a whistle if Regina's front door was open. She often left it ajar if she was working in the living room, but the white iron gate surrounding the property always remained locked. Eddie reported in those days for the local news service E-consulta Veracruz, which Rodrigo Soberanes ran from his office in the port city. Eddie would offer Regina the interviews and quotes he had collected that day for the wire, in case they were relevant to whatever she was working on for *Proceso*. She would say "yay" or "nay" as he ran down the list of news items, sometime rejecting all of them outright by declaring *Todos son pendejos!* "They're all assholes." But more times than not, Eddie would arrive home to a phone call from Regina, who had realized during his short walk from her house that she needed a quote or piece of audio after all.

Like Lev, Eddie said he never thought he was competing with Regina. This camaraderie extended throughout the group. I asked Rodrigo Soberanes one time why the bond among them remained so strong long after Regina's death.

"We were all Regina-ized," he said, laughing. "*La chaparrita* cast a very long shadow."

I asked him what that meant.

"If we had met each other under other circumstances, we probably wouldn't have become such good friends," he said. "We got to know each other in a context where trust was very important. She shared with us—me, Polo, and Eddie—the incidents that made her so distrustful. Lev had a lot of the same experiences. If Regina trusted the other three, I knew without a doubt that I could as well . . . That, and we all liked to drink a lot of beer."

Of all her "children," Polo was the one who stuck by her the most. Eddie said she had a special bond with Polo, which included her being the hardest on his copy, because she saw the most talent in him. Polo and Regina met so regularly that her women friends teased her suggestively about their relationship. But it was nothing like that. To him, she always remained the *maestra*. He had never even seen the inside of her house. The one time she invited him in for coffee, he politely declined, feeling too intimidated. His reverence for her was that complete.

This was why, in the days after her killing, there was no one more shocked than Polo to learn that investigators were homing in on *him* as the suspect.

CHAPTER 7

Case Closed

April 2012

IN JANUARY 1996, REGINA covered the political fallout surrounding the arrest of drug capo Juan García Abrego, onetime leader of the Gulf Cartel, now serving eleven consecutive life terms in a federal prison in West Virginia. An opposition politician who she interviewed, Fidel Robles Guadarrama, accused the Mexican government of whisking García Abrego off to the United States in a rapid extradition, thus avoiding any need to investigate his ties to top Mexican politicians, including the Veracruz governor Patricio Chirinos. The state representative called it "decomposition of the state, impunity, and an arbitrary manner for applying the law," Regina wrote in a front-page article.

Despite the passing of sixteen years and major changes in Mexico's political system, Robles Guadarrama could easily have made the same statement when the state prosecutor's office and forensic investigators entered Regina's home, allegedly to solve her murder. Even though "democracy" had come to Mexico, there had been little change to the institutions needed to support a democratic country. They were still designed and operated, despite the overthrow of the PRI, as mechanisms to keep the ruling party in power. Nowhere was that truer than in the state and federal prosecutors' offices. The justice system, in particular, was used more to vanquish enemies and bury political problems, like embarrassing cases, than to solve crimes. In this context, any kind of government investigation was not meant to find justice, but rather, to make the hubbub go away.

Mexican president Felipe Calderón managed to get a judicial reform passed in 2008 that was moving slowly and reluctantly. Investigators had received mounds of training in forensics and evidence collection, a lot of it paid for by the U.S. government through the embassy. They lifted fingerprints and took DNA samples and detailed every inch of a crime scene. But there seemed to be no awareness that the information collected was meant to build a case. The preferred investigative tool for nailing a suspect continued to be torture. Prosecutors' cases rarely correlated with the scientific evidence. It was much easier to resort to the old method of concocting a version of what happened and then beating someone into admitting to it, whether they had done it or not. There was one catch: With the justice reform, confessions extracted under torture were no longer admissible in court, and judges were now forced to throw out substantial numbers of cases. Suspects were let go if they could prove they had been beaten, or worse, into giving confessions.

The other main tool for prosecuting a criminal case in Mexico was what the magazine *Horizontal* called "the crime of being a victim": "They are impugned for their own misfortune, for walking alone at night, wearing a miniskirt, hanging out with questionable characters, consuming alcohol or drugs or both." Part of building a criminal case in the Mexican court system was proving that the victim had been complicit in their own fate. That way, there would be little outrage when they didn't receive justice.

Such was the case on the evening of April 28, 2012, when investigators began their work at Calle Privada Rodríguez Clara No. 208, where a dead woman was stretched out on the bathroom floor. They carefully documented the scene, measuring the dimensions of every room and every detail regarding the location of the body, which was lying "northwest to southeast with the cephalic region [the head] touching the bathtub." Her face pointed southeast. They documented the sofa and chairs stacked with books, papers, and reporter's notebooks and the packing boxes for a Toshiba computer and an LG flat-screen monitor. Shelves were stuffed with books, magazines, audio cassettes, and CDs, as was the victim's desk, which also held her appointment calendars and a printer. There was a cup of liquid that appeared to be coffee. Another bookshelf was stacked with more papers, magazines, a DVD player, and an Apple iBook. There was a dust mark and dangling cables indicating that a TV had once sat atop another set of shelves. Under one of the side tables in the kitchen were a five-gallon water jug, cleaning liquids, and bottles of soda and beer, full and unopened. There was food on the counter, and the coffee maker was still on. In the bedroom were more books, videocassettes, and CDs; a television on the bureau; and two music players. Regina's purse still contained her bank cards. In the bathroom, clothes were soaking in two buckets, and a third contained water and a rag. There were signs that Regina had put up a fight, judging from the bruises on her torso and arms, and that the attack took place in the bathroom, because objects on her bedroom dresser remained undisturbed. There was an empty Modelo beer bottle in the bedroom but no mention, in the first sweep, of other beer bottles.

Two days later, Laura Borbolla, the federal attorney general's special prosecutor for crimes against journalists, came to Xalapa. Impeccably dressed and tall in her platform heels, Borbolla spoke rapidly and knew the law like a professor. She had a charisma that made journalists feel like she was sympathetic to their plight. But getting results was another matter, and for that reason, they dubbed her one of the *menos peor*, or "less bad," as Mexican prosecutors went. Most Mexican bureaucrats, particularly in the attorney general's office, spent much of their energy explaining all the things that kept them from doing their jobs. Laura Borbolla adhered to that as well: not enough investigators, not enough money, not enough training or institutional support to go against organized crime forces, which paid top dollar for the best attorneys. She wasn't wrong. And she at least tried. She knew the journalists personally and attended events to support them. In the case of Regina Martínez,

Borbolla had no trouble suspecting the killing was related to Regina's work.

She showed up at the crime scene to determine if the case qualified as one the special prosecutor should take on. Under the law at the time, the state was charged with prosecuting common crimes such as robbery and murder, while a federal prosecutor could file a separate case under the statute that made attacks on journalists a federal crime. Then the two agencies did their investigations in conjunction with each other.

When Borbolla entered Regina's house, she encountered a crime scene that could only be described as a mess. There were several empty beer bottles, and someone had fingerprint-dusted them so heavily that they destroyed any potential saliva samples that could have yielded DNA. Borbolla's investigators found a blood sample on the toilet that the state had missed entirely. The food on the stove and the laundry soaking in the bucket had not been tested for anything. The forensics team from the state botched the fingerprint collection, producing only partial prints that were not good enough to make matches in the federal database. Only one print from the entire house was usable. It matched no one on file.

The same day she arrived, before any evidence had been analyzed, State Prosecutor Amadeo Flores Espinosa announced that the likely motive was robbery, because a laptop, a flat-screen TV, telephones, and personal items were missing. Leaks started to appear in the local and national press, the ones I had read, about Regina having known the killers and partied with them until late into the night. In a meeting with state prosecutor Flores, Borbolla asked for evidence and forensics collected in the case. One thing was immediately clear: They had no intention of giving it up.

She hesitated to say publicly whether the lack of cooperation was due to bureaucracy or a cover-up. Privately, she had seen a lot of corruption in the prosecution ranks. The federal attorney general had representatives in every state. But in matters of attacks on journalists, Borbolla found that they were so tightly tied to the state authorities that her own colleagues were undermining her investigations. This was definitely true in Veracruz. She told me of one case she handled there regarding a nonfatal attack on a journalist. When her investigator showed up, the state secretary for public security, Arturo Bermúdez, sat him down and said, "How can we resolve this?" The top cop in Veracruz, charged with maintaining law and order, was asking the federal attorney general's representative how much money it would take to make the complaint go away.

A day or two after Borbolla, Jorge Carrasco, *Proceso*'s reporter on the case, showed up. Like Regina, Jorge had devoted all his adult life to journalism—investigating, traveling to the most delicate corners of the country, and holding government officials to account. He had developed a reputation for being professional and meticulous. And he built himself into an expert on security—the number one issue under President Felipe Calderón—with exceptional sources in the government, military, and those who operated on the edges as informants.

He had been at home with his partner, fellow journalist Peniley Ramírez, and their five-month-old son, putting photographs in an album, when he got the phone call that late April afternoon. *Proceso* assistant director Salvador Corro asked if he could confirm reports that Regina was found dead. The whole *Proceso* staff was on it. Peniley had worked as a journalist in Veracruz and had a number for the governor's spokeswoman, Gina Domínguez. Gina answered right away and said it was true, that it had happened the night before, and the method was very violent. Jorge was the first to confirm Regina's murder for *Proceso*. From that moment, according to journalistic tradition, it was his story.

Jorge saw the same mess as Laura did. It was like trying to find the truth in a thick cloud, and the local press was part of the fog machine spewing speculation by the day. As he started his work in Veracruz, reporters came around unsolicited to tell him things, anecdotes that supported the official version, gossip about Regina. Walter Ramírez was one. Alberto "El Gato" Morales, Regina's former boyfriend, was another. Jorge sensed they were lying, either because they wanted to be part of the story or because the government had sent them to confuse him. He never knew for sure.

This case is going to be very difficult to clarify, Jorge thought. *Why don't they want to give any information?*

He had no evidence that state authorities were involved, but their behavior made him suspicious. They gave the same message the governor had when he received *Proceso*'s top editors: The state had all the authority and would be totally in control of what happened to the case.

There was something else complicating Jorge's reporting on Regina's assassination. *Proceso* was a party to the state's criminal complaint. In an inexplicable move, director Rafael Rodríguez made Jorge the magazine's legal representative on the case at the same time that he was assigned to cover it. It was a mystery why Rodríguez didn't see the blatant conflict in a reporter covering a case to which he was also a party. There was never an explanation, leaving me to think of the old saying that doctors make the worst patients. Media editors make the worst news subjects. They don't know what to do when they become the story. I had seen it many times in the news organizations where I had worked in the United States.

Jorge didn't protest, because that just wasn't his style. He was a team player. The conflict put him in the situation of having access to all the court files, but being prohibited by law from reporting on them. Everything about criminal cases at that time in Mexico were private until a verdict was rendered, and to publish details was to break the law. Ever the responsible reporter, Jorge wrote around the edges of the details. He wanted to make sure not to do anything that would give the state the ability to blame *Proceso* for ruining the case. He recognized that it would be too easy an opportunity for a state prosecutor's office already looking for a quick way to end the whole uncomfortable mess.

As the case representative, Jorge gave the investigators information and tried to get them to pursue certain angles related to Regina's work. They ignored him entirely. Instead, they focused on depositions from Regina's friends, including Rodrigo Soberanes, Lupita López, and Norma Trujillo. The interviews were aggressive, focusing on Regina's personal life and habits. They asked some of her colleagues to submit fingerprints. Mariela San Martín, the seamstress, told a friend that she was scared. She had been inside Regina's house to measure for curtains. They could find her fingerprints.

Investigators asked Regina's friends and acquaintances if she had ever been threatened, and people said no. With that one question, they put the subject of her work aside and drilled into her personal life.

Word about the aggressive depositions got out, and reporters who knew Regina started to take lawyers along with them to their interviews. Attorney Claribel Guevara accompanied Norma Trujillo. The questions focused on what Regina did in her spare time, what she did for entertainment. The line of questioning immediately struck Guevara as peculiar. It seemed designed to divert the entire investigation away from all the articles Regina had published that made her "uncomfortable" to authorities. The questions came with a lot of bias and pressure: What places did she frequent in her spare time? What alcoholic drinks did she like? What did she talk about? They asked Lupita López if Regina had used marijuana or other drugs and what her house smelled like. Lupita was puzzled. "There was no particular smell," she answered. "Or maybe like coffee, if she made coffee."

"Are you sure she didn't go out drinking at night?" the investigators insisted. "Are you sure she didn't drink at home?"

They pressed Lupita to think twice or three times about her answers, to reconsider everything she said, to doubt herself to the point of confirming their version of the facts. Lupita held firm. She and Regina didn't socialize, Lupita insisted, and when they did meet, the topic of discussion was the news.

The questioning effectively intimidated a group of people already terrorized and uncertain about what was going on around them. The journalists were asked for personal information—their home addresses, marital status, the names of their parents and children—information that could be used to make them targets as well. They left the depositions feeling more like suspects than witnesses.

Claribel Guevara became incensed and called a press conference to publicly decry the interview tactics. The state attorney general's office was running in circles with its investigation and deposing only other reporters, she said. The reporters were complaining about the long hours of interrogation and the unorthodox methods they endured.

★

WITH FOUR JOURNALISTS dead in a week, *Reforma* pulled Lev García out of Veracruz for security, but not before the governor, Javier Duarte, sent word that he wanted to speak to him. Lev didn't want to go. He was a little scared and angry, not only at the crime, but also at the fact that whenever a reporter wanted to speak to the governor, they were ignored. He wanted to ignore Duarte in return. He consulted with his editors in Mexico City, and they told him to go.

The two met later that day in Casa Veracruz. Duarte greeted Lev with a hug and invited him to sit down. Lev maintained a professional demeanor and the polite behavior that is the Mexican custom, even when dealing with your enemies.

Duarte went straight to the point: "I had nothing to do with what happened to Regina," he said. "I'm the person who is most concerned that nothing happens to journalists. Not a single one. How would I benefit from such violence?"

"I'm not the person you should be talking to," Lev answered. "The way you've run your government and the bad policies of the communications office make it very difficult for people to believe you.

"I believe you," he continued, lying, "but there are many who don't because you've hidden a lot of information."

Shortly after, Lev left town.

But there was one journalist who refused to leave Xalapa: Polo Hernández. His editor at Notimex asked him to go to Mexico City, also for security, but Polo was angry, and he wasn't going to let anyone drive him out without knowing what had happened to Regina.

People around Polo were starting to worry because he questioned the government's role the night of Regina's murder. And investigators were looking for an easy target. The narrative was emerging: Regina was killed by someone she knew, perhaps even a boyfriend. All the witnesses were asked what they knew about Polo.

Walter Ramírez seemed happy to keep reinforcing the state's story line that Regina had been killed by a lover. In fact, he testified that a friend told him that she was dating Polo. Walter also testified that he too was intimate with Regina for a time in 1996 and knew all her routines. He said he would go to her house for dinner and talk, get really drunk, and sometimes dance salsa—providing a narrative that would strangely mirror the state's reconstruction of what happened the night of her death.

This made a lot of Regina's friends angry, and many refused to speak to Ramírez. To them, he was spreading malicious gossip to help the cover-up. There were rumors that he was going to publicly call for Polo's arrest. Claribel Guevara also could tell from the line of questioning by the state that they were gunning for Polo, and she sent him a warning. His editors at Notimex found a way to lure him to Mexico City under the guise of a workshop he was required to attend. Once he got there, they forbade him from returning to Veracruz. He was in Mexico City when word came that he was the target of the state's investigation.

Polo phoned Article 19, a free-speech advocacy organization that worked on behalf of reporters, and the Committee to Protect Journalists, where Mexico representative Mike O'Connor chalked out a defense plan. O'Connor, a veteran war correspondent and classic curmudgeon, found a perfect fit as the CPJ's advocate for Mexican journalists and freedom of expression. Tall and white-haired, with a gravelly voice from years of smokes and drinks, O'Connor was fierce, funny, and irreverent. He wasn't afraid to talk back to powerful people, a total violation of protocol in Mexico. The Mexican correspondents loved him so much that they jokingly referred to him as their dad.

O'Connor realized immediately that if Polo returned to Xalapa, he would be arrested. Once that happened, they would have no control over his fate. So O'Connor did what he always did in these cases: He made a lot of noise, let the Mexican federal government know that an American, backed by a large American NGO, was watching. Because of the threat of the investigators in Veracruz, Polo was put into the federal protection program for journalists that O'Connor and CPJ had pressured President Calderón to expand just two years earlier. Through several emissaries and conversations, O'Connor and the representatives at Article 19 convinced Veracruz authorities to let Polo be deposed in Mexico City by federal agents.

A few days before the deposition, authorities leaked to friendly media outlets that they had identified Regina's killer and that it was a crime of passion. The local newspaper *Imagen del Golfo* reported that the autopsy revealed a bite on the victim's neck, allowing investigators to make a match with the perpetrator. "With this forensic evidence, they established that it had to do with a crime of passion or 'personal motivations,'" the newspaper reported.

Carlos Loret de Mola, a high-profile Televisa news anchor who was often leaked official information, wrote in his weekly newspaper column that the Regina Martínez case was about to be solved—and that the outcome would generate a lot of controversy. Though he didn't print the name outright, his sources indicated that they were closing in on a suspect and that it was fellow journalist.

Per the state's instructions, federal agents ordered a mold of Polo's teeth, to see if it matched the "love bite," and prints of his shoes for a match with a bloody shoe print found in Regina's bathroom. In the end, they couldn't beat Polo's alibi. He had ATM receipts, phone records, and dozens of witnesses from a wedding who could say he was in Córdoba, a three-hour drive from Xalapa, during the period from when Regina was last seen closing her gate to the hour she was found dead. After the deposition, Polo returned quickly to Xalapa to collect a few things from his apartment with his beloved terrace and never returned. Years later, he still called it the best apartment he ever had in his life.

With the elimination of Polo as a suspect, investigators had to move on, though they continued to posit that the killing was related to Regina's personal life. Other witnesses testified that Regina had beer bashes. A handyman she had hired to do odd jobs told investigators he bought her ten-quart beer bottles every week for the parties she threw on Thursday nights. He said she complained about how her journalist friends would never spring for beer. On Saturdays, he would return the empties and bring her another ten full bottles.

Investigators drew up a victim profile, writing that Regina was very private and told her neighbor Isabel Nuñez that a lot of people didn't like her because of the stories she wrote. The report said that just before her death, she experienced a mood change "to a state happier and more enthusiastic . . . from some outside source, perhaps the start of a new relationship or meeting someone who was very important to her." The report went on to say that investigators had found the "following psychological evidence" in her home: soaps to eliminate cellulite and age spots and a variety of almost-new high heels. Regina also had hired some workers to remodel her house and get rid of the mold stains on her walls.

With the failure to pin the murder on Polo Hernández, a star witness appeared, coincidentally. And he had tales of another alleged boyfriend. His name was Diego Hernández Villa, and he was a known drunk who hung out at his mother-in-law's house, around the corner from Regina's, often sitting on the concrete steps leading out of the neighborhood canyon to drink beer or *caña*, cheap alcohol from fermented sugarcane.

Diego Hernández told investigators that he had recently run into an old drinking buddy, a man nicknamed "La Bola," who was about fifty years old, with straight hair slicked back with gel and cheeks puffy from excessive alcohol. La Bola worked as a shoeshine and a carpenter and lived in a shack on a vacant lot nearby, with an old mattress on the floor. He liked to sing. The previous time Hernández had seen him, La Bola asked if he had any marijuana. But now, Diego noticed that La Bola was cleaned up and well dressed. Diego testified that there was no alcohol on his breath and that La Bola told him that he had made a turnaround because he had a girlfriend, a reporter who lived near Diego's mother-in-law.

Diego Hernández Villa went on from there. He said that as he sat drinking on the concrete stairs the night Regina was killed, he saw a man pass by who he knew as "El Jarocho," a stocky five-foot-three sex worker with straight hair and tattoos covering his forearms, who he guessed was about twenty-eight years old. Diego knew him from Jarocho's wife, who ran a cigarette and candy stand at night in downtown Xalapa. El Jarocho slept during the day and worked all night, turning tricks in Parque Juárez and often robbing his male clients of their cell phones, watches, and other small items. He was violent, Diego said. One time when they were drinking, Jarocho showed Diego the knife he used to commit his robberies.

On the night of the murder, Jarocho was with another man of similar build and look, but Diego didn't know him, only that he was known as "El Silva." Diego said El Silva hadn't been in the neighborhood long and had the markings on his arms of a *pepenador*, a person who collects and sells trash. This man also had recently been let out of prison. There was a third man with them, who Diego knew as "Paleta Payaso." At times, Diego would go drinking with them, he said, but that night, the three men kept walking and didn't speak to him. They headed in the direction of Regina's house. He guessed this was around nine thirty or ten at night.

Investigators hauled in La Bola, but he, too, had an alibi: his actual girlfriend and his brother. He said he went shopping in the afternoon that day, then went home to a room he had in his brother's house, and stayed all night and the next day. It was his birthday, he said, and he stayed inside to avoid the temptation to drink. He told authorities he vaguely knew Diego Hernández—but only by his first name and only enough to say hello on the street. He said he didn't know Regina; nor had he ever been inside her house.

So, they started to focus on the other men that Diego said he saw near her house that night. In October 2012, the state attorney general announced a surprise breakthrough: A suspect was in custody. Jorge Antonio Hernández Silva, aka El Silva, had confessed to being in the house the night Regina was killed.

El Silva was a petty criminal who lived on the streets and turned tricks for a living.

According to El Silva, Regina's love interest was El Jarocho, the sex worker and street criminal. Jarocho had met Regina in a bar and started a relationship with her, according to El Silva. He planned to go to her house that night to rob her. The two arrived at Regina's house at around 10 P.M., and Jarocho threw rocks at her window from outside the iron gate. She appeared at the door in a bathrobe and asked them to wait a few minutes while she changed. She later appeared in jeans and a floral blouse to let them in. Jarocho greeted her with a kiss on the cheek. He asked her to get some beer, so she left the two in her house to go to the corner store, locking the door behind her. (The suspect testimony and the investigators' version of what happened failed to address the fact that forensic investigators found two unopened quart bottles of beer under Regina's kitchen table, indicating that if her guests wanted beer, she already had some on hand.) Once she "left to buy beer," the testimony said, Jarocho started rifling through the drawers in her bedroom, looking for valuables. Regina returned about thirty minutes later with quart bottles of beer. Jarocho opened the beers and handed each a bottle. Then he asked Regina to put on some music, and the two began to dance.

"Why haven't I heard from you? Why haven't you come to see me?" Regina asked Jarocho as they danced. They retreated to the bedroom, where they began to argue. Jarocho grabbed her. Regina broke away and ran to the kitchen for a knife. When Jarocho tried to grab her again, she slashed him in the arm. He pulled a pillow off the bed in self-defense and knocked the knife to the floor. Then he pinned Regina's arms behind her back while El Silva punched her three times in the ribs and stomach, El Silva testified.

"Where's the money? Where's the money?" Jarocho shouted as his arm bled. He grabbed a rag and pulled it around Regina's neck. "Where's the money? Where's the money?" He tightened his grip. Then he took a set of brass knuckles from his pocket and punched her in the jaw. Regina struggled to fight back and loosen the rag around her neck. Jarocho dragged her into the bathroom, knelt by the toilet, and dunked her head several times in the bowl.

"Are you going to tell me where the money is?"

"It's under the mattress," Regina gasped.

El Silva lifted the mattress and took out a wad of bills. "I found it," he told Jarocho, who continued to tighten the rag around Regina's neck. Once she stopped moving, he took the rag and tried to clean the blood on the floor from his arm and from the blow he delivered to her face.

Then he tossed the bloody rag over her head, leaving her faceup on the bathroom floor. Jarocho then ran to the kitchen for a black garbage bag, and he and El Silva loaded the flat-screen TV into it. They filled another bag with other electronics and cell phones and then left the house. When authorities picked up El Silva six months later, he still had Regina's wristwatch and cell phones. The other items had been hocked for money.

Regina's killing was a crime of passion *and* a robbery, the authorities concluded.

There were major problems with the state's case, however. As soon as El Silva got before a judge, he said he had been tortured into confessing. He was abducted by several men who he believed were members of the AVI, the Veracruz Investigations Agency, and held for a week in what they ironically called a "safe house," he testified. He was beaten, waterboarded, given electric shocks, and threatened. He signed his confession with a fingerprint, because he couldn't read or write. They said if he didn't sign it, they would kill Theresa, the woman he called Mom, who cared for him when he was young and living on the streets.

El Silva told the judge that he was nowhere near Regina's house the night before her murder and had nothing to do with the crime. María del Rosario Morales Zárate, El Silva's sister who had a son with El Jarocho, testified to Laura Borbolla's federal investigators that she, too, had been abducted by strange men, along with her five-year-old son. She told a story very similar to El Silva's, saying she was held for a few days in a safe house and threatened. They said they would take her son away if she didn't agree to testify that Jarocho had confessed to the murder.

There were also major problems with the testimony of Diego Hernández, the star witness, something I wouldn't discover until years later.

Jorge Carrasco watched the staging of this fictional play with a personal sense of rage. He knew Regina. He knew every turn in the case. He knew that authorities had concocted a lie. Reporting on it had been particularly difficult. The entire apparatus of the state was against him. Anytime Jorge interviewed anyone on the case, he had the sensation that he really didn't know who he was talking to. Who were they working for? On whose behalf? But there was little he could do. He was a plaintiff in the case.

His hands were tied.

★

ABOUT THE TIME the Regina Martínez case was being wrapped up, at least according to authorities, Mike O'Connor from the CPJ told me he knew a reporter who was looking for work in Veracruz. I needed a reporter there, as our former correspondent was still too terrified to cover anything but hurricanes. I knew if O'Connor recommended him, he would be good. I made an appointment to meet him. He came in my office and sat on the saggy brown futon I had inherited—I'd been unable to convince the Associated Press that I needed new furniture—and talked against the full-length window overlooking the Angel of Independence monument, one of the most iconic views in Mexico City.

The reporter said he had fled Veracruz because of the violence there and had spent a year in self-exile in Mexico City. Now he wanted to go back home, and he was looking for a way to earn money as a journalist. I hired him on the spot. Then I asked him if he knew anything about the Regina Martínez case.

"She was a good friend of mine," the reporter said.

I was excited to learn this. "What happened?" I asked. "Who killed her?"

"The government," he said.

I was taken aback. In all the drug violence and cartel wars, it hadn't occurred to me that the state could be behind some of these journalist assassinations. "How do you know?" I asked.

"We can't prove it," he said. "We just know."

There is nothing more tantalizing to a journalist than the words "we can't prove it." From that moment, I wanted to find out what really happened to Regina Martínez.

The reporter's name was Rodrigo Soberanes.

PART II

CHAPTER 8

The Young Radicals

Sometime between 1956 and 1963

A T THE TIME Regina Martínez was born, Mexico was living a period of great modern prosperity and growth, often referred to as the "Mexican Miracle." Though the PRI still draped itself in the banner of the Mexican Revolution, it had turned the corner from being the party of workers' and land rights to being the bureaucratic and oligarchic machine that would rule the country for four more decades. Starting in the 1940s, the postrevolutionary presidents—two from Veracruz—pushed industrialization, urbanization, and economic expansion. Metastasizing cities, high-rise buildings, grand public works projects, and manufacturing marked a thriving Mexico when on September 7, 1963, Regina arrived, the third of nine children. At least that was the birthdate on her tombstone. There was evidence that she was born years earlier, probably more like 1957.

On one of my first trips to Xalapa, Lev García wanted me to see the place where Regina was born, and he drove me to Rafael Lucio, about eight miles outside of town. Rafael Lucio, which dated back to 1586, was officially incorporated by a Spanish viceroy as San Miguel del Soldado in 1735. Then, in 1932, it became a municipality named for a famous nineteenth-century Xalapa physician, Rafael Lucio Nájera, who had treated presidents and isolated a particular form of leprosy.

Rafael Lucio was the unpolished and unromantic Mexico, the neoclassical town palace without the bas-relief, the basilica with faux adornments stamped out of stucco, and weeds pushing through the cracks of the town square made from concrete, not cobblestone. The "social network" of the day still stands, a covered brick gazebo at the center of town, protecting a collection of concrete laundry sinks from the midday sun. The women gathered to scrub their clothes and gossip at the sinks, which drain into the same water trough.

The story goes that from Rafael Lucio, the Martínez family moved about 150 miles north, to Gutiérrez Zamora, a city of about 24,000 people set amid the lush, humid flatlands near the mouth of the Teco-lutla River, which empties into the Gulf of Mexico. It is the center of the Totonacapan region, named for the indigenous Totonac people who Cortés encountered when he landed there in 1519, and near Papantla, where he came upon the vanilla plant and eventually exported an exotic flavor previously unknown to the rest of the world. Regina's maternal grandmother was from Gutiérrez Zamora and didn't speak Spanish, only Totonac. The town resembled Rafael Lucio, with the identical city hall and provincial feel.

The only issue with Lev's tour was that Regina wasn't born in Rafael Lucio, and she hadn't grown up in Gutiérrez Zamora. She made up the entire story, including her birth date, as an adult—as a journalist, more specifically. That way, no one could go looking for her family as a way to get at her. The only thing true about her early biography is that she was born in a small city, a little larger than Gutiérrez Zamora, in the Sierra Madre Occidental, like Rafael Lucio. She spent her entire child-hood in the same place, in a spare one-room house built by her father. It wasn't in Veracruz.

Yet Veracruz still had an influence on the family, as Veracruzano Adolfo Ruiz Cortines was president around Regina's more likely date of birth and practiced a brand of control on dissidents and the press that she would know well one day. Ruiz Cortines was followed by Adolfo López Mateos, president from 1958 to 1964, a popular orator who completed the party's transition from its revolutionary roots. Under López Mateos, the PRI vanquished both the Communist opposition and the labor agitators after a massive railroad strike during his term paralyzed the country. Teachers and oil workers also took their turns in the streets, but the PRI responded with clubs and torture (killing at least one union leader) and appointed people to top union positions who would keep workers in line.

As was its hallmark, the PRI ruled by both carrot *and* stick. Alongside sending the army to bust up strikes, or assassinating activists like peasant leader Rubén Jaramillo and his family, the PRI built roads and bridges, improved public education, and increased wages and health benefits—particularly for state workers.

(One time, I was traveling a spectacular stretch of road in an isolated part of Sinaloa state when we came upon a treacherous mountain pass famously known as the Devil's Backbone, a nine-thousand-foot elevation with a severe drop on either side of the road. At a scenic overlook nearby was an enormous stone billboard, in the middle of nowhere, thanking López Mateos, who was president when the road was completed in 1960, because he GAVE IT IN SERVICE TO THE PEOPLE. Before the road was built, residents of the tiny villages had traversed the area on donkeys. Such was the reach of the public relations machine of the 1950s PRI—advertising in the remotest of mountain passes.)

Diseases like typhus and smallpox were eradicated. There was a growing middle class. And López Mateos, who loved to travel, touted Mexico around the world as a country emerging from decades of provincial protectionism after so many invasions from abroad. With the dark curly hair and good looks of his famous countryman, actor Anthony Quinn, López Mateos was also a consummate womanizer. His staff joked that he woke every day asking, *Que hacemos hoy, viaje o vieja?* which translates roughly to "What do I want today, a trip or a woman?" He would become the role model for a future PRI president and fellow womanizer, Enrique Peña Nieto, whose campaign Regina would cover a half century later.

But beneath the relative calm and prosperity of the López Mateos administration were the rumblings of a coming tectonic shift: the country's quest for civil and human rights, and for freedom from the yoke of autocracy. Under López Mateos, Mexico saw the beginnings of opposition political candidates from *within* the PRI. Student uprisings were bubbling a full five years before the 1968 army massacre of untold numbers of pro-democracy demonstrators at the Plaza Tlatelolco in Mexico City, one of a handful of key events that set Mexico squarely on the path to overthrowing the PRI.

Regina would be defined by, and a chronicler of, this dramatic shift.

Despite what presidents did on the national or international stage, the Martínez family, like most Mexicans, lived in a conservative society closed off from the rest of the world in the 1960s. It would be another thirty-plus years before the North American Free Trade Agreement flooded Mexico with electronics, washing machines, and many of the cheap products you could find in the average Walmart in the United States—not to mention Walmart itself, now one of the country's biggest employers. Back then, even in the towns away from the ranchos, life was without conveniences and days were filled with manual labor. Everyone had to pitched in.

The Martínez children learned austerity, a trait Regina mimicked in adulthood. (She lived frugally, didn't own a car, but saved a lot of money. Even on her small salary, she died owning her modest bungalow and leaving a generous bank account.) Money was scarce when she was growing up; sometimes food as well, though the family always had at least a pot of beans, fresh tortillas, and coffee, lots of coffee, which was like milk for the children. The Martínez clan had to work from an early age, the boys selling gum or delivering shoes for the cobbler and the girls taking jobs in the local shops. The older siblings cared for the younger ones. The babies followed Regina around, and she relished being their protector. Those who failed to comply with the house rules had to reckon with the stern Florencio, who never liked seeing his children playing or at rest. They always had to be working.

But the nine siblings, each a year apart, found plenty of opportunities for play, especially in sports. The tiny Regina turned out to be particularly talented at basketball, able to slip among the taller kids without detection to make her shots. She wanted to be a journalist from the time she was young. When she was a teenager, she led her siblings in making their own newspaper, *El Diario*, which was printed at a local press where her older brother worked. Each sibling had a job: One was in charge of the *nota roja*, "police report"; another, the society page; and all of them sold copies on the street. The editor in chief, of course, was Regina. Later she worked at a local radio station, reading horoscopes on the air as *La Chica de las Estrellas*, "The Girl of the Stars."

From her father, Regina got her long upper lip, her strict manner, and her strong opinions. Florencio taught his children honor and ethics, never taking a handout from anyone, even if it would help the family. He was a chauffeur for the Puebla politician Manuel Ávila Camacho, who then invited the young man to come to Mexico City as his driver when he was president of Mexico in the 1940s. Florencio turned him down. Instead, Ávila Camacho got his beloved employee work as a driver for a regional director of the bank Banamex. At a time before armored trucks, Florencio transported money, and there was never a peso missing. Regina once told a friend that it was a testament to her father's honesty that he made it to his retirement. Bank employees often were let go for stealing. These were lessons that grounded Regina in her life and her journalism, where she worked long hours and rejected bribes.

From her mother, Regina got her heavy eyelids, her smile, and a regard for those in need. No matter how little the Martínez family had, her mother taught them to share with those who had even less, another trait Regina carried into adulthood. Regina was always finding odd jobs around her house for people who needed work, and she patronized the locals who tried to make a little extra money on the side peddling yogurt or tortillas door-to-door. Even if she didn't need a shoeshine, she still gave the shoeshine man a few pesos.

Ángel saw his older sister as a rebel, not with her parents but with her destiny. A girl from a humble family, half indigenous, was not expected to attend the university or to roam the halls of government writing about malfeasance and the heavy hand of the PRI. Yet, from the time she was a child, Regina wanted something bigger for her life. There was no money in the Martínez family for college. Regina was the only one of nine who willed her way into the University of Vera-cruz to study communications, earning and paying the tuition herself. "She always wanted to better herself, leave town, build her own life," Ángel told *Proceso* after her death.

In 1982, while Regina was still in the university, the Mexican economy collapsed. While some sectors of the country had flourished to that point, the public debt, economic inequality, and inflation ran rampant. The peso in 1982 was devalued by 50 percent. This was the part of the "Mexican Miracle" that families like the Martínezes lived: struggling in the face of prosperity, only to suffer the most in the crash.

Growing up, Regina saw the injustices visited by the PRI and thought writing about them would be the best way to have an impact.

★

FAR AWAY IN Mexico City, in a working-class neighborhood, a young boy was getting the same idea. Ultimately, his path would cross Regina's, they would become colleagues at *Proceso*, and he would end up being the lead investigative reporter on her murder. Jorge Carrasco, the fifth of six children, grew up in an apartment in Colonia Mártires de Río Blanco, a plain barrio in the center of the city, not far from where the country's patron saint, the Virgin of Guadalupe, is believed to have appeared to the indigenous Juan Diego, and where the Basilica of Guadalupe now stands. The son of an electrician and a cleaning woman, Jorge grew up in a small world, his dreams not reaching much beyond the narrow streets of ill-kept stucco homes and low-rise apartment buildings.

He got the idea to attend college from his older siblings and enrolled in the high school prep program of the National Autonomous Univer-sity of Mexico, a public university often called the Harvard of Mexico. It was free to those who qualified, and thus a great engine of upward mobility for Mexicans to this day. His studies were in the relatively new College of Science and Humanities, which was intended to be a center for free thought in an authoritarian country. It was established to quell the social unrest after the massacre at Plaza Tlatelolco. The Mexican government denied the shootings, and to this day, it has never given an accurate number of the casualties. Not only was Jorge's college born from that massacre, but many of its professors had been students in the movement nearly a dozen years before he entered in the fall of 1979. The bent was decidedly Marxist.

Jorge absorbed the radical ideas, read the underground media, and became very critical of his government, but without taking on the political mantle of Marxism. He saw the infighting among student groups divided by their levels of orthodoxy, and he wanted no part of it. There was little notion of a free press. The students adhered to publications of Marxist propaganda.

Instead, he learned in history classes about democracy and the importance of a free press. All his classes, professors, lectures, and debates with other students revolved around doing journalism differently from what was being done at the time. He had read *Proceso* since high school, one reason he decided to sell subscriptions to it door-to-door to earn money for college, pocketing 20 percent of everything he sold.

Then, one day, one of his history professors held up a copy of the magazine in class. "*Compañeros*, history doesn't teach the past, it teaches the future," he said. Then, looking to the magazine, he said, "This is history. This looks to the future."

An image of Fidel Castro was on the cover, and the article was written by Julio Scherer, a man who Jorge had no idea would have such an impact on his life. Mexico's preeminent independent magazine was only three years old at that point.

While he was still in college, Jorge worked at the state-run news agency, Notimex, clipping newspaper articles for the archive. It was what journalists in predigital times referred to as the morgue: endless metal file cabinets filled with envelopes of yellowing articles organized by subject and date. It was how pre-Google reporters researched their stories. Jorge read every newspaper he clipped, and again, the experience led him to a new world: what was going on in other countries, the political tendencies of the various newspapers, and how much the vast majority of Mexican media depended on the state.

After a brief foray into sales for Notimex, Jorge won a competition for an editing slot on the international desk. Eventually, he became a reporter covering international news, and in 1989, he was named the wire service's foreign correspondent in Chile. The Pinochet dictatorship was collapsing after sixteen years in power, and authoritarian governments around the world were falling like the Berlin Wall. Though it wasn't yet Mexico's time, Jorge took deep note of the transitions he was witnessing.

★

AFTER COLLEGE, REGINA spent time in Tuxtla Gutiérrez, the capital of Mexico's southernmost state, Chiapas, where she was taking note of another reality in her country. Her exposure to indigenous communities that lacked education, health care, and often clean drinking water, along with her own upbringing, made her passionate about covering social causes. She also started building what would become a vast index of sources in closed, marginalized communities, the ones who normally didn't welcome an outsider reporter from the city.

When she returned to Veracruz, Regina looked for work where she could. She tried government communications when she couldn't find anything else, and hated it. Finally, she landed a job with Cuatro Más, a state-run television and radio station, as the wire editor, the person who scanned the news agencies for stories and then rewrote them in TV script style.

When then-Governor Fernando Gutiérrez Barrios left Veracruz to become interior secretary for President Carlos Salinas in 1988, his successor sparked a power struggle for control of the state TV channel. A new news director emerged, an up-and-coming contemporary of Regina's who went on to a successful television career. The young director took a walk through the state TV newsroom and wondered aloud why a television station didn't have better-looking employees. Regina was let go a short time later, a dismissal she was certain was related to her dark skin and indigenous features. She later wore her sacking as a badge of honor, openly bragging to friends about the day she was fired for not being pretty enough for television.

But she was unemployed with no place to go. A friend invited her to share her one-bedroom apartment while Regina looked for work.

In her spare time, she went jogging and kept her tiny stature very fit. The months passed until Regina finally landed a job at a brand-new local newspaper, *Política*, joining just months after it was founded.

It would be another decade before the paths of Jorge Carrasco and Regina Martínez crossed. But they were of the same generation, idealistic, eager to be part of a new movement to break the hold that the PRI government and business interests had on the media. They had not the slightest idea what they were in for.

CHAPTER 9

The Mouth of the Wolf

1946

IN LATE 2010, just before Javier Duarte took office as governor of Veracruz, a company called Logistica Estratégica ASISMEX, S.A. de C.V. was incorporated in the Port of Veracruz, offering administrative, accounting, human resources, and financial services. The owners were modest people living in marginal neighborhoods, and they established the firm with 50,000 pesos in assets, about $4,000 with the exchange rate at the time.

In 2011 and 2012, Mexico's national election season, Logistica Estratégica received at least $104 million from unknown sources, and distributed nearly $1.4 million of it to various political campaigns, the vast majority to that of PRI presidential candidate Enrique Peña Nieto.

In early 2012, two Veracruz state officials were stopped in an airport in Mexico state, where Peña Nieto had been governor. They were carrying $2 million in cash in a briefcase and a backpack. The men said the money was a last-minute payment for expenses for various state festivals and that the vendors would only accept cash. They were arrested, and the money was confiscated. Rival political parties said the Veracruz cash, too, was destined for the Peña Nieto campaign.

Among its many contributions in shaping Mexican history, Veracruz was key in developing an important tradition under the PRI: political corruption. It seemed that each of the state's governors over the decades took it to greater levels. And it was one of Regina Martínez's favorite subjects of inquiry as a reporter, starting with the government of Patricio Chirinos in 1992 through four administrations up to and including Duarte's. She was looking into the Duarte administration's finances in early 2012, the year she died. She hadn't discovered that Logistica Estratégica was a shell company set up by Duarte and his associates, according to what's now known. But perhaps her nosing around made them nervous.

This kind of grand-scale public corruption was decades in the making in Mexico, dating at least as far back as the 1930s, with its designers hailing from Veracruz. Miguel Alemán Valdés started the trend as governor in 1936, but he raised it to the level of fine art a decade later, when he was elected president of Mexico.

Alemán was born in Sayula, Veracruz, to a humble family. His father fought in the Revolution and made it to the rank of general. At one point, the general moved his family to Mexico City, where Miguel attended prep school and later studied law. In his late twenties, he created a pact with his high school friends, known as H-1920, in which they pledged allegiance to one another for life. It was this same group that would go on to receive government contracts and live lavishly on the public dole during Alemán's presidency.

Public enrichment reached "stunning new proportions" under Alemán, by some accounts, as he amassed "an astounding personal fortune" under borrowed names while in office. His cronies benefited handsomely as well. During his administration, the U.S. government received a dispatch from its Mexico City embassy entitled "Political Gangsterism in Government." The subject was "shady businesses" involving drug smuggling, pimping, and extortion by people close to Miguel Alemán.

In many respects, Alemán set the tone for the PRI for the coming decades. He was the first civilian elected president in Mexico after a string of post-Revolution generals from the ruling party, which was founded as the National Revolutionary Party in 1929. He was also the first to be elected under the party's modern name, "Institutional Revolutionary Party," its title suggesting the strangely paradoxical notion that a revolution could be institutional. In fact, Alemán started the party's move away from its revolutionary ideals to its nondoctrinaire platform of corporatism, stability, and control. He emphasized business and tourism, opening the country to foreign investment; quashed union strikes; and withstood an unpopular devaluation of the peso—all familiar events in subsequent PRI regimes.

Alemán also founded or fostered what became known as the PRI's state-sanctioned criminal enterprises, the ones that disappeared enemies and spied on people. These included one of the most corrupt security bodies in Mexico's history, the Federal Security Directorate (DFS, for its initials in Spanish), a secret police that he created for his personal protection and to spy on rivals and dissidents. The U.S. government reported at the time that the number one and two officers of the DFS were both suspected of dope smuggling.

Alemán also had close ties with pistoleros, Mexico's old-school gunslingers for hire, who eliminated rivals based on political and business interests. One associate, Manuel Parra, was connected to the murder of Veracruz governor-elect Manlio Fabio Atlamirano, opening the door for Alemán to become governor in 1936. Parra was also suspected in the killing of opposition senator Mauro Angulo during Alemán's presidency. Altamirano's assassins were part of a group known as La Mano Negra, or "the Black Hand." Among the group was a man named Marcial Montano, who allegedly drove the getaway car in the Altamirano murder and became close with the Alemán family.

Alemán was well known for employing various means of coercion on the press, practically inventing the system of *chayote*, or giving money and gifts to control media coverage. "He donated land in the exclusive Lomas de Sotelo district west of Mexico City to a hundred journalists from the big nationals. He also organized a state loan of 730,000 pesos to build their houses," Benjamin Smith wrote in his book *The Mexican Press and Civil Society, 1940–1976*. "By the end of the decade, half the journalists on the presidential beat lived on government-donated land."

Not satisfied with only media control, Alemán went after the political satirists, shutting popular theaters and harassing publications where writers practiced the time-honored art of satire as a way of getting around presidential censorship.

Alemán also set in motion the process for the creation of Televisa, a monopoly and the biggest television network in Latin America, which served as a kind of private state television and propaganda arm for the PRI. Years later, Alemán's son, Miguel Alemán Velasco, would become head of the network.

After he left office, the former president drove his yacht around Acapulco, which he had a strong hand in developing as a tourist destination during his presidency, and entertained starlets. He was listed as one of the world's richest men. His successor, Adolfo Ruiz Cortines, though a fellow Veracruzano who served under Alemán, felt a need to launch an anticorruption campaign to counter the previous regime.

Other Veracruz politicians played a big role in taking the state's brand of politics to the national level. Fernando Gutiérrez Barros headed the secret police during Mexico's Dirty War in the 1970s (a conflict between the government and left-wing student and guerrilla groups) and later served as interior secretary under Carlos Salinas, one of the few Mexican presidents considered to be more corrupt than Miguel Alemán Valdés.

But even in its audacity, government corruption was kept in check under the PRI, ultimately by the imperial powers of the president. When Mexico started having real electoral competition, and the PRI lost in 2000, the president no longer had that grip on the political system. This void meant that the political class at the state and local levels could maintain the business of institutionalized corruption, but without the former centralized limits. The kickbacks on a government contract, known as *diezmos*, for the customary 10 percent involved, grew to 20 percent or even double the cost of the contract.

At the same time, the nature of the drug cartels changed, as the business became exponentially more lucrative. Mexico, practically since the 1940s, had been a main producer of marijuana for the United States' illegal drug trade, plus low-grade heroin known as black tar. But everything changed in the 1980s, when the U.S. Drug Enforcement

Administration tried to shut down the Colombian cartels' cocaine-trafficking routes through the Caribbean into Miami. Some enterprising Mexican drug lords, specifically Miguel Ángel Felix Gallardo, saw an opportunity in moving a much more profitable product, Colombian cocaine, through Mexico. Known as "El Padrino," the former cop founded Mexico's first modern multinational drug cartel.

Veracruz was initially controlled by the Gulf Cartel, an organized crime group born on the Texas-Tamaulipas border that dated back to the 1930s and U.S. Prohibition. But with the example of El Padrino, Gulf Cartel capo Juan García Abrego took cocaine smuggling to an entire new level, and his route went through Veracruz.

Public officials always got their cut from the trafficking of contraband. But by the 1990s, stories started to pop up in *Política* about officials sticking their fingers in this new growing business themselves. Rural mayors were caught cultivating industrial-size fields of marijuana. Campesinos complained that land that had been deeded to them for farming was overrun by narcos landing Cessnas full of cocaine on remote dirt airstrips, while authorities turned a blind eye.

Capos lived quietly among the elite. Drug lord Félix Gallardo had a vacation ranch in Veracruz, as did his partner in crime Rafael Caro Quintero, who is still wanted by the United States for the murder of DEA agent Kiki Camarena.

In May 2002, when Miguel Alemán Valdés's son, Miguel Alemán Velasco, was governor of Veracruz, the Mexican military arrested Jesus Albino Quintero Meraz, a top lieutenant in the Gulf Cartel, in an upscale subdivision in the port. The home where he was living without disturbance was just a few doors from the private home of Governor Miguel Alemán Velasco. The speculation started immediately: How could the governor's security and intelligence forces not know that his neighbor was one of the country's top fugitive drug traffickers?

As the story went, Quintero Meraz had been running cocaine from the Caribbean in conjunction with Mario Villanueva, ex-governor of Quintana Roo state, home to the resort city of Cancún. When the governor left office in 1999 under suspicion of drug trafficking, Quintero Meraz was forced to move his operations to Veracruz.

Governor Alemán Velasco depended for protection on his secretary of public security, Alejandro Montano, the grandson of La Mano Negra pistolero Marcial Montano, who had been close to Miguel Alemán Valdés, the president. Protecting the Alemáns had become an intergenerational family business for the Montanos. In late October 2004, *Reforma* published information from the deposition of Quintero Meraz, who testified that, indeed, Alejandro Montano was protecting the cartel leader in Veracruz. He never faced charges.

One particular Veracruz governor was better than others at taking full advantage of the model set by the former president Miguel Alemán. Fidel Herrera Beltrán, who succeeded the president's son, Miguel Alemán Velasco, as governor, was born in 1949 in Nopaltepec, Veracruz, a tiny town inland from the petrochemical port of Coatzacoalcos. Though there is little written about his early years, people in Veracruz say he grew up poor—hence his oversize appetite for the spoils of his position. According to his official biography, Herrera earned a law degree at Mexico's premier National Autonomous University and later studied at the London School of Economics, opportunities not normally afforded to the poor in his day.

Those who know him describe him as intelligent, very ambitious, and a populist to an extreme. As Veracruz governor from 2004 through 2010, he had an aide who carried a suitcase of money on his state visits—everything in cash, which couldn't be traced—and Herrera handed out bills to those who had suffered natural disasters or had other needs. He wrote contracts on napkins. One politician, who was visiting a house Herrera used to receive people, told me he got lost while trying to find the bathroom and ended up in a room with thirty to forty cardboard boxes. When he lifted the lid on one, out of curiosity, he saw it was filled with cash. "If the amount of money I saw in that one box was in the rest of them, it was a lot of money," he told me.

Herrera had a group of political protégés from the time he was a federal congressman, a tight group of four college students who exhibited the proper characteristics, obedience, and loyalty. One in particular helped him finance his populist machine: Javier Duarte. Duarte had a doctorate in economics—he wrote a thesis on the perils of corruption for the state—and served as Herrera's subsecretary of finance and administration. In his position in finance, he saw a way to secure a larger slice of public funds: municipalities taking out huge amounts of federal- and state-backed loans to be repaid in the long term. With mayors serving only three-year terms, they could pass the debt onto future administrations. The money was set for specific public works for each municipality. But it offered governors a way to skim money via friendly builders and suppliers. Since a majority of the cities went along, the result was a giant basket for Fidel Herrera to spend as he saw fit, aided by local contractors, under the guise of developing local infrastructure.

When it came time for Herrera to pick a candidate from his loyal following to succeed him as governor, Duarte got the nod. Though he wanted to govern in the strong-arm tradition of the PRI, Duarte lacked the charisma and the iron fist that allowed Herrera to get away with whatever he wanted. Despite the opacity in everything he did, people liked Herrera, who was a glad-hander and made people feel important. They didn't like Duarte. He was a chubby, unattractive man. People called him *baboso*, "idiot." They said he was a drunk and that the state was actually being run by the head of communications, Duarte's spokesperson, Gina Domínguez, who was tough and had an air of authority.

During Duarte's six-year term, eighteen journalists were killed in Veracruz. Intimidation of the press was rampant. Police beat reporters covering protests and confiscated their equipment. There was a general shutdown on information coming out of the state. In one of the more egregious displays of irony, Duarte's lieutenants roughed up news photographer Roger López at a 2015 event called by Duarte and the federal subsecretary for human rights specifically to promise safety and free expression for the press in Veracruz.

★

WHEN I FIRST started looking into the story of Regina Martínez's murder, the standard line was that drug cartels were killing journalists. But I started to see and hear something else. Mexican reporters said they

feared the government more than the cartels. In 2015, the federal government's own unit for protecting journalists did a national study of the
killings that said that 40 percent of them were committed by state actors.
This number shot to 80 percent when they looked at the cases from
Veracruz. This meant that the people charged with investigating these
murders were often the perpetrators of them. This might explain why
government officials were so quick to dismiss these cases as having
nothing to do with the journalists' work.

In 2017, I took a fellowship at the University of Notre Dame to do
more research on my fundamental question: Why had democracy in
Mexico become so dangerous for journalists? I proposed working with
Guillermo Trejo, a political scientist I encountered quite by accident.
I am an alumna of Notre Dame. While I was in Mexico City, a friend
invited me to a dinner party for a fellow graduate who was in my class
but whom I hadn't known during school. When we met, my class-
mate, Steve Reifenberg, encouraged me to apply to study at the university's Kellogg Institute for International Studies. "Of course, you will
want to study under Guillermo Trejo," Steve said. "He specializes in
violence in emerging democracies."

I didn't even know that was a thing academically, but it was exactly
what I needed.

When I finally met Trejo, a tall Mexico City native in his forties
with a thick mop of curly hair, we had an instant meeting of the minds.
He was understated, genteel even, yet he conveyed conviction and
passion in his calm classroom voice. His work took him to some of the
most dangerous corners of Mexico, and it was not just for peer-reviewed
journals. Trejo believed that research, facts, and evidence could be used
to push change in his home country.

Trejo had published academic articles on Mexico and violence that
I hadn't seen elsewhere, explaining, among other things, how the cartels
had become "de facto authorities," as the *Diario de Juárez* had claimed
in its 2010 front-page editorial after a journalist there was killed.

The story for Trejo and his coauthor, Sandra Ley, began in 1989, the
year the PRI lost its first statewide election, the governorship in the

border state of Baja California. The political system was finally cracking open, and Mexico was moving toward political "alternation," meaning that any one of three major parties could win an election at the state or local level.

When new parties started winning elections, as in Baja California, it upended the PRI system that had been in place for decades. This included protection for the state-sanctioned criminal agencies, and also for the drug traffickers. Feeling a new vulnerability, the cartels formed their own militias and went to war with the state and one another to protect their territories. There was no viable state institution in place to stop them—quite the contrary.

Under the PRI system, the overseers of organized crime were state security forces and secret police. These were the high-ops government people with the best surveillance equipment and spy training. The PRI allowed these security forces to take a cut of the cartel profits, as long as the party got its fair share. It was considered a perk of sorts to keep powerful, highly trained enforcement agencies from turning on the regime.

The most notorious of these agencies was Miguel Alemán Valdés's Federal Security Directorate. During its forty-year history, the DFS was known for human rights violations and drug running. It reportedly had close ties to the CIA during the Iran-Contra covert operations and created dossiers on journalists, opposition politicians, and top entertainers, including crooner and international star Juan Gabriel. A tape of the torture and interrogation of DEA agent Kiki Camarena contained the voice of a former DFS official. It was finally disbanded in 1985, after its leaders were linked to some of the biggest crimes in the country, including the assassination of Mexico City journalist Manuel Buendía in 1984. The final DFS director, José Antonio Zorrilla, was arrested in 1989 and charged as the mastermind in that case.

When the DFS disbanded, the agents didn't go away. Many joined the new domestic security agency, the National Intelligence Center (CISEN, for its initials in Spanish) or were absorbed into other areas of government. Some took security officer positions in the various states, where they continued to run protection rings for whatever cartel controlled the region.

Ernesto Ruffo, the first opposition governor who won Baja California, told Guillermo Trejo years later that when he took office, he suspected that the state police and the local representatives of the federal attorney general's office worked on behalf of the drug traffickers. When he fired his state police chief, violence exploded in Tijuana, the border city with the largest number of daily crossings between Mexico and the United States.

Early opposition governors from the states of Jalisco, Michoacán, and Guerrero told Trejo similar stories. Lázaro Cárdenas Batel, son of opposition presidential candidate Cuauhtémoc Cárdenas Solórzano and grandson of General Lázaro Cárdenas, one of Mexico's most beloved PRI presidents, campaigned for governor of Michoacán in 2001 on the economy and immigration as issues. His state had been in drug trafficking and marijuana production for decades, but it didn't affect the constituents. When Cárdenas Batel won and replaced all top and mid-level people in the state attorney general's office and state police, he was stunned by the sudden outbreak of warfare. The new governor's closest collaborators were offered bribes. Some were assassinated, as the cartels sought to reconstitute their protection networks.

While free and fair elections were an important step toward democracy in Mexico, they were only one part of what needed to change. The old corrupt institutions, the ones created to serve the PRI instead of citizens—the ones that controlled and protected organized crime—needed to be replaced with ones that could support a democratic system. They needed to be transparent and independent. Outside of a new federal elections commission, this didn't happen.

Without anything like police or judicial reform, criminal enterprises that were previously controlled by an authoritarian PRI had a free-for-all. Security agents from the old system could now cut their own deals with the criminals, or leave government outright and run their own criminal organizations. Some of Mexico's most notorious capos were former state police, and their militias, highly trained ex-military.

The early violence from these warring groups in the 1990s and early 2000s didn't affect average Mexican citizens. Most Mexicans felt they could live their lives undisturbed. Members of high society grew accustomed to the nouveau riche narcos living among them. You knew those two boys in your daughter's private school were the sons of El Chapo Guzman, but no one said anything. You knew the new families moving into Monterrey's exclusive suburb, San Pedro Garza García, were the wives and children of members of the Gulf Cartel, but no one said anything. As long as you didn't bother them, they didn't bother you. This was allowed to build for years, until Mexicans saw their tolerance of cartel families backfire in a most disturbing manner.

The terrain for journalists turned deadly first. It began in the early 2000s, mostly in small towns near the Mexican-U.S. border, where the cartel presence and the threat from political regime change were most overt. The national press in Mexico City felt like spectators to these attacks. What was happening in outlying areas, particularly the border, was another world, one that didn't affect them. Jorge Carrasco used the famous Martin Niemöller quote about the Holocaust to describe the complacency he and his colleagues felt:

> First, they came for the socialists, and I did not speak out—
> Because I was not a socialist.
> Then they came for the trade unionists, and I did not speak out—
> Because I was not a trade unionist.
> Then they came for the Jews, and I did not speak out—
> Because I was not a Jew.
> Then they came for me—and there was no one left to speak for me.

No one was coming for them, at least not yet.

The Calderón presidency's attack on drug cartels made the violence worse. The federal government had gone from protector to adversary, forcing the cartels to look to local and state governments for protection. The killing of local journalists skyrocketed: four in 2007, six in 2008, eight in 2009, ten in 2010. At the same time, another trend emerged: attacks on candidates for local office. Between 2004 and 2018, there were 178 current or former mayors murdered in 24 of Mexico's 32 states. More than half the killings were in towns of 20,000 or fewer people, and 88 percent in towns of 70,000 or fewer.

The conventional wisdom said that cartels in Mexico were all business, not political. We continued to parrot this idea in the press, saying that the extent to which cartels got involved in local politics was totally related to moving product. Guillermo's research showed otherwise: The interests of politicians now in competitive races for office overlapped with those of drug cartels who needed local cooperation. In this new multiparty electoral system, politicians needed money to win. While campaigns under Mexican law are publicly financed with spending caps, there is plenty of cash funneled under the table that is never publicly accounted for. You can see it everywhere: T-shirts, buttons, rallies, entertainment, food, and giant painted signs reaching the most remote parts of the country. Suddenly, there was a new synergy between cartels who needed control and politicians who needed cash.

Those who wouldn't cut deals or who stood in the way of cartel control found themselves in the crosshairs. Starting in 2007, Veracruz under Fidel Herrera and later Governor Javier Duarte was among the top three deadliest states for mayors or mayoral candidates, not just journalists.

As early as 2008, Regina Martínez was writing about this phenomenon for *Proceso*. Eighty-three mayors in Veracruz had been extorted that year for tens of thousands of dollars each by the Zetas, she reported, with many mayors forced to raid city coffers to pay them off. As was his style, Herrera's number two, Interior Secretary Reynaldo Escobar, impugned the mayors for giving in to the narcos instead of going to their aid and prosecuting organized crime, she wrote. The article was accompanied by a huge photo of Fidel Herrera.

Under "democracy" in Mexico, the relationship had flipped. Instead of a central government controlling the cartels, the cartels now controlled local and state governments. Or, as Guillermo Trejo put it, they used targeted killings and violence against candidates and civilians to shape the political order, thereby becoming "de facto political rulers." The narcos didn't run for office per se; they didn't need to.

The reality of the new world order was that politicians and organized crime could create whatever relationships they found mutually beneficial. Sometimes it was elected officials in the service of narcos. Sometimes it was government leaders contracting organized crime to help maintain their political power. Rather than parallel or adversarial entities, government and organized crime in Mexico functioned as an "ecosystem of coercion, corruption, and criminality," Trejo concluded.

He had a name for what he saw in his data: the gray zone.

When I was a Kellogg fellow, I also met Juan Albarracín, one of Guillermo Trejo's doctoral students at the time. Albarracín studied how politicians and criminal groups forged relationships in so-called democratically elected councils in the urban outskirts of Río de Janeiro. Though his work was in another country, what he found mirrored exactly what was happening in Veracruz and other Mexican states.

The work of these criminal rings extended to stealing massive amounts of public money, and it was big business, involving cooperation and collusion on many levels.

The situation required a fundamental rethinking of the traditional notions of both organized crime and the state. In Veracruz, where the seeds were planted decades earlier, the two had become indistinguishable. "We seldom think of the misappropriation of funds as a criminal activity, but it is," Albarracín told me. "And the criminal politicians are incredibly organized."

For journalists, candidates, or activists, you could talk about drug cartels or you could talk about political corruption—but anyone who tried to expose the convergence of the two did so at the risk of being rubbed out.

Albarracín also had a name for what he observed in his studies: the new organized crime.

CHAPTER 10

Sidelined

WITH *Política*, REGINA had stumbled into the perfect job. She found a kindred spirit in the owner and cofounder, Ángel Leodegario Gutiérrez Castellanos, known throughout Veracruz as Don Yayo. Like Regina, Don Yayo was tough, unsentimental, honest, and revered by the people who worked for him. He was born with a stub for a left arm (a defect that would later become part of his character) into a rural family with lots of land. Despite his Spanish lineage on his father's side, Don Yayo was guaranteed the pure blood of a Veracruzano through his mother's indigenous roots and from growing up in one of the most stunning and storied regions of the state, Los Tuxtlas, a jungle mountain range of volcanos. His village, Tres Zapotes, was where two of the famous colossal heads from the three-thousand-year-old Olmec culture were found. The area drew tourists from all over Mexico and beyond for its breathtaking natural scenery and shocking waterfalls. Nearby, Laguna Catemaco was another famous attraction, for its island of imported research monkeys and a main street of *brujos*, "shamans," who wear doctor's lab coats and treat patients in their offices by appointment. Mel Gibson filmed much of his movie *Apocalypto* in Los Tuxtlas.

Don Yayo, tall with thinning black hair and a mustache, was a successful man. Though he grew up on a rancho without electricity, his family moved to the city of Tlacotalpan so he could attend school, where he wore shoes for the first time. His education ended in law school in Mexico City, at the Autonomous National University, with classmates who would shape their era: Miguel Alemán Velasco, son of a former president; and politicians Porfirio Muñoz Ledo and Mario Moya Palencia. Don Yayo knew farming and business and enjoyed singing and poetry, but mostly he knew politics. In true postrevolutionary fashion, he was a journalist *and* a PRI operative his entire adult life. Before *Política*, he had founded another newspaper, *Diario del Sur*, in Acayucan, about two hours southeast of where he grew up. When he wasn't running the two newspapers, he served as a judge, prosecutor, state congressman, director of the state government press office, and state party chair for the PRI. He was also a public notary, a lucrative side job that the state often reserved for party loyalists. Notaries could make official anything you asked them to.

When he founded *Política* in Xalapa in 1987, Don Yayo still loved his party, but not the way it was governing, seeing corruption and ineptitude on a regular basis. He wanted to create a newspaper dedicated entirely to political issues. Not only that, he wanted to practice a new kind of journalism to counter the controlled press of the time, to create a publication that served the governed, not the government. There was no media like that in Xalapa, though he had as an example the combative *Notiver*, Veracruz's largest newspaper, based in the port. It was run by Alfonso Salces, who emigrated from Spain to work in *La Parroquia*, the coffee business of his uncles, before starting the newspaper in the 1970s. The paper sold out on the street every day, and Don Alfonso had the money to print whatever he liked. But *Notiver* was pure tabloid journalism. Don Yayo's charges joked that, with *Política*, he wanted the *New York Times* but with the bite of *Notiver*.

Don Yayo set out to establish a newspaper that was "antisystem," according to his daughter Yolanda Gutiérrez Carlín. He told his reporters they could cover whatever they wanted—certainly unusual for Xalapa and most of the rest of the state. The reporters were young and eager, running on the euphoria of being a moth-eaten band of misfits who could make powerful men—yes, almost entirely men—dread opening the newspaper in the morning. Don Yayo was deft at handling his party colleagues at the same time that he slung mud at them on the pages of his newspaper.

Regina dove in, focusing on the marginalized people who made the news at the time only in positive stories about government handouts that said nothing about the conditions in which the people lived. She interviewed the indigenous, the peasants, and the union workers, all of whom had never had a voice in the traditional press.

Regina's reporting was legendary among her colleagues—so much so, that when I first heard of it, I was sure it must be an exaggeration, an assassinated journalist being lionized by her peers. In death, people become at least a small bit mythological. And the quality of journalism in the provinces was marginal at best, the standards by which they reported even more questionable.

After a bit of a runaround—*Política* wouldn't give me access to its archives—I found editions of *Política* in the state's public archives in Xalapa and personally reviewed almost twenty years of the newspaper. Not only were Regina's friends *not* exaggerating, but I was astounded by the level and the volume of what she had written. And it wasn't only me. I hired an assistant in Mexico to catalogue all the articles I had amassed. She spent most of the job, hours and hours, completely mesmerized reading every piece Regina had written. "Nobody was writing things like that in Mexico at that time," she told me. "Especially not in the provinces."

Regina covered hunger strikes, antihunger marches, and political violence. She reported on campesinos drinking contaminated water; rural communities demanding vaccines for a measles outbreak that killed twelve; cancer-causing elements in the marine life in the discharges from Laguna Verde, Mexico's only nuclear power plant; and children learning in open-air classrooms because the government had failed to construct schoolhouses. She wrote a three-part series on exploitation, layoffs, and contract violations affecting union workers at the giant Mexican brewery Cerveceria Cuauhtémoc Moctezuma, producers of Dos Equis and Sol, in the Veracruz city of Orizaba. In one installment, she wrote that wives of some laid-off workers had turned to prostitution to make ends meet.

All that just in the first eight months of 1990.

The offices of *Política* sat for thirty years atop a bookstore and pharmacy facing the vast side wall of Xalapa's main cathedral, accessible by a passageway through a bald mini-mall and up a flight of stairs to what in Mexico is the first floor. Next door was the television studio, where Regina spent much of her time with the TV director, Don Yayo's son Ricardo Gutiérrez.

Initially, the newspaper printed only one thousand copies, compared to the establishment press, like *Diario de Xalapa*, which had circulations of more than forty thousand. But because *Política* was the vanguard, and Don Yayo was open to trying anything, it regularly sold out, and copies were shared many times over. (At its peak, the printing was eight thousand copies.) *Política* was the first newspaper in Xalapa to put biting political cartoons on the front page. It was also the first newspaper in the conservative Catholic community to have a sex page, which came about quite by accident one December, during the annual holiday news lull. One night, Salvador Muñoz, the number two editor, had scoured the wires and filled the paper with everything he could find, but he still had a blank page. It was the late 1990s, when e-mail spam was taking off, and Muñoz was receiving lots of e-mails about sex, erectile dysfunction, venereal diseases, the Kama Sutra, and "discovering your erotic sixth sense." In desperation, he decided to use them to fill the hole on page four of the newspaper.

The next morning, when the paper was out, he got a call from Don Yayo. Muñoz braced himself for a chewing out. After Don Yayo lectured him for ten minutes about decency, the community, and how the señoras would be scandalized, he said, "You know what? I want a Page Four like that every week!"

"Yes, sir" was all Muñoz said.

Later that day, when he saw Don Yayo in the office, his boss glee-fully asked, "How did you manage to piss off my wife so badly?"

"What do you mean?" Muñoz asked.

"With that Page Four," Don Yayo said. "She wanted to take you straight to hell."

Page Four solidified *Política*'s perch as required reading in Xalapa. Soon, other newspapers were adding sex pages.

Compared to *Notiver*, the largest newspaper in the state, Don Yayo's budget for *Política* was more like pocket change. The newspaper was printed in sepia tone, a cheaper ink. Sometimes he would have to call in chits or borrow from the newspaper in Acayucan to make his payroll. Payday was sacred and couldn't be missed. At one point, Don Yayo sent his accountant to the newsroom to find ways to cut expenses. The accountant proposed eliminating free coffee for the reporters. The staff complained, but none louder than Regina. (Everyone knew she made the coffee when it was too strong for anyone else to drink.) Don Yayo relented, and the free coffee stayed.

He took care of his staff, which at one point reached forty-five people. The newspaper had a photo technician who was known to come to work drunk. One day, assistant editor Raciel Martínez (no relation to Regina) was waiting on deadline for photos that never came. He knocked on the darkroom door. No answer. He knocked again. No answer. When he tried to enter, he found the technician passed out, his body blocking the doorway.

Martínez called Don Yayo, who ordered him to send the technician to his office. "Stop messing with that shit," he told the technician. But he refused to fire him. Instead, he required the technician to check in with him every day before entering the darkroom, so he could verify his sobriety. In his own way, Don Yayo created an employee assistance program, with antidoping measures for his staff.

Regina thrived in this tough-love newsroom. She quickly earned the nickname "Macha," for her gruff manner. Others called her "Doctora," because she always seemed in charge. Many saw her rene-gade style as part nature, part Don Yayo nurture. She was special to him, almost like a daughter, but so were the handful of other journalists who were willing to the push the boundaries. Don Yayo was impressed with Regina's knowledge of indigenous communities and her contacts in Veracruz.

She would come in from assignments, hair sticking to her sweaty forehead, and regale Salvador Muñoz and Don Yayo in the most exciting and colorful way with what she had discovered. Then she would sit down to write it in the dry officialese of journalism of the time. "We've just heard the best version of *that* story," Don Yayo would joke.

Regina was almost always the last one to turn in her stories before the presses ran, and they were often way too long. They became known as *reginazos*, which translates roughly into "enormous Reginas."

Ya entregaste, Macha? the editor Raciel Martínez had to ask several times on deadline. "Have you turned it in?"

Salvador Muñoz, too, would beg and beg for her copy, and sometimes, by the time it came in, there would only be a small hole left in the newspaper. He would have to trim the article to make it fit. Inevitably, the next day, there would be an eruption.

"Why did you cut that?" Regina would demand of him. "It was the most important part."

"If it was most important, Regina, why did you put it at the bottom of the story?"

While most reporters barely left their desks, writing from government press releases and telephone calls, Regina traveled all over for stories. She was often accompanied by photographer and cartoonist Alberto Morales. They went everywhere together, making an odd pair, tiny Regina next to the burly and bearded Alberto, who measured about six feet tall. After some time working together, they became a romantic couple.

Regina ventured to the remotest parts of the state, to the scenes of government conflicts with farmers, coffee growers, and peasants that had previously been carried off without a hint of scrutiny. Her friend and rival Andrés Timoteo told of traveling long hours to the mountain pueblos of Veracruz to get a story, only to find when he arrived that

Regina had already been there. "Give our regards to Regina," the locals would say as Timoteo headed back to Xalapa.

The changing politics in Mexico also dominated Regina's coverage. In the months leading up to Veracruz's 1992 gubernatorial election, voters in the small pueblos, normally PRI strongholds, were fleeing to the Party of the Democratic Revolution, or PRD. The new party was founded by Cuauhtémoc Cárdenas, son of Lazaro Cárdenas, one of Mexico's most beloved PRI presidents. But the younger Cárdenas became fed up with the corruption and broke away from the PRI. Regina's stories questioned the legitimacy of PRI candidate Patricio Chirinos's victory in the governor's race in the face of voting irregularities. The PRD accused the PRI of using premarked ballots and falsified voter credentials to win, according to a front-page *Política* headline with Regina's byline that July.

Don Yayo then sent Regina to cover political uprisings in Michoacán, Cárdenas's home state, where the PRD was staging massive public sit-ins to protest what they said was a stolen gubernatorial election by the PRI. While Chirinos in Veracruz served his term, the winning PRI candidate in Michoacán was forced to resign two weeks after taking office. The PRI would not allow a special election and appointed another party member to be governor of that state. But in exchange, the ruling party conceded more and more electoral reforms. The political upheaval and energy in the whole country was adrenaline for Regina, whose main target was always the PRI.

She roughed up Governor Chirinos in the pages of *Política* during his entire six-year term with her two favorite recurring themes: illegal money grabs and human rights abuses by a party struggling to maintain its power. By 1994, the once-dominant PRI was under pressure from growing defections to opposition parties. Then came the full-blown revolt by the Zapatista Army of National Liberation in Chiapas against the federal government and the abuses they would suffer under the North American Free Trade Agreement. Regina went often to Chiapas to cover it.

Miguel Ángel Yunes, Governor Chirinos's number two, who ran the state from day to day, was also a favorite target of Regina's. She exposed his heavy-handed tactics against indigenous and peasant communities in the name of keeping the Zapatista rebellion from spilling over into Veracruz. In one of the most notorious cases, Regina wrote about land evictions by state police and pistoleros in the community of Ixhautlán de Madero. The expulsion left eleven people missing and at least two men dead in a river. Police blockaded the dead men's families from retrieving the bodies of their loved ones. Yunes denied that the casualties even existed, saying only that two state policemen had been killed in the area, but without explaining why or how.

Witnesses told the National Human Rights Commission that the two men were captured by state forces and severely tortured. Yunes's crackdowns in the rural communities of Veracruz led to several human rights investigations, though the toothless organization never held anyone accountable. Regina covered all of it in detail.

One summer night in 1994, she was still in her cubicle in the newsroom at nine thirty, as was her custom, when the telephone rang. A strange male voice was on the line.

"I'm going to give you a story," he said.

"Who is this?"

She heard silence, and then "I want to give you a story."

"Where are you calling from?"

A noise came through the receiver, some kind of interference on the line.

"Excuse me, where are you calling from? I can't hear you."

More silence. Then the man spoke very softly. "Go to La Parroquia on Ávila Camacho and look in the men's bathroom, behind the toilet tank." Then the caller hung up.

Regina went to the café with Alfredo Morales, who could check the men's bathroom. The cavernous restaurant was nearly empty, with only three of the dozens of tables occupied. She chatted with the waiters and the cashier, who knew her from the *Política* office, just around the corner, until Morales emerged from the men's room with a yellow envelope. It contained a Sony cassette tape and a message on fax paper. The tape held what seemed to be telephone conversations between Governor Chirinos and officials in the Secretaría General de Gobierno, the department run by Yunes, talking about using public money to host a campaign visit by PRI presidential candidate Ernesto Zedillo, illegal under Mexico's new election laws. Officials were mapping out how to do this "without leaving a trace," Regina wrote in her article. The fax paper explained that the leakers, who said they couldn't give their identity for fear of reprisals, had sent a series of recorded phone calls to Alianza Civica Veracruzana, a civil society organization formed to advocate for clean elections. The leakers referred to themselves as "mere mortals, but with the capacity to inform from inside."

"While you're trying to investigate who did the spying, you might want to also look into who was violating federal election laws," they wrote.

The same caller had notified other Xalapa dailies, but by the time they reached the café bathroom, they found nothing. The tip was already in the hands of Regina Martínez, whose story ran in *Política* the next day and put her, once again, at the center of a political furor. The article set off a media frenzy. Alianza Civica Veracruzana filed a formal complaint that the governor's office had used state resources to help a political campaign, including a state helicopter to transport the candidate.

The PRI's stranglehold had weakened so dramatically that insiders were no longer fearful of whistle-blowing, and the Mexican public was starting to demand transparency. The fledgling independent media was the tiny dog exposing Veracruz's fiery wizard, and it was Regina's name on some of the most potent stories: that state employees were being pressured to vote for the PRI, for example; or that international aid from the World Bank and the United Nations slated for roads, latrines, and granaries in poor communities was going to the party instead.

The stories were not well received by a power structure used to quashing dissent. Regina was barred from press conferences and from receiving state press releases. She wore this, too, as a badge of honor.

★

DON YAYO AND his staff in general suffered for their independent reporting, especially under the administration of Chirinos, which Don Yayo felt was particularly corrupt. In retaliation, the government took away Don Yayo's lucrative notary designation. Sometimes the punitive measures were more overt. One day, Miguel Ángel Yunes appeared in Don Yayo's office steaming over a column that Salvador Muñoz wrote about the governor offering his condolences to the family of a young woman who had been murdered.

"Instead of offering condolences, why don't you give us security in the streets?" Muñoz wrote.

After Yunes left, Don Yayo summoned his number two. "Did you write this?" he asked.

Muñoz nodded.

"You made Yunes mad. He wants your name, address, everything. They'll do some ugly things."

"What do we do?" Muñoz asked.

"You need to leave and go to Acayucan."

"When?"

"Right now."

Muñoz went home and told his wife they were moving that day to a town four hours south, where Don Yayo had founded his first newspaper. Salvador remained working for the newspaper there for three years, until the end of Chirinos's term.

The close of the 1990s brought good fortune for *Política*. The new governor, Miguel Alemán Velasco, the son of former Mexican president Miguel Alemán Valdés, was a good friend of Don Yayo's from their law school days. Government advertising in the newspaper improved, along with the paper's budget. But reporters wondered if the newspaper would lose its edge and become too cozy with the new administration.

Regina was especially concerned. "So, we can't *madrear* Miguel Alemán?" she asked Ricardo Gutiérrez one day, using a Mexican verb that literally means "to mother," but that in slang means "to fuck somebody up."

"You can, but it has to be for a good reason," Gutiérrez replied.

He encouraged her to become director of information as a way to cope with the editorial change in *Política*'s leadership. The newspaper's director of information received all press releases and government communiqués and assigned the news stories. Regina's stint at the job made her even more of a legend among her admirers, who remember her sitting at the director's desk and politely accepting the submissions people brought in the front door, the kind that most official newspapers printed verbatim. Then, after they left, she would ceremoniously throw the press releases into the trash, exclaiming, *Pinche propaganda!*

By the early 2000s, Regina also had become a contributor to the magazine *Proceso* in Veracruz. With the abysmal salaries paid by local media, it was customary for the better correspondents to work for national publications too. Regina, Lupita López, and Andrés Timoteo were all correspondents for the Mexico City newspaper *La Jornada* at one point. Regina's collaboration with *Proceso* started when the magazine decided to publish a southern Mexico edition. When that was folded for lack of money, she stayed on, getting paid per story while keeping her day job at *Política*.

She managed to *madrear* Miguel Alemán with no interference from Don Yayo. In one of her more talked-about stories in *Política*, she discovered that Alemán was traveling around the state in a $17.3 million Cessna Citation X, the same model of plane, she noted, owned by actor Sylvester Stallone and champion golfer Tiger Woods. Where was the money coming from for such elaborate transportation for a public official? The Secretaría General de Gobierno said the jet was owned by Alemán. The governor, in turn, said it was owned by a private company—not the state—that leased it to the governor for $2,500 an hour. He accused Regina of overzealous reporting.

If the jet was rented, Regina asked, why did it have a mural of El Tajín, Veracruz's most famous archaeological site, on an interior wall? Why would a company buy one of only sixty-two Cessna Citation Xs in the world just to rent it to the governor of Veracruz? Every time Regina asked questions, the officials waffled, both about the ownership of the jet and how much state money had gone toward flying Alemán around in luxury. What's more, she discovered that Alemán had used the jet to ferry the PRI candidate for president, Francisco LaBastida, in clear violation of election laws.

Another of her famous stories was her coverage of an accident involving local police preparing for a giant festival at El Tajín. The festival was created by Alemán himself to highlight the state's cultural riches. Some three hundred police officers were ordered to jump up and down on a giant platform erected for the fair to make sure it was sound. The platform collapsed, killing one and injuring thirty-three officers. While other reporters covered the accident from official sources at the site, Regina went to the hospital to interview two men who suffered severe cranial damage in the fall. She was the only one to report the victims' harrowing account. One of the injured officers described thinking of his two children as he fell sixty feet, certain he would die. She also was the only one to report that the victims were receiving no help from the state for medical bills, despite the governor's promise, and that the order for such an insane act had come from the state secretary of public security, Alejandro Montano. Montano was a periodic figure in Regina's stronger features.

In early 2003, she had a bylined story based on a leak of U.S. embassy documents to the newspaper *Notiver*. Dated 2001, the documents outlined a complaint by the FBI to its Mexican counterparts that several unnamed high-level public security officials in Veracruz were taking bribes from the Gulf Cartel, presumably in exchange for protection.

There had always been rumors of public officials getting their cut from the trafficking of contraband, but this was one of the first overt accusations. In response to the protection story, Governor Miguel Alemán published a full-page letter in *Política* and other media demanding that anyone making such accusations come forward with proof. In a separate article, Alejandro Montano called the allegations "political." Still, it was a turning point for a state that, until then, had kept its connections between politicos and narcos out of the public spotlight.

People who know him told me Montano wanted to move away from his legacy as a bodyguard and doorman to the rich and powerful Alemán family and become a powerful man in his own right, from pistolero to *politico*, something he accomplished quite effectively. But he never lost his threatening edge. Polo Hernández remembered attending one of his press conferences and going up afterward to ask some tough question that Regina had sent him to ask, but out of earshot of the other reporters.

He doesn't even remember the topic, only that Montano was irritated. When Montano went to shake Polo's hand, he squeezed it tightly, in a painful grip, grinning and saying, "Give my regards to Regina."

Reynaldo Escobar was another of Regina's subjects. Escobar, a round man whose belt size matched his height, was a cunning lawyer and esteemed professor at the law school. Some called him the best legal mind in the state. He worked for former governor Dante Delgado, including getting him out when he was jailed on embezzlement charges. Escobar had been the mayor of Xalapa, where he was accused of overseeing the growth in bars and strip clubs associated with organized crime, and the number two under Fidel Herrera when drug violence in Veracruz started to take hold.

Regina wrote about Escobar over the years in the context of his city budgets not passing muster with the state auditors and his blanketly labeling victims of violence, journalists and others, as "narcos." She also tied him at one point to Fidel Herrera's questionable finances regarding the state-owned professional soccer team, which was investigated as a money-laundering scheme.

Throughout the term of Fidel Herrera there were rumors that he had sold the state to the Zetas. Then-President Felipe Calderón publicly said as much, though he didn't name Herrera. Escobar ran the day-to-day government for Herrera as the crime wave grew. He ran mostly under the radar. But rumors abounded about his side businesses and ties to organized crime, including what Villamil had reported in the infamous *Proceso* article published right before Regina's death. As with Montano, there were accusations but never formal charges.

In late 2010, when the new governor, Javier Duarte, named Reynaldo Escobar as attorney general, people inside the prosecutor's office were stunned. Regina wrote that Escobar's appointment was in violation of the state constitution, which said the top prosecutor could not come directly from another public position.

Escobar had problems with Regina, according to several sources. One was the opposition legislator Sergio Vaca Betancourt, who I went to interview at one point. Vaca Betancourt loved telling stories about

Regina and how irreverent she was with politicians. He said that one time, she followed a secretary of government—he couldn't remember which one—down the hall repeating, "I'd like to ask a question. I'd like to ask a question." She followed him all the way to his office, where he slammed the door in her face, nearly hitting her in the teeth.

"And guess what she said to him?"

"I don't know."

Chinga tu madre! "Motherfucker." One of the most vulgar things you can say in Mexico. Vaca Betancourt broke into laughter. "That's how she was. She had a lot of problems with Reynaldo Escobar," he said.

"What kind of problems?"

"She criticized him," he said. "One time, during a campaign, I think what she wrote cost him the congress. It was around the time of her assassination. I think it was the same with Captain Montano, who was chief of Miguel Alemán's bodyguards. In reality, she left a lot of resentment."

"And who else? Montano, Escobar. Who else were her worst enemies, do you think?" I asked.

"Well, the very same Fidel," he told me.

Regina's vigorous reporting on Fidel Herrera started before he was even elected. When Herrera was still a candidate, *Proceso* received confidential documents from the Mexico attorney general's organized crime unit showing that Herrera was the subject of a federal investigation for alleged ties to organized crime groups operating in Veracruz. The documents cited a photograph of him with José Luis "El Azul" Esparragoza Moreno, then a top lieutenant in the Sinaloa Cartel, that was found in a raid of a narco ranch in southern Veracruz a few months before the 2004 gubernatorial election. In a preelection story for *Proceso*, Regina and José Gil Olmos wrote that the organized crime unit wouldn't confirm the authenticity of the leaked documents. Herrera, when asked about them, called the accusations old news. "I'm a man of laws, clean, known, and recognized," they quoted him as saying.

★

REGINA'S STORIES WERE nonstop. She discovered 7,500 *aviadores*, or "aviators," Mexican slang for people who are on the public payroll but who perform no discernible work. According to her report, the *aviadores* collected three hundred million pesos in salaries, and they included the wife of a federal legislator. Regina acquired state fiscal records showing the purchase of millions of dollars in hospital equipment in the last three months of Chirinos's administration that was either never installed or never functional. Seven months after one of Veracruz's major natural disasters, she tracked down donated relief supplies intended for the victims (food, clothing, drinking water, and bedding) sitting in twenty-four government warehouses.

At one point, Miguel Alemán came looking for Regina at the newspaper office, saying he just wanted to talk. When she arrived at the office that day, her colleagues were frantic to tell her that the governor was looking for her. In polite, old-school Mexico, no one was rude to the governor. But Regina had no problem turning down the most powerful man in the state. She knew that such "talks" usually led to offers of money or positions in exchange for silence. She made it a strict rule that she would speak to politicians only if it involved a story. "I don't need to talk to him," she said. "If I do, I'll call him."

Other reporters followed in Regina's footsteps, and when they ran into trouble, they reached out to her for help. One was Norma Trujillo, who in the 1990s was chasing tips about a brewing public health crisis around homeless teens in Xalapa who had been infected with HIV. In her reporting, Trujillo met a young teen who had been abandoned by his parents at age six and drafted into child prostitution by age seven. His name was Jorge Antonio Hernández Silva.

A woman named Theresa fed and cared for him at times when she found him sleeping in her doorway. When Trujillo met him, he was fifteen years old, strong, stocky, and combative, going in and out of juvenile detention for petty crimes. During one stint in jail for robbery, he tested positive for HIV. Health officials panicked. They had no regimen for treatment and knew little about the disease. Fearing he would pass it to the other juvenile inmates and cause an epidemic, they put him back on the street—without medication or any information about his condition. Health officials said he wouldn't live a year. Trujillo wrote a story about the state's treatment of the young teen, noting that at least 10 to 15 percent of some three thousand street children were carrying the virus for AIDS.

When her investigation was published in the newspaper *Diario de la Tarde*, state officials accused her of fabricating it. There were no street children in Xalapa with HIV, they said.

Her credibility under attack, Trujillo sought out Regina for support. Regina was outraged at the treatment Norma was receiving over the story, and she used her biggest weapon against the critics: Regina convinced *Política* to publish Trujillo's story as reinforcement, giving it a wider audience and influence.

Jorge Antonio Hernández, known as "El Silva," was part of an elaborate community of children, mostly boys, who lived on the streets of Xalapa. Some slept at a shopping center construction site. Others stayed in flophouses like the Hotel Greco, just five blocks up the hill from *Política*'s offices. They would pool whatever change they had to crowd into a room for the night and then make a living stealing and selling their goods to the hotel managers running a racket. Many of them offered sex in Parque Juárez at night. The boys stuck together for security. They also had support from some Jesuit priests who started a nonprofit group, Movimiento de Apoyo a Niños Trabajadores y de la Calle, or Matraca, which provided clothing, food, and classes at different points around the city. The young priests of Matraca were trying to secure rights for the children working and living on the streets.

Norma Trujillo's and Regina's reporting on the issue helped sway public opinion and put pressure on the state legislature, which eventually passed the Ley Matraca, "the Matraca Law." It codified for the first time the human and legal rights of children, both in families and living on the streets. Among other things, it guaranteed their right to health, safety, education, and legal protection, and it required public employees to report children living in abusive situations or face sanctions.

Arturo Marinero was a young mental health counselor in the mid-1990s working for Matraca when he met El Silva. The teenager couldn't read or write, was very disheveled, and was addicted to sniffing paint thinner and glue. The street kids would come by for clothes and supplies and eat at the Matraca dining room downtown, which also had tutoring, games, and a hot shower. Marinero and his colleagues would organize events for the kids, such as holding a Christmas celebration in the construction lot where many of them lived. El Silva, too, would show up for help, but he was always on the outside. He was incapable of making friends and often turned violent against the other kids, who avoided him. He slept alone in doorways or in Parque Juárez at night.

Marinero and his staff put a premium on making Matraca a safe haven, and they tried to accept everyone. But El Silva's aggression was a problem. After a while, the other kids stopped coming if he was at the center. Marinero and coworker Alfredo Castillo gave him warnings and reminded him of the rules: no violence. Castillo was particularly firm with the kids and emphasized to El Silva that he needed to control himself if he wanted to use Matraca's services. But he couldn't. After El Silva started a fight with another kid, Castillo, who wasn't a priest but who had the demeanor of one, grabbed El Silva by the shirt and put him against a wall. "You will not touch another child, or we are going to call the police!" he yelled in his face.

Norma Trujillo found El Silva much quieter, punctual, and respectful. She and three other reporters put their money together to buy him food. She went many nights to Parque Juárez, where he and the other male prostitutes worked, and accompanied him to his medical appointments, to make sure he was receiving the public health benefits he was entitled to for treating HIV.

A short time after Trujillo published her story in 1994, El Silva disappeared. She and others assumed he had succumbed to his disease. She was dumbfounded when the polite abused teen she knew appeared eighteen years later as a prime suspect in Regina's murder.

★

FOR THE MOST part, Regina had covered drug trafficking only when opposition leaders accused the PRI government of harboring narcos.

Her journalistic acumen included knowing exactly what topics to avoid for security reasons. Drug trafficking was one of them. But the tide of news swept her there anyway, as both the cartels and the cocaine transport business in Mexico grew.

Regina's career was affected by another force out of her control: the death of Don Yayo in 2001. He suffered from cirrhosis and had stopped coming to the office near the end, though he still kept up his newspaper column, which he normally dictated to his secretary. When his number two, Salvador Muñoz, went to visit him one day, Don Yayo asked him to take the dictation instead of the secretary. Muñoz knew his death was inevitable, even though he and Don Yayo both pretended that they would continue in this way for years to come. Soon, Don Yayo was too ill to take visitors, but Muñoz would still call.

"You're coming back, right?" Don Yayo asked during what would be Muñoz's last phone call.

"Of course," he answered, then started to cry.

"Why are you crying?" Don Yayo asked. "Don't be a *pendejo*. You'll always be the number two editor. You'll always be my second in command."

"I wasn't crying about that," Muñoz explained to me, recalling the conversation sixteen years later. We were sitting in a coffeehouse in Xalapa, where the grinding of beans at times became so loud that I was worried my recorder wouldn't pick up his story.

At this point in remembering his years at *Política*, Muñoz choked up. He apologized and asked for a minute to compose himself. When he had, he said, "He was someone special, like a father, a boss, a teacher . . . For me, the newspaper *Política* was a workshop in journalism more than a newspaper. It was a place that allowed you to do things, to try things, including something totally new, like putting a political cartoon on the front page. In those days, everyone was accustomed to photos. And with the personality of Alberto Morales, who was really bold for that time, to put cartoons that really poked a finger in the wound, that hurt the politicians. It was a surprise. A marvel."

When Muñoz walked into the newsroom after Don Yayo's death to greet his widow, Yolanda Carlín, he said, "Whatever help you need,

Señora, I'm at your service. Whatever you need me to explain about the newspaper."

"You have nothing to explain to me," she answered curtly. "I know how to run a newspaper."

From that day, the tone of the irreverent *Política* started to change, and not for the better.

Under Yolanda Carlín, Salvador Muñoz was replaced as subdirector by Gustavo González Godina, a friend of the Gutiérrez Carlín family and an editor who encouraged publishing the government's official line. Under the new management, Regina increasingly became a problem for the newspaper. She lost her position as director of information, which González offered to Rodrigo Soberanes, her protégé, while she was still in the job.

Soberanes told Regina about the offer. He could tell she was hurt, even though he had turned it down.

Her trust in anyone around her had already been shattered. Several years earlier, she learned that her boyfriend, Alberto Morales, had been paid to inform on her to the government, telling them what she was working on. The betrayal was devastating. She no longer made phone calls at her desk for fear of being overheard.

With the arrival of Governor Fidel Herrera in 2004, after an election that also had its irregularities and was ultimately decided in the courts, *Política*'s relationship with the government became even cozier. Herrera was known to splurge on the media, including individual journalists, to buy good coverage. (The Veracruz state government consistently refused any public records requests asking how much taxpayer money was going to the press. They said it was confidential information. But in June 2016, media outlets published a list of payments that showed the government of Duarte owing *Política* $180,000, although it didn't specify for what or during what time frame.)

Regina was unfazed and continued with her critical stories. While they caused tension at *Política*, *Proceso* had no problems publishing them. In late 2004, at the end of Miguel Alemán's term as governor, Regina and *Proceso* colleague José Gil Olmos wrote a long article calling his administration a disaster.

"Just to make the finances of his government more or less clean," they wrote, Alemán "asked the local Congress, at the last minute, for the approval of a loan of 3.5 billion pesos. During his government, Veracruz ranked second nationally in poverty rate behind Chiapas, according to data from the Ministry of Social Development. It has also recently become one of the leading 'exporters' of illegal workers to the United States, according to the PAN [the opposition party] and local businessmen. In addition, corruption scandals involved members of his cabinet, excessive spending on airplanes, festivals, and payroll, as well as complaints against members of his family for alleged acts of corruption."

The directors of *Política* maintained their rosy coverage in direct rebuttal to their own reporter. The newspaper marked the end of Alemán's controversial tenure with a front-page photograph of him and his wife under the headline SATISFACTION FOR A MISSION ACCOMPLISHED. Another time, he was pictured on the front page with newspaper director Yolanda Carlín and her daughter Yolanda Gutiérrez Carlín, all wearing wide smiles.

But as Fidel Herrera took over and 2005 commenced, the gangland violence in Veracruz was growing in a very public way. Three people were killed in a shootout that authorities attributed to a "settling of scores" between factions of the Gulf Cartel. Journalist Raúl Gibb Guerrero was fatally shot eight times in an ambush after receiving threats, and Veracruz saw more narco killings in the first three months of the year than had occurred in the entire previous year. The federal government sent the army to try to quell the violence. Still, the crimes continued. The remains of a businessman and his chauffeur were found in a suspected hit by organized crime.

Regina tried to leave the stories on drug violence to her colleagues. The only crime stories she was passionate about were the killings of journalists, which rose right alongside the drug violence. Probably more than her colleagues, she saw this as a personal threat to her future and her livelihood. She reported that in just one week of April 2005, Mexico saw two journalists killed, including Gibb, while another went missing. Under the headline NARCO PLAGUE THREATENS FREEDOM OF EXPRESSION,

Regina quoted Reporters Without Borders demanding that the federal government guarantee protection for the media.

Proceso in particular was feeling pressure in the new environment in the form of libel lawsuits, or at least threats of them. Its correspondent was kicked off the presidential plane. Correspondents in Oaxaca and Tamaulipas states were kidnapped as an intimidation tactic and later released. A correspondent in Michoacán was threatened. The magazine saw what it viewed as a campaign by the Calderón government to link *Proceso* with organized crime.

The Mexican government had a habit of doing "perp walks" whenever it caught members of drug gangs. It would display the suspects and their guns, drugs, communications equipment, and anything else confiscated in a bust for the media to photograph. Two times, they displayed copies of *Proceso* along with the contraband, implying that they had found copies of the magazine in narco hideouts, and said that one drug lord ordered his underlings to buy *Proceso* every week. Government officials said a protected witness testified that narcos were paying one of *Proceso*'s correspondents. The editors found it a dangerous ploy and filed a complaint with the National Human Rights Commission.

★

REGINA CONTINUED WITH her same topics, like the 3.5-billion-peso loan Miguel Alemán requested just before leaving office. According to her scathing retrospective of Alemán's six years in office, the loan was to cover the deficit Alemán was leaving, despite having accomplished no public works or services other than part of a highway. Her focus on state budget irregularities brought her an unlikely ally, Miguel Ángel Yunes Márquez, a young opposition state legislator on the congressional audit committee and the son of Miguel Ángel Yunes Linares, who Regina had often skewered when he was the government secretary under Patricio Chirinos. The younger Yunes was willing to ignore her disputes with his father when he discovered that Regina was the only reporter in the state interested in complicated subjects and in poring through documents to get a story. He began leaking Regina financial documents from the audit committee.

At the end of the Fidel Herrera administration, Regina wrote the same story again of a governor's request for a huge loan just before leaving office, only this time it was 10 billion pesos. She quoted opposition legislator Sergio Vaca saying he was offered a bribe of 1.5 million pesos to vote yes on the loan. He said he refused.

Regina loved her scoops. Publication days were her holidays, the rare times she was openly radiant, walking around with a copy *Proceso* in whip hand. While the reality remained that investigative reporting had little impact on Mexico's elected officials or their habits, there was joy in tweaking a power structure that felt entitled to do what it wanted while placating the masses with handouts and lies. In one such story, Regina found a lucrative business connection between Governor Fidel Herrera and a textile magnate nicknamed "the Denim King," who was linked to a pedophile ring involving some of the country's wealthiest and most powerful men.

When Regina started on her exclusive report, Kamel Nacif was already in all the newspapers for the scandal known as Mi Gober Precioso. A year earlier, in 2005, the investigative reporter Lydia Cacho had published a book, *The Demons of Eden*, about a pornography and prostitution ring involving young girls in the resort city of Cancún. In it, she outlined associates of the ringleader, Mexican businessman Jean Succar Kuri, who had already been tried and convicted to 112 years in prison when the book was published. Nacif was named in the book as a close associate of Succar's, even paying for his criminal defense. Another associate was Mario Marín, the governor of Puebla state, in central Mexico.

In the Wild West of impunity that is Mexico, Nacif and Marín decided to kidnap Cacho in 2005 and smuggle her to Puebla to faces defamation charges because of her book. She was captured in Cancún, beaten, and threatened with rape. The scandal went viral when the Mexican press was leaked telephone recordings of Nacif and Marín congratulating each other for "whacking the head of that old bitch."

Mi gober precioso, Nacif said to Marín. "My dear governor."

Nacif was Herrera's business partner, Regina discovered. They had cooked up a scheme to sell electricity Nacif could generate in shuttered textile mills in Veracruz. According to Regina's article, Herrera pressured eighty-nine municipalities to buy their electricity from this new utility, promising a 10 percent discount in electric bills. Meanwhile, the profits would go to a company in which Nacif was the sole administrator.

Regina's favorite part of the whole story was the headline that appeared in *Proceso* referring to Herrera as EL OTRO GOBER PRECIOSO (THE OTHER DEAR GOVERNOR). Herrera was furious. That week's edition of *Proceso* disappeared from the Xalapa newsstands. Regina loved the cat-and-mouse game, calling her colleagues around the state to see if the magazine had been pulled from other cities as well.

Herrera called the story "reckless, unfounded," an attempt to attack the credibility of his administration. "You will not be successful," he was quoted as saying in *Política*, Regina's own newspaper, which refused to print the original story—only Herrera's rebuttal.

Even as she was sidelined for her critical stories, Regina maintained her talk show for *Política* television, run by Don Yayo's son Ricardo Gutiérrez, who remained loyal to her. She still scored the week's newsmakers for the show: whatever politician was in the spotlight or a top official or literary figure visiting Xalapa for an event. In September 2006, her guest was state representative Alejandro Montano, who she had covered over the years for his alleged ties to narcos and, more recently, as the person who, as head of public security and in charge of transit authorities, had given lucrative taxi concessions to members of his family. Montano was considering seeking higher office and willingly accepted the TV interview. Afterward, as he shook her hand, he thanked Regina for the opportunity to appear. "The next time I see you, I'll have to invite you for a *pan de muerto*," he said, referring to the special Mexican pastry made only during November's Day of the Dead celebration. Rodrigo Soberanes, who also worked at the TV station, heard the exchange but thought nothing of it, until he saw Regina's face. It had gone white.

"Did you hear that?" she said. "He just threatened me!"

By 2007, Regina had become just too uncomfortable for Yolanda Carlín, who maintained a very close relationship with Fidel Herrera. He and his wife appeared on the front page of the newspaper with Carlín when Herrera was a guest speaker at the twentieth-anniversary celebration of *Política*'s founding. Regina became persona non grata in her own newsroom. *Política* stopped publishing her stories. They wanted her to quit, but she waited to get fired, because under Mexican law, the newspaper would have to pay her a severance—money *Política* didn't want to expend. She came to work every day, did her reporting, and wrote stories that never saw the light of day in *Política*, but that she was also sending to *Proceso*.

Though they both worked for the magazine, Jorge Carrasco and Regina had not yet met, but he was about to get to know her. There is a famous saying in Mexico that there are three untouchables: the president, the military, and the Virgin of Guadalupe. Regina was about to take on two out of the three.

CHAPTER II

Reginazos

February 2007

O N A CHILLY late-February afternoon, seventy-three-year-old Ernestina Ascencio left her hut in the Veracruz village of Tetlatzinga with her two dogs to herd sheep in the rocky soil of the Zongolica, a remote mountainous area about a four-hour drive from Xalapa. When she didn't return, her children went looking for her. Her daughter found her lying in a ravine, near death, just outside a military encampment. She had been raped and beaten. She muttered one thing in her native Nahuatl: "The ones in green."

She clearly meant soldiers.

She died the next day, February 26, 2007.

The federal government had sent a battalion to the Zongolica from the Twenty-sixth Military Zone near Xalapa, and about two hundred soldiers had set up camp near Tetlatzinga the day before, about three hundred yards from where Ernestina was found. Residents of the tiny indigenous community, where many speak only the native Aztec language Nahuatl, were so incensed with the news of Ernestina's death that they gathered and surrounded the military encampment, threatening to exact justice themselves. (Lynching is not uncommon in Mexico's remote communities.) The mayor got them to back off, but he called Governor Fidel Herrera and told him he needed to come immediately to avoid a conflict with "the worst kind of consequences."

Herrera arrived by helicopter the next day, but he couldn't address the community because of his tight schedule. He told the mayor that he could be sure they would pursue the criminals to the fullest extent of the law and that the Mexican Army would want the same. He also promised two school buses and road repairs for the community, paid his condolences to Ernestina's family, and left.

The indigenous community for years had complained of abuses by the military that regularly patrolled the Sierra, mostly in search of guerrilla groups. They implored government officials to remove them. No one knew exactly why the army continued its patrols: The Dirty War was long over. The most recent plea was a letter earlier that same month to the military base in Orizaba saying community members could no longer tolerate the abuse and invasion of their land. The complaints included soldiers stealing firewood, arbitrarily detaining people, taking over private property, and harassing and sexually assaulting local women. According to one local mayor, families stopped sending their daughters to school for fear of what would happen to them while they walked in rural areas alone. The response? "This brutal killing," said Julio Atenco Vidal, director of works and development for the town and a lifelong activist for indigenous rights.

Regina's first report, with details of the crime, appeared on Sunday, March 4, 2007, *Proceso*'s publication day. There was another competing story that day: the Villarín horserace shooting near the Veracruz airport that killed Zeta leader Efraín Teodoro Torres and launched the state's deadly cartel war. But it was the attack on Ernestina Ascencio that dominated the news that day.

Within the next few days, Regina had made the drive to Tetlatzinga. Already, government representatives had started distributing groceries and bicycles to the angry residents in the municipality, Soledad Atzompa, where the town was located. As she arrived in the small village, Regina saw crews of masons with sacks of concrete, bundles of rebar, and cinderblocks already at work on the houses that Fidel Herrera had promised Ernestina's family. The elderly woman had left five children and thirty grandchildren.

Regina made it to the plywood hut where Ernestina had lived and listened to the details of what had happened from her son Francisco as he sat across from her on the dirt floor. Candles cast a glow on an image of the Virgin of Guadalupe, part of an altar erected in Ernestina's memory; the altar was surrounded by bundles of white flowers in plastic buckets on the floor.

"We're still in the novena," Francisco said in a mixture of Spanish and Nahuatl, referring to the nine days of prayer to help the deceased pass from purgatory into heaven.

A biting wind broke through gaps in the uneven boards. Tetlatzinga, a community of only 168 families, was seven thousand feet in altitude and shaded by pine trees. The inhabitants' main source of income was fashioning rustic furniture from the local wood.

"The first thing I saw was my mother's dogs and sheep," Ernestina's daughter Marta told Regina. "They were wandering. The dogs took me to where she was lying. She could barely speak. But she was able to say they were soldiers. They had beaten her and tied her up. Then she asked me for a drink of water."

Ernestina's sons had to load their mother into the bed of a small pickup to get medical help. Because the area is so isolated, they first took her to the nurse in town, who said they needed to get her to another town, where there was a doctor. Driving over a winding mountain pass, they reached the doctor, who said she needed the regional hospital in Río Blanco. In all, it took ten hours to get Ernestina to the hospital. She died there the next day.

Regina interviewed the medical examiner at the hospital, who said Ernestina had broken ribs, cracked vertebrae, lesions on her body, and vaginal and anal tears consistent with sexual assault. The cause of death was a fractured skull and anemia from a hemorrhage in the anal canal, Regina wrote.

Everyone assured the family that the authorities would find and prosecute the culprits. Fidel Herrera called it "a horrible, murderous assassination of a native of Veracruz, Mrs. Ernestina Ascencio, who was brutally violated and her body thrown onto a hillside, there, in a hole."

Investigators from the National Human Rights Commission came and said the evidence looked consistent with a sexual assault. The military encampment was shut down, and the troops were ordered back to the main base. The case first went to the state's special prosecutor for sex crimes and crimes against the family, and word got out that four soldiers had been arrested.

Then representatives of the federal government arrived, and the story changed.

★

LIKE CARLOS SALINAS, who was accused of stealing the presidential election from Cuauhtémoc Cárdenas in the late 1980s, Felipe Calderón had a credibility problem when he took office on December 1, 2006. He won the race against the leftist candidate, Andrés Manuel López Obrador, by a hair, and many accused him, too, of having stolen the election. López Obrador supporters camped out on Mexico's City's Paseo de la Reforma, blocking the main thoroughfare in protest for months. Calderón was inaugurated in a rapid, two-minute ceremony in the congressional chambers, while rival lawmakers brawled to try to stop his swearing in. He had secretly taken the oath the night before, in case he didn't make it into the chambers.

Just ten days into his term, on December 11, 2006, Calderón shocked the country by sending 6,500 troops to his home state, Michoacán, to battle drug cartels, which he said had taken over. The government needed to act decisively, he said, to prevent organized crime from overrunning the country. The move puzzled many. Calderón had campaigned to be the president of jobs, to fix the Mexican economy as the exodus of migrants to the United States was at its height. Most Mexicans at the time didn't consider security a huge problem. In fact, when Calderón took office, Mexico was experiencing its lowest murder and crime rates possibly in the history of the country, certainly since an official count had started in the early 1990s. The murder rate hit its lowest point in 2007, when homicides per one hundred thousand people fell from a peak of nineteen in the 1990s to eight, not far off from the U.S. rate of six that same year.

People could only speculate that Calderón wanted to appear tough, in charge. In January 2007, he outlined a five-point plan to improve security, and it centered heavily on the Mexican Army. He held the army up as the most trusted government force, which he dispatched to the streets, he said, because so many local police organizations had become corrupt and were colluding with criminals. Now it was February, nearly two months into his ambitious plan, and the top story in the country was about army soldiers raping and beating a helpless, elderly indigenous woman.

There was a dispute among a competitive gang of reporters—Regina, Andrés Timoteo, and Norma Trujillo—about who broke the Ernestina Ascencio story. But the person who owned the story was Regina Martínez. She wrote every detail and turn in the case for *Proceso* in articles that appeared for weeks on consecutive Sundays, producing one exclusive after another.

★

AFTER PROMISING JUSTICE, the army changed its story to say it was not soldiers, but rather, men *dressed* as soldiers who had committed the crime. As proof, the commander of the post issued a public statement saying they had examined the genitals of four officers and seventy-nine troops and none had exhibited injuries consistent with sexual activity "for at least seven days before the events they are accused of." The commander later tried to withdraw the statement, Regina reported, saying it was not official, but it had already been widely distributed.

As the days went on, the story continued to shift. Not only were there no longer soldiers involved, but suddenly, there was no evidence of a crime having been committed at all. The arrests the local residents had heard about didn't exist. Eleven days after Ernestina's death, the head of the National Human Rights Commission, Rodrigo Soberanes's uncle José Luis Soberanes, ordered her body exhumed for another examination. He said the result wouldn't be ready for weeks. Yet, four days later, President Calderón told a Mexico City newspaper that Ernestina Ascencio had died of chronic untreated gastritis.

The National Human Rights Commission's report agreed that there was no evidence of sexual assault and that the broken bones and other injuries had been caused by the jostling that occurred as her family carried her to the hospital in a pickup truck. The commission slammed the local medical examiners who did the original report, citing "omissions and inconsistencies." The medical examiners, including Juan Pablo Mendizábal, were suspended by the Veracruz attorney general.

Residents of Soledad Atzompa and the Zongolica were predictably outraged, claiming a government cover-up. There were at least a dozen witnesses who had seen Ernestina's condition as she was loaded onto the truck bed. And no one believed that her daughter Marta had been lying about what her mother said to her as she lay dying.

For the first time, Regina's reporting was directly challenging the veracity of the highest authorities in the land. With each edition of *Proceso*, she reported a new chapter in the absurdities put forth by the federal government. How had President Calderón gotten a cause of death in four days when the Human Rights Commission had said its inquiry would take weeks?

"We don't know if the president gave his opinion without knowing the case and made a mistake or tried to protect the army," Javier Pérez Pascuala, the mayor of Soledad Atzompa, told Regina. "If so, it's very disturbing conduct for the head of our nation."

The Human Rights Commission gave another cause of death: "acute bleeding from her digestive tube." The head of the regional hospital gave yet another reason for her fractures, saying her ribs were cracked when she went into cardiac arrest, and medical workers tried to revive her using chest compressions. Regina asked the state's special prosecutor if he had been pressured to change his story. He said no.

"We Mexicans are very screwed if the [Human Rights Commission] caves to the perverse interests of the army," Regina quoted the indigenous rights leader Julio Atenco as saying. "It's the only reliable institution involved in the case, and now they're saying there was no rape."

The suspended medical examiner, Mendizábal, wouldn't speak to anyone in the press, but he sent a written statement only to Regina. He listed his twenty years of experience and his university training and maintained that the work had been carried out "with full adherence to the law and without serving any petty political, economic, or other interest." Regina's report that the original medical examiner stood by his work, despite state persecution, was yet another exclusive.

There were rumors of other cases of abuse by soldiers. Reporters tracked down a girl who they heard was raising a child who had been fathered during a rape by a soldier. The rape victim had turned away a crew with cameras, but when Regina arrived, she decided to speak. The girl was only twelve when she was raped by two soldiers while walking to school on a rainy day through the mud. She knew nothing about sex or pregnancy and had gotten her first period only three months earlier. After a time, she started to feel kicking in her stomach. Her mother was dead, and she was sure her father would throw her out of the house. Her godmother took her to the local group that advocated for indigenous rights, which in turn alerted the governor's office of this and other abuses. Regina wrote exclusively in *Proceso*:

> Three months after Carmen's daughter was born, in early 2002, the OINSZ leadership, headed by Juan Carlos Mezhua Campos and Celfa Méndez, arranged a meeting with then-Governor Miguel Alemán to ask him to intercede "so that high army field commanders coordinate with civil authorities and thus avoid further abuse in the region."
>
> There, says Mezhua Campos, "we told Gov. Alemán what had happened to the girl, and they promised that they would help her to at least live in peace." In all, 20 cases of abuses committed by soldiers against civilians in the Sierra de Zongolica were presented to Alemán. The most serious, stresses the now leader of the PRD, "was the rape of the 12-year-old girl who became pregnant."
>
> They gave the girl a medical exam and detected anemia. Then they gave her groceries and baby clothes and sent her

home. Days later, when Carmen's father had already accepted Maria del Carmen's return with her daughter, "a group of 20 armed soldiers broke into his house, threatening and frightening the victim and his family," Mezhua said.

The teenager remembers that the military "went to the farm where I was working. There was a downpour. They took pictures. I ran for my girl, covered her with a quilt and ran to hide, but they followed me.

"They told me to leave them alone, because I was hurting them by saying they had raped me. They told me to stop pursuing it. I didn't answer them. I just crouched down, hugging my girl, and they kept taking photos."

Regina's ultimate bombshell in the Ernestina Ascencio case was a photograph leaked from the morgue. The image was of Ernestina, deceased, lying on a white tiled medical examiner's table with a bloody head wound—an odd thing to find on a person who had died of gastritis. (Some countered it was blood from the autopsy). The photo was published in *Proceso*.

Regina reported that the Interior Ministry corralled Ernestina's family and convinced them to stop speaking to the press. Ten weeks after Ernestina's death, the Veracruz state prosecutor also announced that the elderly woman had died of natural causes and had exhibited fecal blockage and internal bleeding. The case was closed. The family would not comment.

The forty communities of the Zongolica were in shock and promised to carry the case to the Inter-American Court of Human Rights. The Veracruz Civil Organizations Network issued a statement: "They used the power of the State to encircle the family and create an official version to exonerate the army. And the state government preferred to give them an out, a negotiated exit, showing the state to be nothing more than an appendage of the presidency."

Regina's final story on the case ran under the headline EL GOBER-NADOR SE DOBLA (THE GOVERNOR CAVED). It was another blow to Fidel Herrera, and it was circulating to the entire country via *Proceso*.

Despite the outcome of Ernestina Ascencio case, Regina's reporting did have an impact. Less than a month after the case was closed, the Mexican Congreso de la Unión took up a bill to change both the constitution and the military code to give civil authorities the sole responsibility for prosecuting crimes committed by the military against civilians. They cited the death of Ernestina Ascencio as one of the motivating cases for the bill—"the lack of transparency, arbitrariness and impunity with which an issue can be treated when the institutions agree to do so, in this case, because it had to do with the intervention of the army."

The Ernestina Ascencio story was the last straw for *Política*. The newspaper wouldn't publish any of Regina's stories on the killing—and, finally, Yolanda Carlín let her go. Carlín fired her own son Ricardo Gutiérrez on the same day. Regina and Ricardo both hired the same lawyer to fight their dismissals. In the end, Regina was able to negotiate a severance package with Carlín that allowed her to buy the modest bungalow she had been renting.

With her departure from *Política*, Regina went from a correspondent for *Proceso*, paid by the story, to having a full-time contract, writing for the magazine but also filing daily reports for the *Proceso* news service, APRO. She continued with her theme: public corruption and human rights. But as time went on, Regina again was pulled into writing about drug violence.

The environment for reporting in Veracruz continued to get worse. Reporters Without Borders issued a press release demanding action on two robberies that occurred in the home of Regina's colleague Andrés Timoteo, one of the other major reporters on the Ernestina Ascencio story. His laptop and a USB of archives were stolen. When police showed up to investigate, they told him the thief would have done better to steal the ceramic set he had in the living room. When Timoteo returned home later that day, the ceramic set also was gone. He moved out.

What Regina didn't tell the advocacy groups, or anyone, was that her home, too, had been broken into and her laptop stolen.

At one point, Fidel Herrera, like Miguel Alemán, tried to reach out to Regina to have a "talk" about her stories. He decided to go through one of her longtime friends who worked for Ranulfo Márquez, his director of civil protection. The friend reached out and invited Regina to have breakfast with her, Herrera, and her boss, Márquez. Regina reluctantly agreed, but on the day of the breakfast, they waited for Regina, and waited. Finally, the friend called her to find out what had happened.

"I can't bear to do it," Regina said.

The second in charge for Herrera when he and Regina went head-to-head was Reynaldo Escobar.

★

IN LATE 2008, two decades into their careers, Regina and Jorge Carrasco's paths finally crossed. He was asked to fill in when *Proceso*'s assistant director went on vacation, and he worked directly as Regina's editor, though over the phone. He already knew her distinguished reporting, and he found her easy to work with. She wrote a lot, and she would cover any subject, the perfect correspondent. Many of her stories were published by APRO, which acted as a wire service for media around the country. The subscribers in Veracruz who were unwilling to publish their own critical stories simply printed Regina's. It was an arms-length protection for them from the government censors and a way in which Regina's stories got the widest distribution, putting her at the forefront statewide for critical journalism.

She was noticed, and not in a way she liked. Two years before she was killed, a Veracruz newspaper columnist, Carlos Lucio Acosta, was leaked a list of "uncomfortable reporters" compiled by the state government. Regina was on it. The leaked document said those listed should be investigated "because they weren't magnifying the political, economic, cultural, social and religious work" of Governor Fidel Herrera. The document was styled like instructions, as if to a team, saying they were to investigate the listed journalists' public and private lives and collect personal data, including their sexual orientation, social acquaintances, and sources. The instructions also mandated that state spies find out the reporters' political leanings and whether they had ties to Herrera's political enemy, Miguel Ángel Yunes, and the opposition party, National Action Party, or PAN, its Spanish initials.

"The information provided to this reporter by a source who asked not to be identified, indicated that along with the format to collect personal data, the project operators are provided with computer equipment, software, and video recorders for spying," the columnist wrote.

The year 2011 brought more violence to Veracruz. It started with newspaper columnist Noel López Olguín being abducted by gunmen in the southern part of the state. His body was found three months later in a mass grave. It was also the year that the two *Notiver* journalists, Milo Vela and Yolanda Ordaz, were assassinated.

At about this time, Lev García wrote a small story about Javier Duarte and his family showing up forty minutes late to a performance of the Youth Orchestra of the Americas in the Veracruz State Theater. The concert was held up until they arrived. When Duarte entered, the crowd whistled and booed solidly for several minutes, with some yelling, "What an embarrassment!" The booing stopped only when the musicians took their seats onstage and prepared to play. Lev wrote that Duarte had learned well from his political mentor, Fidel Herrera, who got booed in 2004 for showing up thirty minutes late to a symphony performance. Again, the musicians were made to wait. When Herrera finally entered that hall, the conductor asked for a round of applause for the governor, to which the audience started whistling and booing. One concertgoer yelled that they were being asked to applaud a "thug."

Reforma published his article at the bottom of the front page.

A few days later, Lev was working at his bar El Conspirador when he noticed two men outside looking at his motorcycle, a black Honda VTX 1300 cruiser. He went to see what they wanted. They started chatting him up, admiring and asking questions about the bike. Something about them seemed off—the way they were dressed, the way they spoke, more like hired hands than motorcycle enthusiasts. He thought maybe they would try to steal the bike, and he asked a friend to keep an eye on it. Polo Hernández came by the bar that night, and as on many nights, he stayed until closing. When a couple of employees finished and headed home, they noticed that the same two men were waiting outside in a white Nissan, a Tsuru, the model known in Mexico for being used by taxis and criminals. One of the employees called Lev to warn him. The rest still in the bar, including Polo, hatched a quick plan. No one called the police, because there was a good chance the perpetrators *were* the police. The first group who had left waited outside in a taxi while Polo and others called a second taxi. The bar faced two streets, Allende heading downhill, and a second one that climbed the hill to Parque Juárez. The two taxis waited on the uphill road.

When Lev left the bar, he hopped onto his bike and faced it the wrong way down the street, avoiding the Tsuru and making a sharp turn onto the uphill road, where he sped off. The two taxis sped after him as protection. The Tsuru followed in pursuit, driving on the sidewalk at one point to get around Polo and his friends in the two taxis.

Meanwhile, Lev headed to a house uphill where he and his friends had planned to meet. Two beloved things in life, his bike and his friends, had saved him. He escaped what he assumed was a kidnapping attempt, or maybe an assault designed to scare him. But on the part of whom? It could have been narcos who wanted to demand a ransom, something that was happening to business owners around the city. Or it could have been the government in retaliation for something he wrote. After consulting some friends, he decided it wasn't narcos, because they would have walked into the bar and just taken him. These guys were so inept that they must have been hired by the government. But for what? Lev could only guess it was because of the front-page article about Javier Duarte getting booed at the concert.

When Lev told his editors what happened, they pulled him out of Veracruz and sent him to work in another state for a time. Meanwhile, two men matching the description of those who had chased him showed up outside the house of someone close to Lev in Mexico City, watching from a taxi without plates.

After about six months, *Reforma* decided it was safe for Lev to return. But after Regina's death, when they had to pull him out again, the newspaper published a story, top of the front page, linking Erick Lagos, Duarte's number two in charge of running the state, to organized crime. The article cited the deposition of a Zeta regional leader known as "El Lucky," who said the cartel paid Veracruz police and prosecutors thirty million pesos a month in bribes and that the cartel's contact with the state government was a man named "Lagos."

Lagos responded with a rebuttal the next day, saying he was surprised at how prominently *Reforma* had placed "the declarations of a presumed criminal." A key government and party official when Lev was kidnapped, Lagos may have been on to something. It wasn't unheard of for large media outlets to send messages via stories when their reporters were under attack: "We know it's you, and we know what you're doing." Lagos vehemently denied the accusations.

In September, Regina and Jorge Carrasco had their only byline together, a cover story on the thirty-five bodies dumped in broad daylight—the story I had asked Regina for help on. It meticulously described how Duarte had rapidly lost control of his state to criminal forces, and it called his first year in office the most violent in Veracruz history. The Zetas cartel was even torturing and killing marines, the elite forces based in Veracruz who Calderón had dispatched to fight the drug war. The article announced the appearance of a rival group, the Jalisco New Generation Cartel, whose stated mission was to wipe out the Zetas.

As a result of the wave of violence, Reynaldo Escobar stepped down as state attorney general after less than a year on the job. He cited "personal reasons."

The next month, Regina wrote for *Proceso* how dangerous it had become for journalists in the state, under the headline VERACRUZ: THE HIGH RISK OF INFORMING. She quoted a member of the PAN opposition party saying when investigative reporters "start to find some threads that do not suit some politicians, they repress and threaten them." She described the government painting the dead journalists as narcos and the psychosis that had set in among Xalapa residents, terrorized by the violence and uncertainty.

She also agreed to be interviewed by an organization of journalists, though she wanted to be anonymous.

Regina called 2011 the most difficult time of her career in terms of repression, censorship, and fear. In November, she met with Jorge Carrasco in the offices of *Proceso* in Mexico City. "No more," she said.

"Do not assign me any more stories on drug cartels, please. It's becoming way too dangerous. I don't want to do it anymore."

Jorge still remembers how insistent she was.

"I'll write about drug violence only if it's official information that I can pass on to you," she said. "But nothing else. I can't do it. I'm done."

That Christmas, Regina returned to Xalapa from her family vacation to cover another giant shootout, the third major gun battle in Veracruz that year. Criminals attacked a series of passenger buses, then came under fire from Mexican soldiers. Eleven civilians and five gunmen were killed.

When Regina arrived at her house, she discovered that someone had broken in, without a single lock or her iron gate having been disturbed. They stole more than three thousand dollars in cash she had in the house, money she was planning to use to buy a mini-SUV that Lev was selling. Whoever took the money had gone straight to her hiding place without disturbing anything. There was something else odd: Her bathroom was steamed up as if someone had just showered there, and her decorative soaps were squashed.

A few days later, Mariela San Martín, the seamstress, called. She had last been at Regina's in early December to get measurements for curtains. She had tried and tried her number, finally reaching her after Christmas. "I've been trying to reach you. I have your curtains," she said.

★

WHEN MARIELA SHOWED up at Regina's door, Regina said she had something to tell her. "I don't want you to tell anyone. I've already told the magazine. Someone broke into my house." She said not a lock had been broken, and she told Mariela about the soaps. "I guess I made a bad investment," Regina said. "I've been spending to make all these repairs, and now I don't feel safe living here."

"Get a dog," Mariela urged her. "At least he'll bark or let you know if something is wrong."

"Naw," Regina said. "When they come to kill me, they would just kill the dog, too."

"Think, Regina, think. Who has a key to your house?"

She thought for a moment. Then a look of recognition came over her face. She didn't answer Mariela's question.

Regina's friends took the break-in as an ominous message "that they can get into the most intimate area of her house," Rodrigo Soberanes said.

The locksmith who came to reinforce her locks said the break-in was a professional job.

★

AFTER LEV GARCÍA returned to Xalapa in early 2012, he began to stick closer to Regina, Rodrigo Soberanes, and Polo Hernández. They started a system of check-ins with one another, whether they were out on a story or in for the night. They now realized how exposed they were. All were single, lived alone, and were very protective of their personal lives and information. Given the events of the last six months, they decided it would be prudent to form their own circle of protection. Regina wasn't very good at it, but she would answer if texted—except on weekends. She wanted her friends to respect her time to herself, and they agreed.

The friends started reporting stories together, planning to publish in their various media on the same days, so no single person could become a target for a controversial piece. Regina and Polo collaborated on a story about a shootout, allegedly between federal forces and cartel operatives. According to official reports, eleven gunmen were killed and another eight detained. One of the men killed was named Joaquín Figueroa Vázquez, fifty-three, who was coincidentally the father of a young woman who was Polo's friend. The woman called Polo to tell him that her dad was a diesel mechanic, not a cartel gunman, and that the state had fabricated the story to cover up for its killing of innocent civilians. For safety, Polo and Regina investigated the claims together. They produced a damning report under a double byline that ran in media outlets all over the state. Among other things, they found that Joaquín was returning to Xalapa from Córdoba with two other coworkers in a white company van when he failed to heed a military checkpoint. But when the family saw photos of the three murdered men from the scene, their bodies were in a different vehicle, a black truck, and all three had large-caliber guns alongside them. What's more, the men who had supposedly been killed in a gun battle with soldiers and federal police had been beaten in the face almost beyond recognition. Figueroa had received a single shot, execution style, to the back of his neck. The story pointed to federal forces manipulating a crime scene to cover an extrajudicial killing of innocent people.

This piqued Regina's interest. How many other innocent people had suffered the same fate and been passed off as criminals? she wondered. Even though she was done covering cartel violence, she couldn't help thinking like a reporter.

The friends continued to pool their efforts in the spring of 2012, including after Enrique Peña Nieto announced his candidacy for president and made a campaign stop in the Port of Veracruz. Regina and a group of other reporters carpooled with Lev to the port to cover the event.

Jenaro Villamil had come from Mexico City for *Proceso*. He was covering the presidential race nationally and was preparing a report for the Sunday magazine. Because he didn't know the state that well, Regina sat at his shoulder during the event, pointing out the local politicians and people of import who greeted and dined with the man who, in a matter of months, would be elected president. They stood in a gallery above the luncheon, where everyone could see them working together.

Villamil had received leaked documents about two Veracruz PRI politicians, Reynaldo Escobar and Alejandro Montano, who attended the event and were running for the national congress. The documents showed that Escobar was suspected of allowing the Zetas to take over Veracruz, with the testimonies of fourteen protected witnesses as the source of this information. Other documents showed that Montano owned a newspaper, nine buildings, a house worth more than $1.5 million, and nearly four acres of land in a subdivision under his wife's name—all on a public servant's salary.

Villamil offered Regina the documents because Veracruz was her beat.

"No," she told him. "They came to you. You take the story."

When Regina and Lev García returned to Xalapa the evening after the Peña Nieto event, the reporters went their separate ways, Lev to his favorite cantina, Los Álamos, to write his story. His own bar would be too distracting.

Los Álamos was a classic hole-in-the-wall, rustic, with white plastic chairs, tables covered in picnic cloths, and walls painted with wild, monstrous images of a graphic novel. As soon as he settled in, Lev got a call from Regina. She had some information she needed to verify. He invited her to the cantina.

"Naw," she said. "You're there with all your friends, and I don't feel like talking to them."

"I'm here by myself."

In no time, she was pulling up a plastic chair at the only table with a Wi-Fi signal. Lev was a bit surprised to see her; she hated going to cantinas. She carried only her telephone and asked if she could borrow Lev's computer to write her story.

"You go first, because you have to get yours in quicker, and lend it to me after," she said. "I'll edit my notes in the meantime."

She had ordered a beer, but it sat untouched while she wrote. "When she worked, the rest of the world around her didn't exist—just her, her voice recorder, and her computer," Lev later told me.

When they finished writing, she seemed in a rare mood to talk. "So, Lev," she started, "have you decided to settle down yet?" She was referring to his rotating romances.

He laughed. "No. And it's not because I'm not looking. I just haven't found her yet."

"You should think about that, about settling down. Stop the craziness."

The two rarely talked like this, but Lev was open to it. He trusted her.

"You know, I've been thinking," she continued, "about slowing down a bit. Cutting back on my work. Maybe writing about other things. Maybe doing something else entirely."

Regina said she admired Lev for having a life outside work. He had his bars, his bike, his girlfriends. She had consecrated her life to journalism. "I want a personal life. I want a partner," she said. Then she paused. "Can I tell you something that you promise never to repeat?"

Lev nodded.

"I've met someone."

Lev listened without reacting.

"It's making me think," she paused, "about having something solid, something serious, a family life. I don't want to keep dedicating one hundred percent of my time to this job."

Lev didn't ask any questions. With his friends, he left the reporter's notebook in the bag; he just listened. He wondered if maybe that's why such a hermetic person like Regina chose him to share her confidential information. He assumed her new love interest was someone he didn't know, because if it had been one of their close friends, she would have had her catbird look. She loved it when she had gossip or a scoop that she knew everyone else wanted to know. It always showed on her face.

"Hey, do you remember I told you that I have a nephew?" she said, changing the subject.

Lev had only a vague recollection.

"Guess what he wants to be?"

"I don't know."

"A journalist. What do you think?"

Lev broke out laughing. "Don't let him! You don't have to look any farther than us to know that!"

The two friends laughed heartily.

"Do you ever think of making a change, of leaving journalism?" she asked.

Lev knew her question was in the context of his near-kidnapping and his need to flee the state for a while. A lot of his friends were asking him the same question. Why, after all that, had he returned to Xalapa and the same work? What he endured stirred all of them to reflect, to think about the risks they were taking and to what end. Of course, it had crossed Lev's mind, too, that it might be wise to do something else.

"I don't want to die doing journalism," he told her. "But I can't seem to stop doing it, either."

"I know; it's hard to leave," she said.

They both laughed, but this time more compulsively, out of resignation to what their lives looked like, to the reality that being a good journalist in Mexico at that time meant sacrifice. It was not what they intended, but they both had put other things in life on hold out of necessity.

The two accomplices smiled at one another across their beer mugs.

Regina knew that Lev wasn't going to leave reporting.

Lev knew the Regina wasn't going to cut back.

The following Sunday, alongside his story about the Peña Nieto campaign, Jenaro Villamil published a bylined report on the leaked documents and accusations of corruption against Escobar and Montano. When the story came out, copies of *Proceso* were nowhere to be found on Veracruz newsstands. It was April 8, 2012. Regina called her editors in Mexico City to report that, once again, someone had disappeared the magazine.

Apparently, state officials were not pleased.

CHAPTER 12

The Cover-Up

April 2013

JUST A YEAR after Regina's murder, El Silva, the former child prostitute, was convicted as an accomplice in the crime. Meanwhile, El
Jarocho, the alleged killer, was nowhere to be found. According to El
Silva's false testimony, Jarocho had left town eight days after the murder,
but not before confessing to killing Regina to his wife, Rosario, when
she demanded to know how he had cut his arm. But Veracruz authorities didn't seem to be looking for Jarocho; they had their man.

For those closest to the case, the ultimate insult came when the state
concluded that Regina's murder was a crime of passion.

Rodrigo Soberanes was in despair. Regina had disappeared on the
weekends to create an impervious wall for her own protection. Now
investigators had used that wall against her to say that she led a double
life.

Proceso writer Jenaro Villamil was also in despair. He was convinced
that Regina was killed because of his story about Montano and Escobar,
not anything she wrote.

Jorge Carrasco, the chief correspondent on the story and Regina's
one-time editor, found the whole outcome offensive. It was an affront

to him, the magazine, and the memory of Regina. It was an insult to their intelligence, as if authorities were outright laughing at them. Once the case was complete and went to a judge, Jorge no longer had to worry about his reporting hurting the investigation. He was done writing around the edges of the bad telenovela—the serious reporter and her secret double life—that the state had created to explain away Regina's death.

Jorge thought about his last conversation with Regina, in late 2011, when she said she no longer wanted to cover organized crime in Veracruz. The atmosphere had become too dangerous. He knew that, too. Still, he was ready to pick up where she had left off: to expose every gap, every contradiction, every manipulation of the evidence in her case by this group of government officials who, for whatever reason, felt the need to cover their tracks.

This was a confrontation now.

His gloves were off.

★

IT WASN'T ONLY Jorge Carrasco who wasn't going to let the Regina Martínez case go away. Given El Silva's testimony that he had been tortured into confessing, El Silva's pro bono lawyer, Diana Coq Toscanini, started the process to get his conviction thrown out under the justice reform. Laura Borbolla's office got federal investigators to administer the Istanbul Protocol, the UN standard for documenting evidence and effects of torture.

The judge ignored the new law on testimony from torture and sentenced El Silva to thirty-eight years in prison. Five days after El Silva was sentenced, Jorge dropped his biggest story, taking apart every inconsistency in the case. It ran under the headline WE DON'T BELIEVE YOU: A COVER-UP OF A SENTENCE.

The story said not a drop of blood or DNA found at the scene could be traced to El Silva or El Jarocho; nor the one useful fingerprint. No alcohol was found in Regina's blood, only coffee, even though the official story said she was drinking beer with the two men. El Silva was sentenced before the judge could see the results of the Istanbul Protocol.

The alleged robbers left many valuables untouched, including a laptop, a printer, and Regina's credit cards. El Jarocho was never charged, even though he was considered the murderer and was a fugitive. Although he had been in prison three times, there was no record of his DNA or fingerprints to match against the evidence. They tested Jarocho's five-year-old son for a possible DNA match with the blood samples at the scene; it came back negative. Prosecutors didn't include Jarocho's prison records in the case file, nor did they provide them to other states when asking for help in detaining him. Investigators never asked Jarocho's wife for one of his shoes to see if it fit the bloody footprint in Regina's bathroom—though, they did ask several journalists to supply their shoes. The chief prosecutor overseeing the case, Consuelo Lagunas Jiménez, said Jarocho was a lookout for the Zetas, but she never followed this line of investigation; nor did she follow multiple requests from *Proceso* to investigate Regina's work as a possible motive for her murder. Lagunas Jiménez even got the date of the murder wrong in the court documents.

The *Proceso* article was damning. Borbolla backed it up with her own examples. Among the items the robbers left in the apartment was a brand-new sound system still in its box. She said Regina's cell phone stayed active for two days after the murder and could be located via a cell tower in Xalapa. But Veracruz investigators—in a state that regularly spied on politicians and journalists—claimed they didn't have the technology to track it. The police said they found Regina's watch in a pawn shop, but the owner, who knew El Silva and Jarocho, said neither had ever pawned a watch there.

Jorge finished the story early in the week before publication and let it sit for a few days. When he read it again, before he sent it to the editors, even he was astonished at what a hard-hitting piece it was. It had flowed out of him. It was easy to write. He had all the details. It was the right time to be merciless. It had been a year, and still nothing was certain.

He looked at the article one last time on Friday. He also appeared in a debate on the radio program of Carmen Aristegui that morning, dismantling the case. Then he took off with Peniley and their son to spend a weekend in Cuernavaca, a popular leafy suburb of haciendas and second homes. It was Mexico City's Hamptons, the place people went to get out of the smog and traffic, a place that boasted the best climate in the world. They had rented a house for a big party with friends. Some of Jorge's colleagues from *Proceso* were with them. His story on the Regina case was posted on the Internet on Saturday and appeared in the printed edition on Sunday. After the radio interview on Friday, Jorge and Peniley were both nervous about the reaction. On Sunday, their son left with a family member so they could spend a few days in Cuernavaca alone.

That same day, the reaction to the article came. Jorge started getting messages on his BlackBerry from a source: "I don't know what you wrote this weekend. I haven't read it. But it was received very badly by the government of Veracruz. There was an urgent meeting that included security officials, the chief of operations for state police. They're coordinating with the Zetas to find you. They've requested all your personal information from the federal database."

The source continued texting: "These are the addresses they have for you."

"They instructed the team looking for you to be aware that they don't appear on surveillance cameras in Mexico City."

Later, the source texted an image of Jorge's driver's license. They had pulled that, too.

"They," according to the source, was a group of current and former Veracruz state officials, including Duarte spokeswoman Gina Domínguez; Interior Secretary Gerardo Buganza; José Nabor Nava Holguín, head of AVI, the state investigations agency; and José Antonio Villegas Rosas, a former head of AVI, who quit because he was under investigation for ties to drug cartels. "This asshole doesn't understand and keeps publishing things about us," one of the participants reportedly said. "We're going to have to do something to him to make him calm down."

Laura Borbolla's office confirmed that the people named had gathered in the same location around the time of the alleged meeting by the pings of their cell phones made to the same tower. There were two meetings, according to the cell records, one in the upscale Xalapa neighborhood of Las Ánimas and another in the offices of the state police.

Jorge and Peniley were stricken. Their son was already miles away in Mexico City, and it was too dangerous to return to the city to get him. Jorge called *Proceso* editor Salvador Corro and then Rafael Rodríguez, then Julio Scherer. The magazine put out an immediate statement outlining the details of the threat: "Proceso holds the government of the state of Veracruz responsible for any aggression that Jorge Carrasco Aráizaga and his family may suffer from these events."

It was written by Jorge and Peniley, unbylined. He was covering a threat on his own life.

The couple spent two more nights in Cuernavaca before returning to Mexico City, where they stayed with a nephew for a time, rather than returning to their apartment. *Proceso* was in touch with the newly formed federal protection unit for journalists, known as the Mecanismo. While the couple was staying with Jorge's nephew, two strange men showed up in the apartment complex. A neighbor asked what they wanted. They said they were looking for "el ingeniero Duarte," a name that couldn't have been a coincidence.

Jorge was terrified. He pleaded with the Mecanismo to do something, and they sent security guards the next day. This allowed him and his wife the cover to collect their son and a few belongings and get on a plane out of the country.

Whoever was out to get Jorge missed him, but there was a major casualty. With Jorge's extraction from the country, *Proceso* wasn't willing to risk losing another reporter—to the same case, no less. The investigation into the death of Regina Martínez was killed as well.

PART III

CHAPTER 13

Arrancando Motores

W HEN JORGE WAS threatened in early 2013, I was far afield of the Regina Martínez case. We were preoccupied with the changes in U.S.-Mexico relations under new president Enrique Peña Nieto:

> Mexico is ending the widespread access it gave to U.S. security agencies in the name of fighting drug trafficking and organized crime, but President Barack Obama said Tuesday he won't judge the change until he meets this week with the country's new leader.

This was the lead paragraph to one of my stories as Jorge Carrasco was fleeing the country.

I did notice one development in the case out of the corner of my eye: El Silva's sentence was thrown out in August of that year because a court ruled that his human rights had been violated in the legal process. Two of three magistrates in the Veracruz Superior Court voted to overturn the conviction based on El Silva's complaints that he had been tortured into confessing.

At Christmas that year, I ran into the Committee to Protect Journalists' Mike O'Connor at a party. He had written several articles about Regina's case, and I told him I was interested in discussing it with him. We made plans to have lunch over the holidays, but a head cold made me cancel. We rescheduled for the first week of January 2014. On December 29, 2013, O'Connor died in his sleep of an apparent heart attack.

O'Connor himself had a strange experience when he went to Xalapa to investigate Regina's murder. Someone entered his hotel room as he slept and left a box of chocolates in the drawer where he had put his reporters' notebooks. He took this as a message that he was being watched and probably an attempt to scare him. It didn't work with O'Connor, who had covered wars in Central America and the Balkans. When Rodrigo Soberanes asked him, wide-eyed, what he did when he found the chocolates, O'Connor said, "I ate them, *cabrón!*"

Rodrigo loved to tell that story over and over.

Again, I got distracted by the rotary cannon spray of news coming out of Mexico and Central America at the time. Twenty fourteen was the year that forty-three teacher's college students disappeared and that the Mexican Army massacred as many as twenty people who had already surrendered.

In 2015, I finally decided to take up Regina's case in earnest. After five years, my job as bureau chief was coming to an end. The AP, like the military, rotated its troops around the world based on specific assignments, and it liked to see you keep moving. As I was looking around for other opportunities, I became a reporter again.

Rodrigo Soberanes had worked for me for a while by then, as a Veracruz correspondent, and we had developed a good rapport. When I asked him about exploring the case, he said he would consult his friends Lev García, Polo Hernández, and Eddie Romo to see if they would be willing to meet me and hear my idea. Regina's inner circle didn't give interviews or participate in the commemorative marches that had occurred over the years. They knew Regina had hated that kind of stuff. They were reporters, not activists. Rodrigo called back quicker than I expected to tell me they had said yes. He said he would introduce me to them the next time he was in Mexico City.

About the same time, I met Jorge Carrasco. I called him up cold and said only that I wanted to introduce myself. He knew nothing about me, yet easily agreed. It was if he already guessed what I was going to ask, which was quite possible, given how quickly word travels among journalists. We met at Panadería Rosetta, a tiny cave of a breakfast bar in the popular Roma district that overflowed with businessmen, hipsters, and the district's beautiful people waiting on the sidewalk for one of a dozen stools inside. I was surprised at how refined Carrasco was for a journalist, in a coat and tie, though I couldn't help but smile at the patches on his elbows—professorial. There was nothing battle-worn about him. His face was kind and his manner open. He told me he would help me with the Regina Martínez case any way he could, though he didn't have much. Everything he knew he had already published in *Proceso*. He asked me not to tell anyone we were talking. He still felt very much at risk. He arrived to meet me in an SUV with an armed guard.

Events continued to weigh heavily on Jorge. Julio Scherer had passed away just a few weeks earlier, from sepsis. It wasn't entirely a surprise. He was approaching eighty-nine, and his health had been failing. Don Julio had always reminded Jorge of his father—his physical strength, his determination, his zest, how he was unafraid to show affection. When the phone call came, on January 7, 2015, that Don Julio had passed, Jorge felt orphaned, just as he did when he lost his own father. He never thought of himself as one seeking Don Julio's attention, though he loved it when Don Julio read his stories and gave him feedback. They gravitated toward each other organically, first, because they had both covered Chile under the dictator Augusto Pinochet, and Don Julio remained fascinated with the subject. Later, Carrasco's oldest, also named Jorge, was born on the same day as Don Julio's oldest, Julio. The small references built mutual empathy.

This time, however, Jorge felt not only for the loss of someone he personally knew and admired, but for the loss of an icon. Don Julio was *Proceso*, and by then, so was Jorge. He had worked at other top news organization with excellent editors who became good friends, but he never wore the flag as he did at *Proceso*. You put on the shirt, you carry the identity. He remembered his first story, and the first edition when he filled in for the assistant director on vacation.

But after Don Julio was gone, there was great uncertainty. There was no heir apparent. Director Rafael Rodríguez had been with Don Julio from the start, and he, too, was approaching retirement. What would happen to *Proceso*? What would happen to Jorge?

★

SHORTLY BEFORE HE fled the country, Jorge Carrasco met Julio Scherer outside Don Julio's apartment in the Mixcoac district of Mexico City and walked with him to a nearby café. Over two hours of coffee, they reflected on the trauma that had just occurred, that neither had expected nor sought. But it came, and they had suffered. For Don Julio, it reminded him very much of the coup at *Excélsior*, where he was extracted from the newsroom under the threat of violence. Don Julio was punctilious in his manner, and Jorge listened intently. There was always something to learn in any conversation with him, but this was unprecedented. Don Julio told Jorge that when he headed home the night after the coup, he wanted to quit journalism. He didn't like where it had taken him. When he told his wife, Susana, she said, "I'll support you no matter what. But journalism is who you are. What else would you do?"

Jorge had never heard Don Julio, this powerful man with so much experience and mental clarity, speak about a blow that strong, one that could knock you off balance; what that does to your spirit and how it can take you to a place where you question whether you can continue with your career.

Each of them had to weigh the impact going forward.

Jorge wasn't sure in that moment, in that conversation, how he would continue. He had known the job was dangerous. He was covering the assassination of a colleague he knew well. The brutality of her killing had moved him terribly. Still, he was able to maintain outwardly the reporter distance that allows one to write but not feel, that renders reporters heartless at times to the people who encounter us on a story. Becoming the target shattered that veneer. Still, he knew he wasn't going to quit. Reporting was like the priesthood, he and Don Julio agreed, an act of faith, of belief that what you did was essential to society and human freedom. It was a vocation from which you couldn't easily walk away.

But as with a priest, Jorge's divine mission ultimately collided with human frailty.

Jorge and his family spent about three weeks in Paris and Spain before returning to the Mexico City apartment that he bought in 2006, long before his wife and son were even on the horizon. They lived on a short, narrow tree-lined street with well-kept stately houses along one side and an infill of papery 1970s high-rise apartments (that had likely replaced earlier stately homes) on the other. His narrow five-story apartment building looked like an afterthought sandwiched in—some glass, some concrete balconies, and no discernible style. When they returned home, the Mexican government had stationed three federal police officers outside, dressed as civilians.

They quickly learned that they couldn't move without the accompaniment of these men, who were armed but who never openly displayed their weapons. The family remained terrified, and nothing about the arrangement brought any comfort. Jorge was most afraid when he was in the car, a dark SUV that was not armored and where he thought he was most vulnerable to ambush. Rather than secure, the guards made him feel more nervous, because his protectors were prepared for something terrible to happen. Every morning, he and his three-year-old son climbed into the truck for the ride to preschool at the Liceo Franco Mexicano, a twenty- to thirty-minute drive, depending on traffic. His preschooler was unfazed, referring to the bodyguards as "the neighbors."

"Come, we're going with the neighbors," Jorge would tell his son. But for Jorge and his wife, every time they saw the guards, they relived the trauma. In 2014, they had a second child, and even walks with the stroller or trips to the supermarket included armed guards. Every decision needed approval from the state. The only time they felt truly safe was inside the house. They felt free only when the guards dropped them off at the airport to go on vacation.

When Jorge returned to the *Proceso* newsroom for the first time after his brief exile, and with armed guards, he realized he no longer wanted to know anything about the Regina Martínez case or about organized crime in Veracruz, where he had written some of his best stories. He also discovered that he couldn't write—not a word. He spent three months reading and passing time before he could dig into a story again. Even then, he did so very carefully, checking every word, thinking every possible way it could be misconstrued.

He was living in a cell. When he wanted to report a story, especially in a dangerous area, the bodyguards had to go with him, basically killing his ability to work. No reporter can instill confidence in the people he must interview if he's surround by armed men. It was an enormous source of stress and frustration for him and his extended family. His enemies had succeeded: He never wrote another line about Veracruz nor set foot in the state again.

★

NOTHING HAD IMPROVED since Regina's death. If anything, things had gotten worse. Besides the three photographers killed within a week of her murder, another reporter was assassinated and two more went missing in 2012 alone. (They still haven't been found.) Meanwhile, the mainstream Xalapa newspapers seemed to be in a contest for who could write the most flattering headlines about Governor Javier Duarte and the PRI: DUARTE: IMPORTANT ADVANCES IN SECURITY IN VERACRUZ, said one newspaper, *Diario A-Z Xalapa*. DUARTE: VERACRUZ, WITH IMPORTANT ADVANCES IN THE AREA OF SECURITY, the same day in the competition, *Gráfico Xalapa*. When I shared some of those newspaper front pages with my AP editor, he said, "Wow, looks like Cuban state media."

Just two weeks before Jorge was forced to flee the country under a threat from Veracruz, the National Association of Newspaper Editors in Mexico, representing more than one hundred publications, gave Governor Javier Duarte a special commendation for his "commitment to freedom of expression." The award was given for his creating a state commission for the protection of journalists, a toothless agency stacked with his allies receiving generous state salaries. Mexicans called these kinds of acts on the part of government officials a *simulación*, just like the word in English: fake.

In 2014, while Duarte claimed that the state's shootings and organized crime spree had waned significantly, the year opened with the killing of Gregorio Jiménez, a local reporter in the industrial city of Coatzacoalcos. Then another reporter for a Veracruz newspaper was kidnapped and murdered after writing about a criminal cell that was siphoning and selling illegal gasoline.

Each new killing put Jorge and his wife more on edge. Every time, she urged him to leave the country: "We could stay with my family in Miami."

"What would I do in Miami?" he always responded.

By the start of 2015, some fourteen journalists had been murdered or disappeared in Veracruz just in the first four years of the Duarte administration. (Governors in Mexico can serve only one six-year term.) Twenty fifteen began with yet another killing, the particularly brutal murder of Moisés Sánchez, a taxi driver who published his own newspaper, *La Unión*, in a suburb of the port called Medellin de Bravo. In an attempt to deflect the attention from yet another killing, Duarte initially said Sánchez wasn't a journalist. But Sánchez used his self-published newspaper to cover the sad state of municipal affairs, including the city's failure to protect its citizens or pave its streets. He wrote about corrupt police officers in a local drug-dealing ring and was one of the organizers of a citizen group that was planning to start their own patrols, given that no one could trust law enforcement. It was a growing trend at the time for citizens to take up arms in Mexico, where the groups were known as *autodefensas*, "self-defenders."

Two days into the New Year, at least a dozen men with assault weapons kidnapped Sánchez from his home in the evening while he was taking a nap. His remains were found twenty-two days later in three garbage bags on an abandoned dirt road. He had been beheaded alive. A man arrested by police confessed to killing Sánchez on the orders of the mayor's bodyguard, who was also arrested, but who was later let go for lack of evidence. The mayor of Medellin remains a fugitive in this case.

I went to interview Sánchez's son, Jorge, a year after his father's death. When I walked into the house, I noticed one of Jorge's young sons, a five-year-old, looking at me with a grim face while clutching a yellow toy pistol at his side. I didn't think much of it, other than that it was a boy with a toy gun. I later discovered that Jorge's sons were with Moisés and witnessed as their beloved grandfather was violently kidnapped by a group of hooded men with AK-47s. I was a stranger, and this child was braced for the worst.

★

THREE DAYS AFTER Moisés Sánchez's body was found in garbage bags, Rodrigo Soberanes introduced me to Polo Hernández and Lev García for the first time. We met at El Péndulo, an iconic four-story bookstore with an open-air terrace café looking out onto one of the Roma's main streets and thronging nightlife. Rodrigo came first, then Polo, who I realized I had met at Mike O'Connor's funeral. He now worked for *El Economista* in Mexico City, a well-respected financial daily covering general news. The ponytails had long disappeared, but they still seemed youthful. We sat waiting for Lev.

Rodrigo had just told me that he was leaving the country for Chile, where his wife, Brenda, had a scholarship to earn a master's in child development. She was leaving journalism, and they both thought it a good idea to be away from Mexico for a while. Only Lev, who had been pulled out of Veracruz twice under threat, had returned and was still practicing journalism in Xalapa. It was a mystery to me why. But Rodrigo told me that Lev could take over his job at the AP as Veracruz correspondent and that I would be in good hands.

"There he is!" Rodrigo said, peering over the railing to the bookshelves below, where Lev was browsing the collection. I saw the top of a gray head of hair on a man walking with a cane. I was surprised that their group included someone so senior. But as he gingerly climbed the stairs, I saw that he, too, was young, just prematurely gray, and the cane was from a motorcycle accident that had crushed his left leg.

As I watched them greet one another with manly hugs and back slaps and start immediately into their playful insults, I felt I had been let into a private club. But it was a club I recognized: They were much like the characters I had befriended in newsrooms in my day as a provincial reporter in the United States, the overeducated, underpaid wannabe poets and novelists who spawned the catchphrase "journalism is the last bastion for the marginally talented." They had the same irreverence, sarcasm, gallows humor, and appalling wardrobes. Lev García's fashion sense was somewhere between biker and archaeologist. Eddie Romo, who I would meet later in Xalapa, lived in a tiny apartment with a cat, a couch, and a table barely large enough to hold the twenty-seven-inch iMac he used to edit video. His mother periodically slipped a little dough into his bank account if he ran short. These reporters smoked like fiends and told vivid war stories of the times they stayed drunk for days or were chased by vigilantes who thought they were narcos and other wild anecdotes that never made it into their newspaper stories for lack of verification.

I don't know why they opened up to me. Perhaps because Rodrigo told them I was okay, and they trusted him. Or, maybe because they were journalists with an important story that they couldn't tell. At one point, later in our friendship, Lev texted me: "If it had not hit me so hard, perhaps I would be writing the story."

I realized early on that the killing of Regina Martínez had been an attack on them all.

"She was our beacon," Polo said. "Then everything came crashing down. It was something very well planned. They calculated the consequences."

I laid out my idea, and they agreed to help. Because I would be asking them for names and information, and they were working journalists, I wondered if I should pay them for their work, as we did the local collaborators at the AP. None of them wanted money. They said ours would be a relationship built on *chelas*, Mexican slang for "beer." If I was going to get along with them, it would require buying, and drinking, a lot of *chelas*.

A short time after our first meeting, Polo and I returned to the same bookstore/café. It was late, after he got off work. We sat on the terrace under a deceptively crystal night sky at a wooden bar table abutting the balcony railing, where Polo could smoke. The February chill and cloudless sky created an illusion of crispness when, in fact, after three months of dry season in Mexico City, one of the most polluted in the world, what we were breathing was corrosive.

I started with the easy questions—his life story, how he met Regina—and he answered between draws on his cigarette, exhaling through the corner of his mouth. When he got to describing the phone call telling him that Regina was dead, he paused with his head down. After a second, I realized he was crying.

It was here and in subsequent conversations that Polo helped me pick up the threads of a dormant investigation. He started with the background, 2011, when the cartel violence spiked. That's when the harassment of journalists reached a new level they hadn't seen before.

In Mexico, people move fluidly from politics and government to journalism and back. A lot of the spokespeople for government offices or elected officials in Veracruz were former and future colleagues of the press. Some were good friends and had relationships dating back years. Some—in clear ethics violations—took salaries from the government *and* worked as reporters for local media or their own digital news sites. These former and future journalists working for Duarte started turning on their colleagues. They tried to paint all working press as colluding with the narcos. And as the journalist assassinations grew, officials openly used fear to try to keep reporters from doing their jobs. In the case of the three journalists murdered the week after Regina's death, Rodrigo called Polo with the tip he had heard in the attorney general's office: that their bodies had been found. But Polo couldn't use the source, so he called Miguel Valera in the governor's office to confirm it. "The only way you would have that kind of information is if you knew the killers," Valera responded, implying that Polo was somehow involved.

Polo said reporters received such accusations regularly from the government. He was also followed by strange men and had state police with large-caliber rifles milling outside his house when he was still reporting in Xalapa. He was pressured by the state to give up sources, including via a Freedom of Information request filed against Notimex, the state-run news agency where he worked at the time.

Reporters were so used to living under a general intimidation strategy by the government that they had built up callouses. So, it was difficult for them to gauge whether this new treatment was truly dangerous or just more cat-and-mouse games that, for the most part, they could ignore. One thing was certain: The intimidation was so organized and widespread that there had to be a larger purpose at work.

Polo gave an example of the size of the power they were dealing with in the case of the disappeared customs official, Francisco Serrano Aramoni, who had been sent by Calderón to clean up corruption in the port. Many said the two were also relatives.

"So, a cousin of the president disappears, and nothing happens. That means they have more power than the president," Polo said of the forces at work in Veracruz. Then he told me that if I was going to pursue this story, I would be entering *la boca del lobo*, "the mouth of the wolf."

CHAPTER 14

Welcome to Xalapa

2015

I T WAS A good time for me to go to Xalapa. Rodrigo explained that the PRI was gearing up for local elections that summer, and they would be too distracted with backroom dealing around candidates to notice me there. In most officials' minds, the Regina Martínez case was closed and would not cause them any more trouble. Still, Rodrigo cautioned me, I had to tread carefully so as not to "wake the beast."

We had a little time before Rodrigo's departure for Chile for my very first trip to the state. He picked me up at the Veracruz airport. Just outside, he pointed out the road leading to the old racetrack, Villarín, where the 2007 shootout killing the Zetas leader set Veracruz on its violent course. When I finally arrived in Xalapa, Valentine's Day 2015, I didn't find it charming, as everyone had told me I would. I could see only the more treacherous aspects, that the walls had ears and eyes. I was oblivious to the snowcapped volcanoes and the alluring discord of provincial street life, marimbas clinking and break-dancers whirling in the lush shade of Parque Juárez; the redolence of coffee in the nose at any turn. Everywhere we went, I looked around to see if anyone was watching us. In one café, where a man sat down at the table next to ours when others were empty, I asked Rodrigo if he looked familiar.

"Is he following us? Did we see him at the other place?"

Rodrigo shook his head. I felt tense.

Rodrigo arranged for me to meet quietly with the people who knew Regina best, at Café Don Justo, which sits at the edge of Parque Juárez, up a flight of stairs from the street. We all pulled up chairs around a metal table on the café terrace. I met Lupita López, Regina's friend who saw her just hours before she died. She spoke in a low tone and decided that if we texted, we should go by code names. She was "Maria," and I was "Oriana," the name Rodrigo suggested, in honor of the great Italian journalist Oriana Fallaci.

The most entertaining of the group was Monserrat Panes, an ample woman with a gap between her large front teeth, which kept her lips parted in a mischievous smile. Monse, as she was known, was the receptionist at *Política*, the most powerful person in the newsroom, as any reporter knows. She knew the gossip and the tricks to getting what you needed in supplies or help from the top editors. Regina often took phone calls at Monse's desk, so as to be out of earshot of the other reporters. They also bantered back and forth. Regina encouraged Monse to stop obsessing about makeup and her looks. "Read a book," she would tell her. Monse was so trusted that Regina hired her sister to clean her house.

"Her stories were always causing controversies," Monse said with a proud laugh. "No matter what was coming in the legislature, Regina had a copy of it in advance."

Monse let us into the newsroom of *Política*, which was closed because it was a Saturday, and there was no Sunday edition. I walked into a throwback, a 1970s-looking newsroom with shellacked wood paneling, popcorn ceilings, and large wood conference tables. From the front door you could see the archive, rows and rows of leather-bound copies of every issue of *Política* since its founding in 1987. The very first edition of the newspaper was framed on the wall, alongside a faded color portrait of Don Yayo; his wife, Yolanda Carlín; Governor Miguel Alemán and his wife, the photogenic Christiane Magnani, Miss Universe 1953.

Monse's receptionist desk sat just inside the door. The reporters and editors worked in plain office partitions with laminate desktops and soft fabric walls for postings with pushpins.

Regina's cubicle remained empty nearly a decade after she left the newspaper, a blue desktop surrounded by three low gray walls. Rodrigo came to the corner and leaned against the partition as he did in the days when he was a young reporter seeking her help. "I would stand here and stand here, and she would ignore me until she finished her stories," he said.

Later, he wanted to show me the place where Regina used to have lunch almost every day, a mom-and-pop restaurant downtown called Los Alcatraces, where I met Eddie for the first time. The restaurant had classic Mexican décor, clay-red walls with a bright yellow chair rail and tapestries of flowering cacti and indigenous women with Diego Rivera–like bunches of calla lilies, known in Mexico as *alcatraces*. The rustic wooden tables had woven red-and-blue tablecloths. Regina in her day sat in the same seat at the same corner table, with her back to the wall and a full view of both the front door and the patio. She always had to see who was coming and going. Rodrigo insisted that I sit there, in her place, to get the full experience.

There was no menu, just a chicken, fish, or beef plate with rice and vegetables, consommé, fruit-flavored *aguas frescas*, and dessert—three courses for less than three dollars. The restaurant didn't serve alcohol, but the waiter would run out and buy a bottle of Corona just for Regina, because she liked to have beer with her midafternoon meal. The owners adored her. After she died, they erected an altar to her in the restaurant for the Day of the Dead. They were also very protective of her. When investigators came around asking questions, they refused to cooperate. They knew any details they gave about Regina—her habits, her companions, her single bottle of Corona every day—would be used against her.

As I sat in the Regina chair, the three friends launched into their stories: Eddie and the heavy box of documents Regina had sent him to retrieve; Rodrigo having to rewrite a story for her seven times.

Her favorite subject at lunch and everywhere was the reckless spending of the governors. She liked to follow the money and would

get whipped up over the fact that no one could account for all the money
the governors borrowed on behalf of the state. One day, it was Fidel
Herrera building a debt of ten billion pesos, three times the amount
his predecessor had left. "He's bankrupting the state, and nobody's stopping him!" Regina would shout, raising her eyebrows and waving her
hands. Her students Rodrigo, Polo, and Eddie would listen, rapt, with
serious faces to match the gravity she gave the situation.

Lev, for his part, enjoyed the lunchtime show, the tiny explosion of
outrage. After a while, he would start to snicker. "And what are you
laughing at?" Regina would say, sneering at him. Then they would all
fall out laughing.

As the three rehashed these conversations and debates in the restaurant, I noticed why Regina liked the view from the chair where I
currently sat. I spotted a table full of state and federal police officers
eating on the patio, one of whom kept turning her head in our direction with the sound of the conversation. It made me uncomfortable.
Though I didn't personally fear for my safety, I wanted to heed Rodrigo's advice and not wake the beast. It would make some difficult work
a little bit easier if I stayed anonymous. I told the rest that maybe we
should change the subject. They agreed.

But it was as if, for a moment, they could conjure her again. The
only person missing besides Regina was Polo. Lev wrapped up the
conversation this way: "The only thing we know for certain is that she's
dead. Everything else is speculation."

★

THE NEXT DAY, Rodrigo took me to Regina's house, a small stucco
bungalow behind a latticed brick wall. At one end was the large,
white iron gate that opened onto her patio. To our surprise, it looked
as if someone were living there. There was a car parked on the patio
and soccer shorts hanging on a clothesline, with men's tennis shoes at
the front door. Wooden furniture had been broken up and stashed in
one corner of the yard. The electrical meter wasn't hooked up, so we
suspected that whoever was there was squatting. We wondered if it
was Regina's nephew. Supposedly, she had left the house to him. But

why would he be living there without electricity? We knocked on the gate, but no one came out. I took a photo of the license plate on the car to see if we could figure out later who it belonged to. (It belonged to one of Regina's siblings.)

After that, we headed to the cemetery, where Regina had been laid to rest on the hill overlooking Xalapa. We stopped at one of the many flower shops lining the road up to the entrance, and I bought a small arrangement of white and yellow chrysanthemums. After we parked the car, Rodrigo searched for the grave amid the headstones decorated with flowers and multicolored pinwheels. But he couldn't find it. He walked around and around without success, trying to retrace the steps from his memory of the funeral. "Where are you, Regis?" he murmured, using the nickname they liked to call her. Finally, we walked to a maintenance hut and asked one of the grave-diggers for help.

"What's the name?" he asked, opening a registry that was still written by hand.

"Regina Martínez," Rodrigo said.

"The reporter?" The gravedigger closed the book, evidently not needing to look up the plot, and led us up the hill. Rodrigo was amazed. He asked the man how long he had worked there. Twenty years. Did he remember all the names of the people buried there?

"Imagine how many graves he's dug, how many names he's recorded, and he can remember her off the top of his head," Rodrigo said to me. "She appealed to people like him, the simple people."

We stopped at Regina's headstone, which sat right next to the road. Now Rodrigo was baffled. He was sure it had been moved, because he was a pallbearer and remembered carrying the casket from the road into the middle of the large plateau dotted with monuments. I laid my flowers on the headstone. It bore a blue Talavera ceramic cross and a splotch of cement where it looked like something else had been attached and then removed. Another friend later told me Regina's headstone originally had the image of a typewriter, but it somehow went missing. "They steal everything here," she said. Everything about the spot seemed blank, with no spirit of or connection to or inkling of the fierce woman who was buried there. I could feel her ambivalence about her own grave.

Rodrigo remembered the day she was buried, April 30, 2012. The weather was mild, overcast, a lot like it was on the hill the day we were there, though the sun broke through as we stood there talking. It was Sunday, and taxis pulled up regularly to drop off families visiting graves. A man motored his ice-cream cart along the cemetery road. I always marveled at how entrepreneurial Mexicans are, on the one hand, to think of selling ice cream in a cemetery, and how casually festive they were, on the other, to enjoy ice cream in a cemetery.

We stayed at Regina's grave for a while, Rodrigo remembering and me writing furiously in my notebook to the soft whirring of pinwheels, the ones that supposedly spun backward on the day she was buried.

★

BY THE TIME of my visit, Jorge Antonio Hernández Silva, El Silva, whose conviction was overturned in August 2013, was back in prison serving his original thirty-eight-year sentence. The day he was let out for violation of his human rights, Regina's brother Ángel filed an *amparo*, an appeal of sorts under Mexican law, challenging the Superior Court decision. He said he was convinced of El Silva's guilt. "I saw the video where this subject, in a terrible manner, describes the crime he committed against my sister. The magistrates are wrong," Ángel wrote in a letter to the public.

Another court restored the conviction, and in October 2014, El Silva was rearrested. He was found living in a small town in the state of Tlaxcala, where he had shaved his head and mustache to avoid recognition.

Before I left for the airport, we made a stop at the office of Diana Coq Toscanini, attorney for El Silva. I had come up with her name in my research, so Lev called an attorney friend of his who knew her to help make the introduction. In the environment of fear and opacity that ruled Veracruz, it was nearly impossible to just show up without an entrée.

Coq agreed to meet us at her home in Jardines de las Ánimas, an exclusive subdivision in Xalapa where many politicians live. Her office was surrounded by a high stone wall, with her name printed on a metal garage door that also bore signs warning of high-voltage electrical current, watchdogs, and closed-circuit cameras. When the door opened, we were greeted by some small dogs in what was a fashionable stucco-and-tile house behind the wall. We climbed the stairs to her office. Coq, a flamboyant middle-aged woman, was heavy on makeup and leopard and geometric prints. She invited us to sit down and began talking without stopping for the better part of an hour. She gave me a copy of a complaint she had filed with Mexico's Supreme Court, alleging human rights violations in the case of El Silva. She said he was in solitary confinement, and even she, his lawyer, was forbidden from seeing him, a violation of his rights. And because he was HIV-positive, she had no way of assuring that he was receiving proper medical attention and his retroviral drugs. Under Mexican law, if she could prove that his human rights were being violated in prison, he would be freed. The Supreme Court never took up the petition, but Coq mentioned she was also filing it with the Inter-American Court of Human Rights.

She said El Silva was innocent, and that authorities knew where the actual killer, El Jarocho, was living, but had failed to go after him. She also named top state authorities, including Erick Lagos, saying they knew all the inconsistencies in Regina's case, but continued to advocate for El Silva's conviction. She said some of them were even named in his arrest and detention, when he was tortured into confessing to a murder he said he didn't commit. Then she told me I couldn't print any of this—a deal I considered void the following July, when she called a press conference and said everything publicly that she had told me in private.

After that first meeting and another in Mexico City, Coq wouldn't take my calls. I was never sure why. Her response to me, along with the moved headstone, Regina's mystery love interest, and her made-up biography, were part of a list of strange details that kept building in the Regina Martínez case.

CHAPTER 15

What Was She Working On?
Part I

2015

W HEN I TOOK up the Regina Martínez case, the prevailing theory on her murder among friends and colleagues had nothing to do with a crime of passion or a robbery. They believed she had come into the crosshairs of one of two Veracruz politicians, Reynaldo Escobar or Alejandro Montano, because of the *Proceso* story on illegal enrichment and ties to narcos that ran three weeks before her death.

When I went to interview *Proceso* writer Jenaro Villamil about the article, he said he suspected Montano or Escobar immediately.

It wasn't difficult for people to pinpoint Alejandro Montano, grandson of a pistolero and protector of a drug lord, according to the drug lord himself. Rodrigo Soberanes had never told investigators of the time he overheard Montano invite Regina for a *pan de muerto*. He knew the only thing such testimony would bring was more trouble on himself. Regina, meanwhile, had referred to Reynaldo Escobar openly as "that delinquent," something that made her friends a little nervous for her.

Still, the idea that the article on the two politicians had caused her murder didn't make sense to me. There had been many allegations written about both men over their decades in public office, not just by Regina. In fact, many of the stories she wrote were based on leaks of documents to other media—not even her own investigations.

Why would a small inside story in *Proceso* have triggered them?

There were other theories that, to me, were equally implausible:

She was killed by soldiers for uncovering the rape of the elderly Ernestina Ascencio five years after the fact: Those supporting this theory said the Mexican Army has a long memory and was at her home after the murder.

She was killed accidentally: The thugs were sent just to rough her up and send her a message.

She actually *did* know El Jarocho and let him in that night: After all, reporters associate with a lot of questionable characters.

She was killed just to send a message to other journalists to stay in line.

None of these, for me, seemed to be a reason to assassinate a well-known correspondent for a national magazine. It was a drastic measure not taken up lightly, even by criminals.

Threatening a second reporter, Jorge Carrasco, for investigating the initial murder meant, to me, that there was something huge at stake. Yet there was nothing in Regina's repertoire prior to her murder that was anything more than the daily news. She wrote about arrests of drug traffickers and crooked politicians, but just off the police blotter, just as she had told Jorge Carrasco she would do the last time they met.

The only thing that made sense to me was that she had been killed for something she was working on, something someone clearly didn't want published. But what?

Everyone I asked had a different answer to that question.

For Jorge and Lev, the answer was nothing. She had told both of them that she wanted to cut back, to move away from the kind of reporting she had traditionally done. Both of them said, based on their final conversations with her, that they doubted she was getting into anything sensitive.

Both Rodrigo and Polo told me she said she was working on something about the Zetas, an assignment from *Proceso*. A month before she died, Rodrigo said, she told him that the story was "very strong," and "dangerous." He told her to be careful. "You're out there on your own," he said. "If anything happens, *Proceso* is not going to back you up."

Salvador Corro, her editor at *Proceso*, told me that several months before she died, she said that she was working on something that had to do with an ex-governor and corruption. He had no details. They were talking on a phone line that was surely being listened in on, so they avoided specifics. He said he often didn't know what Regina's investigative stories were until they landed on his desk.

Another person close to her quoted Regina as saying, just a couple months before her death, "I finally have the goods to tie Fidel Herrera to the Zetas."

Then there was the incident of the strange phone calls on her Black-Berry. The first person to mention them was Polo. About a year or so before she died, Regina had gotten a new phone, a BlackBerry, from *Proceso*. She cursed the phone, couldn't figure out how to use it, and had to ask others for help. Then strange calls started coming, asking for "Comandante Cobra." Instead of telling them they had the wrong number, she would respond that he wasn't there, in case she could learn something about the nature of this Comandante Cobra. When she told Polo about the phone calls, he told her to get rid of the BlackBerry immediately. It would be too dangerous if the people calling found out that they were getting a reporter instead.

"Are you kidding?" she answered. "Of course I'm not getting rid of it."

Lev heard the same story from her, but he brushed it off as an odd coincidence. He said she mostly laughed about it.

One of Regina's close colleagues, who didn't want to be named, said the calls for Comandante Cobra were numerous. Regina took the information to Miguel Naranjo, a columnist known as El Flechador, "the

Arrowhead," who covered politics and organized crime. Naranjo, after some research, told Regina that "Comandante Cobra" was the narcos' code name for Fidel Herrera and then told her to be careful.

According to one version of the story, Regina told *Proceso* about the calls and somehow discovered that she had inadvertently been assigned a cell number that previously belonged to Fidel Herrera.

According to yet another version, which the source I was talking to had received secondhand, Regina was walking with Mariela San Martín one day, the woman who made her clothes, and they ran into a woman named Ángeles, who was the private secretary to Fidel Herrera's wife. Regina and Ángeles were chatting when Ángeles said, "You need to give me your cell phone number."

"You already have it," Regina said.

"No, I don't. Call me, so I will have it in my phone."

So, Regina dialed, and Ángeles received a call with the readout FIDEL HERRERA.

"Hang on, El Licenciado Fidel is calling me," she said, using the formal title for an official.

"Answer it," Regina said and started to laugh.

Ángeles discovered that the call was from Regina, proving she had Herrera's old cell phone number.

"I've received enough things so I can really do a number on him," Regina allegedly said.

At least five people told me the same story about the phone calls, three who said the story came directly from Regina. *Proceso*'s editors denied knowing anything about the calls.

Finally, I decided to trace the BlackBerry number for previous owners. I had no sources with Telcel, the country's major cell phone company at the time. You need someone inside to leak you the information, as account details are private. So, for six hundred dollars, I hired a private investigator to get me a history on the number. The information came back that the phone number on Regina's BlackBerry had been created in 2008 for *Proceso* and remained as one of the magazine's phone accounts until it was reassigned in 2014. It was never the number of Fidel Herrera. In fact, there was no previous user.

Could Regina have had another cell phone that had the previous number of Fidel Herrera? It's possible. She apparently had two other phones. (I tried to trace another of her phone numbers, but too many years had passed.) But everyone who told me the story of the strange calls said they came on Regina's BlackBerry, which carried the number assigned only to *Proceso* and no one else. According to my investigation of the phone line, the notion that she had Fidel Herrera's former number just wasn't true.

This was the kind of reporting atmosphere I was in, the same viscous soup Jorge Carrasco encountered when he first started reporting on Regina's death. It was going to be difficult to prove anything for certain.

I needed to go to *Proceso* to find out what they knew. I called and made an appointment to meet with Rafael Rodríguez, the director of the magazine in its main office, in Mexico City. The offices of *Proceso* looked like a newsroom out of 1976, the year the magazine was founded, a haphazard arrangement of metal desks piled with papers and reports wherever they fit. The plank floors creaked, and the rooms smelled of book bindings and wood lacquered with time. Bookcases lined the wood-paneled walls, filled with encyclopedias and bound copies of the Mexican magazines *Nexos*, *Política*, *Vuelta*, *Plural*, *Tiempo*, and of course *Proceso*, some defunct, some living, a chronicle of various attempts over the decades at a free press. The journalists also looked as if they had been there since *Proceso*'s founding. Some had been, including Rodríguez. The newsroom was on the first floor, where posters demanding justice for Regina hung on the wall. The *Proceso* website listed a running count of the days since Regina's death, under a photo of her and the headline: DAYS OF IMPUNITY. The number of days was over a thousand when I first approached *Proceso*.

The magazine had come under a lot of criticism for not changing its style since the 1970s, or its manner of investigative reporting. Continuing with the old school of Mexican journalism, the magazine made claims at times without attribution, a historical arrogance from the early days when readers simply had to trust that the journalists had inside sources. In reality, they did have such sources, but there was no transparency about how the information was vetted. It was a holdover from the days when

Mexico's circles were very small and when politicos, intellectuals, and mafiosos regularly intersected, trading inside information over dinners or other social engagements. Often, they were from the same families.

By 2015, you could still read an entire investigative piece in the magazine and not know where the information had come from. Meanwhile, other Mexican media were coming into the twenty-first century of investigative reporting, when the Internet allowed a new level of transparency. Mexican journalists not only documented their information, but they posted the source materials and interviews online for readers to peruse themselves. There was a struggle inside *Proceso*'s own staff from the journalists who wanted to see changes. Jorge Carrasco was one of them. But the old guard prevailed.

Despite the criticisms, I walked into the building feeling I was in the hallowed halls of Mexican journalism. There was no question that Julio Scherer was a national hero.

Director Rafael Rodríguez was a diminutive man with thick glasses and dark hair who had been with Scherer since the beginning. He received me in a small conference room, also lined with bookcases, and was kind and cordial. He said I could use the magazine archives and photographs for free, as long as I credited *Proceso*. This truly was a grand gesture made to a freelancer on a tight budget.

I explained my mission and immediately dove in by saying, "I think Regina was killed for something she was working on."

"I agree," Rodríguez said, so quickly and surely that it surprised me.

"So, what was she working on?"

"We don't know," he said, with eyes that said there was more, but that he wasn't going to tell me.

I decided not to press the magazine's evasiveness at the time. They didn't know me. I was an outsider. And they were *Proceso*. It made sense that they wouldn't open up to me, even though we were all in the same business. That's not how the Mexican journalists in the capital city viewed most of their American colleagues.

But the leads so far had turned up nothing. The former governor and corruption? *Proceso* has nothing more on that. "If we knew, believe me, we would have printed something," Regina's editor Salvador Corro later told me. The Zetas? It turned out that *Proceso* had published a special edition on the Zetas right before Regina was killed. But it was only a compilation of stories that had been published previously, by Regina and many reporters.

Then I discovered a new possible lead. In one of my early visits to Xalapa, I sat down with Julio Argumedo, a freelance photographer, at Bola de Oro, one of a chain of cafés featuring coffee from nearby Coatepec. It had a large outdoor patio with dozens of tables just a block from the statehouse, on the main downtown street. Rodrigo and Lev introduced us because Argumedo, known to the group as Don Jules, had worked with Regina on a story that had never been published. Don Jules had made the photos and turned them over to Regina to go with the *Proceso* report.

My heart was racing as I talked to him. This would be the key to my investigation, the detail that no one else had. Don Jules told me that in 2011, Regina was trying to document how many people were buried in the municipal cemeteries' anonymous mass graves and what percentage had died of gunshot wounds. She wanted to show that the government was vastly undercounting the toll of drug violence. In many cases of drug war dead, families were too afraid to retrieve the bodies, so they ended up in a city's mass grave. She suspected those victims were undercounted, making the impact of President Felipe Calderón's war far higher than officials had reported, Don Jules told me. Burial records from the public cemeteries would be one way to prove it.

Don Jules had followed Regina to cemeteries in Xalapa, the port, and Boca del Río to talk to the administrators and request numbers. Regina had finished the reporting, Don Jules said, and was presumably writing up the report at the time she was killed. He didn't have details of what she found, but he surmised that she got what she was after. All he knew was that he turned the photos over to her and never saw them published, nor did he get paid.

I asked if he had copies of the photos, and he said they were on a hard drive that had been stolen. He couldn't show them to me.

Eddie Romo confirmed that Regina had told him she was on a story that involved tracking down gravediggers in the Port of Veracruz. He wondered how she had continued to be so brave. The mere thought of the story gave him the chills.

Everyone, including us at the AP, suspected that the drug war casualties were being undercounted, and we had tried to pin it down in our own stories. Once again, Regina had been ahead of her peers. She had set out to prove it at least a year before we did. But in early 2015, this didn't strike me as a particularly sensitive story. Documenting the number of people killed by bullets in an anonymous municipal grave didn't seem the kind of subject that would get anyone killed.

I would later change my mind.

For lack of a better theory, I decided to look into what Regina told one person shortly before her death: "I finally have the goods to tie Fidel Herrera to the Zetas." In 2015, when I started this investigation, this idea made the most sense. Another newspaper had tipped me off to this idea.

Three months after Regina was murdered, the *New York Times* had a front-page blockbuster: The Zetas were laundering millions of dollars in drug money in the United States through a horse-breeding and -racing enterprise run by the brother of the Zetas' second-in-command. Though the story didn't mention Veracruz, it turned out that characters from the state played a big role: A petroleum contractor, along with a former city councilman from the port, had carried the money from Veracruz and purchased the horses themselves, so the transactions couldn't be traced to the cartel. Both were indicted by the U.S. Justice Department, though the ex-councilman was later exonerated. It turned out he had been kidnapped and severely tortured into agreeing to carry the money and make the purchases. He was a victim, not a coconspirator. But the other figure, Francisco "Pancho" Colorado, was convicted of using his company, ADT Petroservicios, a contractor of Petróleos Mexicanos (Pemex), to hide the purchases of the horses. Colorado, who died in a Texas prison in 2018, had close ties to Fidel Herrera and had been pictured with him. He was widely suspected of using his businesses in general to launder money for the Zetas.

In 2013, a full year after Regina's death, an ex-accountant for the Zetas detained in the United States testified that one of the cartel's leaders gave Colorado twelve million dollars intended for Fidel Herrera's 2004 gubernatorial campaign. Herrera denied the accusation.

Is this what Regina knew? I wondered. The *New York Times* had discovered the connection ahead of time, because the same day the horseracing ring was broken up and the Justice Department announced the arrests, reporter Ginger Thompson had a front-page, four-thousand-word story detailing the whole sting operation. She said in the story that the *Times* agreed to hold publication until arrests were made.

Did Regina have the story ahead of time as well? Was this her story that tied Fidel Herrera to the Zetas? I spent at least a year talking to everyone I could find in that case, including Ginger Thompson, who knew well what was going on inside Mexico. No one knew anything that could tie Regina to this story. I hit one of many dead ends.

★

ON MY SECOND reporting trip to Xalapa, Rodrigo arranged for me to meet Alonso Martínez, Regina's nephew. Her family hadn't spoken publicly in the three years since her death. They were adamant about keeping press away. But Rodrigo reached out to Alonso to see if he might want to talk. As far as anyone knew, Alonso was the closest person to Regina. He was now twenty-three, and Rodrigo said it was difficult to arrange something because the young man worked at night in *cine*. I thought he meant a movie theater and imagined this young man taking tickets. Later, I discovered he worked in *cine*, as in "cinema," as part of a camera crew filming music videos and other spots. Alonso knew Rodrigo was one of the people his aunt had trusted. He agreed to come to Eddie's apartment one afternoon, where we sat in the tiny living room drinking tall cans of Modelo beer, all except Alonso, who never drank.

At one point, one of Eddie's neighbors passed by and waved to the group through the open window. It was Rubén Espinosa, a photographer who freelanced for *Proceso*, *Cuartoscuro* (Darkroom), and other photo agencies. I didn't notice him, nor the fact that I had seen him just two days before.

Every year on April 28, the anniversary of Regina's death, journalists and activists in Xalapa organized a protest in the main square, Plaza Lerdo, marching with banners and signs that read KILLING JOURNALISTS

WON'T KILL THE TRUTH and WE DON'T BELIEVE YOU, the original words of *Proceso* editor Julio Scherer to Governor Javier Duarte the day after Regina was murdered. This year, 2015, reporters paid tribute with speeches, some simply reading Regina's *Proceso* articles aloud. The numbers had dwindled from one thousand on the first anniversary to three hundred on the next, and now, on the third anniversary, just a few dozen gathered in the central square, named for Xalapa native Sebastián Lerdo de Tejada, who served as Mexico's president from 1872 to 1876. It was the location of all protests in Xalapa, and Regina had spent a lot of time there covering peasant farmers and other dispossessed as they made their cases in front of the statehouse across the street.

Regina's colleague Lupita López, who normally chose to keep a low profile after her friend's death, never shied away from grabbing the microphone at the memorial celebrations. "Three years ago, the journalism profession in Veracruz and the country suffered a great blow. Regina Martínez, regional correspondent of the magazine *Proceso*, was assassinated and her challenging voice silenced, ending her dreams and her mission, a life dedicated to journalism," Lupita opined in her always steady voice, now loud and tinny from a single amplifier as it carried over the clamor of the midday traffic. "It was here on Plaza Lerdo where Regina Martínez adopted the feelings of the voiceless. But she didn't just stay here, comfortably awaiting the demonstrations, but ventured to the mountains and the indigenous communities to see firsthand what they lived, the abuses of the caciques [tribal chiefs], the stolen land, the violent evictions and unfair imprisonments.

"Regina always saw the other side of the news. She scrutinized behind the scenes and brought to light what others did not see. Her capacity for indignation at injustices never left her. She was tireless in the search for truth. She questioned power from the trenches, without being intimidated. She walked with the migrants, with the mothers of the missing migrants, with [human rights activist] Father [Alejandro] Solalinde, with laid-off workers, with those fighting for social justice, with relatives of the disappeared." Beads of sweat had formed through Lupita's makeup as she continued speaking under the laser-like sun of the wide-open plaza.

"She was tireless until the end of her days in the search for truth and justice—until April 28, 2012, when she was killed in her home. At the time, she covered electoral issues and stepped on many toes. She also covered issues of violence and insecurity in the state. But she wasn't allowed to continue. Today, Regina is no longer with us. May she rest in peace and, hopefully, one day justice will be done."

For this anniversary, the journalists decided to escalate the protest and publicly rename Plaza Lerdo for Regina. A gold plaque was ordered, reading, PLAZA REGINA MARTÍNEZ, APRIL 28, 2015, to be affixed to a wide stair leading to the open square. The man gluing the plaque in place was Rubén Espinosa, who was photographed doing so by several people, including me. The display was accompanied by a protest sign: DUARTE, ASSASSIN OF JOURNALISTS. JUSTICE FOR REGINA. The plaque was removed by city crews almost as soon as the protest ended, leaving a white epoxy scar.

At the time, I had no idea who Rubén Espinosa was, but I later saw him running alongside the march with his camera. As was his style, he both covered and participated in protests. Now he had casually walked by Eddie's apartment as I prepared to meet Regina's nephew.

Alonso was short with thick black hair and the long face and features of his aunt, but in a softer, more handsome way. When I explained what I was doing, he said he would have to speak to his father, Regina's brother, Ángel, who handled everything around her death. He said his father had told him to be careful, to think about the consequences of what he might say.

The last time he saw his aunt Regina was Valentine's Day 2012, a little more than two months before she died. They exchanged gifts. Alonso gave her a tiny owl made of obsidian; she collected owls. She gave him a Radiohead T-shirt and a Bob Marley CD and told him that she would be busy for the next two months finishing a report, so he shouldn't come around. But they made a date for May 5, to go shopping just before a family gathering for Mother's Day.

"I'm really deep in an investigation," she told him, "and I have to lock myself in the house and write."

CHAPTER 16

A Pattern Emerges

2015

T HE HIGHWAY FROM Xalapa to Mexico City at times mimics La Ruta de Cortés, the route the Spanish explorer originally followed to conquer the Aztecs in what was then Tenochtitlán. Cortés took a wild, circuitous ride through the mountains before meeting up with what is now the Mexico 140D, popularly known as a *cuota*, an inter-state toll road designed to be safer and better maintained than the local roads. Today, 140D shoots straight over the mountains west of Xalapa and dumps into the Oriental Basin, flat shrubland dotted with mostly dry alkaline lakes between Veracruz and Mexico City. Once the road reaches the border of Tlaxcala state, there are two ways into the country's capital, another arid basin dotted by lakes that the Spaniards drained to create Mexico City. There was the southern route through Puebla, which Cortés took on his march to meet Moctezuma, and a northern one through the city of Tlaxcala, which he took on his retreat.

I drove both routes several times with Lev García, who periodically hitched a ride with me back to Mexico City. I did the same when he was heading to Xalapa. We spent a lot of time together working, but also just talking. On our long drives between the city and Veracruz, I put my voice recorder between us in the console and just listened as the tow-colored fields and mountain forests whizzed by. It was an ideal situation for an interview: boxed together in a car without interruption, insulated by the drone of the highway and the motor.

Other times, we met in bars—or cafés, if Lev wasn't drinking—in Xalapa, the port, Mexico City, and even one time in a seafood shack on a Mexican beach. Lev no longer owned the bar El Conspirador, but he still always seemed to have something going on the side. At first, it was recovering from his accident. The year after Regina's death, he crashed his motorcycle while driving drunk. Doctors were barely able to keep from amputating his leg. Long after he stopped using a cane, it still hurt. With all the difficult things I was asking him to recall, I could never tell if it was the injury or the memories that made him wince and rock back and forth during my interviews.

As with everyone else, I started by asking Lev why he had wanted to be a journalist.

"I wanted to tell stories," he said. People on his mother's side of the family had worked in government and seen the abuses firsthand. Sometimes they had to participate in them to keep their jobs. He had listened to their stories growing up, but never saw anything like what they said was going on on the news.

"When you grow up with people who show you reality, who show you that there are other things going on, you find that interesting. You have a little better vision about life in your country," he explained. "And you think, *Wouldn't it be great to tell the real story, to inform more people, to affect society and the country, to be a counterweight?*"

I had the same question for him as I had for Jorge Carrasco: How could he think of journalism as a way to do good when it was a profession traditionally racked with corruption and sycophancy? Like Jorge and Regina, it turned out Lev was operating on the ideal of what journalism *could* be.

"It's not the profession; it's who practices it," he said. "You can choose to be anything, an architect, say, and be corrupt . . . I believed journalism would be a great life, but I never imagined it would be so complicated."

"No?" I asked, genuinely surprised.

"Honestly," he said, laughing at me and his own naïveté. "I thought it would be a little more noble." He said he thought he could ignore the corruption around him and just go about his business. But it was difficult for him to remain on the margins and not be disturbed by it. He remembered times when, while eating lunch with him, Regina would watch the young reporters come into the restaurant and would say, "I wonder how long before they become *cochinos*"—"rotten."

"These *escuincles* coming into the profession can't even write," Regina had complained another time, using Mexican slang for a little brat. "But they've already learned how to hold out their hands."

I didn't understand why Lev kept returning to Xalapa. Wasn't he tempting fate?

Xalapa is a metropolitan area of nearly eight hundred thousand people, the twenty-ninth largest in Mexico. But as I walked or drove around with Lev, it felt like a small town, *his* small town. He was always stopped on the street by someone, to talk, or nodding or honking greetings to other drivers in traffic. He would shake hands with and slap the backs of the guys, bask in the flirtatiousness of the young women, and launch into lengthy banal conversations about who knew what, who was doing what. He introduced each person as a "very good friend." Sometimes I got annoyed, waiting for these chitchats to end, but I was getting the answer to my question. *This* was how he survived: having lots of allies, people who liked him, people who became his eyes and ears. That's what he said when I asked him flat-out.

"I feel okay here because people know me," he said.

It was also defiance, his way of standing up to a power he ultimately couldn't beat.

"I'll leave Xalapa when I'm ready," he said, "not when *they* tell me to."

No matter how much time I spent with Lev, I always had the feeling that I didn't know the whole story. He had a way of operating from the corner of the eye, the sideline, that made me wonder what he was up to. His phone was always pinging, and he was constantly texting back. Sometimes, I wondered if the messages had anything to do with me. What I did know was that Lev was a one-man news agency. He was constantly getting tips, picking up information, building stories. He also did construction projects on the side. Sometimes he would go incommunicado for more than a normal amount of time, and my mind would fill with wild scenarios based on what little I knew about his life. Accident? Kidnapping? Bender? He always responded eventually. He had left his phone at a friend's house, or he had been installing a sceptic tank and couldn't answer.

Lev had contacts everywhere, and sometimes he took me along to meet them: lawyers who never spoke to reporters, people inside the government. One time, I followed him to an interview at the headquarters of a gubernatorial candidate, and I saw random burly men in sunglasses hanging around the lobby. They weren't official security. *Porros*, I thought, the infamous political goons who, under the PRI, bashed heads to keep people in line.

"Are they?" I asked Lev.

"Most likely," he answered.

I often felt he was holding out on me with regard to information. At times, I *knew* he was. But he never lied, as far I could tell, simply omitted. I gave him the benefit of the doubt that he was just expecting me to be a good reporter. I wasn't going to get answers, even from him, unless I asked the right questions. It wasn't deception but discretion. Like his glad-handing around town, it was one of his survival skills.

There was one thing in Lev's story that puzzled me most: Why hadn't he asked about the person Regina was seeing? Who was it? It seemed to be very relevant information when she ended up dead. At first, he told me it wasn't the kind of thing he would probe anyone on. Later, he told me she *had* told him who it was, but he couldn't tell me because he promised her he would take the secret to his grave.

"What happened to him?" I asked. "Where was he after she was killed?"

"I don't know" was all he would give me.

I was perplexed. I begged him to tell me. This seemed to be such a key piece of information, and he was a reporter. He wouldn't budge. I tried to find out who it was on my own. Again, I went down some rabbit holes. I discovered that Regina had had a relationship with one of Lev's friends and mentors, who later committed suicide. Was it because of what had happened to Regina?

"I know who it is, so you don't have to tell me," I said, partly trying to bluff him to see what he might volunteer. When I shared who I had decided it was, he laughed.

"That would be news to his live-in girlfriend."

He was right. At the time of Regina's death, this man was living with another woman. And his suicide came several years later.

One time, we sat in a simple *fonda* restaurant two doors from my hotel, with Lev drinking horchata because he was on the wagon, and me, lemonade in solidarity. I had asked him to describe the meeting he had with Javier Duarte shortly after Regina died. Lev rubbed his face and started blinking as if he had a tic. He had a hard time describing it.

"The months all blend together between my incident and Regina's death," he said, referring to the attempted kidnapping. "I was drinking a lot, and I can't remember. And I don't see any purpose in going back and trying to."

Then I started in again on Regina's love interest. "Who was it? You have to tell me."

"No, Kathy."

"If you don't trust me . . ."

"I trust you, Kathy. I've told you more than I've told anyone. But I can't on this one."

"Pleeeeease? You have to tell me!"

"Don't abuse me!"

He was clearly in distress, so I had to drop it.

★

PEOPLE SPOKE TO me because they trusted Lev. He put me in touch with the sources who had known Regina best. One was Miguel Ángel Yunes Márquez, the son of the heavy-handed government leader Miguel Ángel Yunes Linares who became Regina's good source. The young Miguel Ángel, nicknamed Chiqui Yunes (or "Little Yunes"), was now mayor of Boca del Río, the upscale sister city to the port. Once the Yuneses left the PRI in a dispute with the leadership, they joined the National Action Party and became the opposition in Veracruz. Regina was one of the only reporters who would cover them; the official press covered only the PRI. Despite their past differences, Regina became very important for the Yunes family.

Lev and I pulled up to the white arches of the Boca de Río city hall, right on the Gulf. We crossed the indoor courtyard and climbed to the second floor, where we were made to sit in a small waiting room. Government buildings in Mexico, especially the older, colonial-style ones like this one, usually had the look of decades of rapid repurposing inside: hollow partitions, flimsy doors, old Naugahyde couches in odd configurations, such as down a hallway, and nothing ever designed or completed. This one was no different, except that everything was white and spare. After a while, we were led into the conference room off Chiqui Yunes's office, another fake space walled off with glass, so anyone could see who he was receiving.

Chiqui Yunes was a slender, bearded man in his late thirties. That day, he looked relaxed in a casual Oxford shirt that was a signature style among many Veracruz politicos: collar open, tails out, sleeves rolled up. When I told him I wanted to know about his relationship with Regina Martínez, he dove into storytelling.

He had met her when he was a freshman state legislator in 2004, at just twenty-seven years old. She treated him skeptically because of his age, he remembered, the young son of a powerful politician trying to build a dynasty. (There has barely been a year since then when there wasn't an immediate member of the Yunes family in office in Veracruz, as mayor, state or federal legislator, or governor, often several of them holding office at the same time.) Regina started to reconsider when she realized Chiqui Yunes was serious about his role as president of the state Congressional Oversight Commission, the auditing committee. "When she saw that we were going to work to bring into the light a lot of corruption scandals, I became one her main sources. They were complicated themes that quite frankly few other reporters wanted to touch."

They included the huge loans, hundreds of millions of pesos, that two governors took out right before they left office, money that disappeared within days without explanation or accounting of where it went.

Chiqui Yunes said he had learned from Regina. "When you have an audit with thousands of pieces of data, not all the data is interesting. She taught me how to choose the information. For what? Why this information? There were certain specific points that I knew could attract attention and bring the spotlight to the subject. Thanks to Regina and what she published in *Proceso*, I was interviewed by all the important media in the country . . . It was the sign of a good journalist, when you have that eye for the things that are interesting to readers and the things that are not."

Lev had proposed that I talk to Yunes because he might know what Regina was working on before she died. He said he didn't. They hadn't spoken, he said, in several years.

I asked for his reaction when he heard that she had been murdered.

He said he was certain in that instant that it was a hit: "I can't say who or how or why. But Regina stepped on the toes of many important people, many political and economic interests. Obviously, it made her a lot of enemies."

Lev also got me an interview with Miguel Ángel Yunes Linares, Chiqui Yunes's father and the former number two under Governor Patricio Chirinos. The elder Yunes received me in his high-rise office on Avenida Paseo de la Reforma, Mexico City's grand main streets lined with banking and insurance skyscrapers, with marble fountains and monuments at every intersection. The full glass windows looked out on the leafy promenade. Yunes greeted me in a suit and tie, much more formal than his son. Twenty years earlier, Regina was slamming him in the pages of *Política* for human rights violations in remote mountain communities and for his one-hundred-thousand-dollar yacht running aground in a known drug-trafficking lane. But he seemed to have forgotten all that when her name came up. Now she was a hero. "This is a case that should be investigated to the core to see if there was a direct intention to eliminate her," he said. "Because Regina had a lot of important information."

"What important information?" I asked. "What did she have?"

"Regina had investigated, for example, the links of Fidel Herrera and Duarte with organized crime," he said. "It's a theme in Veracruz. Everybody knows it. And there are elements to support that these links exist."

Again, as often in my reporting, I felt my heart leap. *He's confirming what the others said Regina said. Fidel and corruption. This is it!*

But then he kept talking: "Regina investigated a lot of things. I don't know what elements she would have had, but evidently they were really afraid of her."

"That's why I'm asking," I said. "What was she working on in that moment?"

"I don't know," he answered. "But surely her work was related to two themes: corruption and links to organized crime. That's where she persevered."

Dashed. He had nothing specific, at least not anything he was willing to tell me.

Yunes was plugged in, but he had also been accused of being as corrupt as any Veracruz politician. I figured there was a good chance he probably knew exactly who had ordered Regina's assassination. Even though, in theory, Yunes could smear his archenemies in the PRI, like Fidel Herrera, with information about a political hit on a reporter, Veracruz was a small world. People were always changing sides, and even enemies had backdoor agreements. Politicos would rail at their rivals in public, then all show up to the same wedding or rodeo on the weekends. If Yunes knew anything, sharing it wasn't necessarily in his best interest.

★

OVER THAT SPRING, I also spent a lot of time with Regina's nephew Alonso, who wanted to respect his family's boycott of speaking about the case, but he also thought that maybe by helping me, he could find out what had really happened. We connected immediately. He was a youthful old soul, a vegetarian who didn't drink or smoke, the son of two yoga instructors. Before I knew it, we were more like friends. Alonso asked my opinion on various life issues while introducing me to local artists and writers, such as the poetry of Veracruz's Rubén Bonifaz. He read aloud to me his favorite passages from the sixteenth-century Spanish poet and playwright Félix Lope de Vega. He showed me the music videos he worked on. As time went on, he moved to a more professional production house and even started writing his own short feature films. He would ask me what I thought of the story lines.

We frequented the most discreet places we could find in Xalapa, so no one would know he was speaking with me, for his security. Family members had been followed and harassed as if the state feared they might know something. We met for lunch in whatever vegetarian restaurant Alonso chose, or at one coffeehouse we liked that was tucked above a side street off the main square. You couldn't see the sign unless you were looking for it, and then you had to climb a narrow stair to reach the café. The dark stairwell gave way to a cheerful establishment with a sunny patio. We met there a lot because there were hardly any patrons and because the owner was friendly. Like most twenty-three-year-olds working in the art world, Alonso was nocturnal and had difficulty showing up on time. But I always had work to do and didn't mind the wait.

I treaded lightly with him on the subject of Regina. He, Lev, Polo, and Rodrigo were one big case of post-traumatic stress disorder, each with his own way of coping and none ever seeking professional help for the trauma Regina's murder had caused him. Alonso said he still had trouble believing she was gone, and he still ached for her guidance.

Sometimes, he came to Mexico City to film a music video. He was more anonymous in the big city, and that's where I felt more comfortable asking him to talk. That's where he opened up about Regina.

Alonso's own parents split when he was very young, and he grew up with his dad, who remarried and had more children. Alonso got along okay with his stepmother, but he never quite felt part of the new family. Regina's house was his refuge. He was the only person who knew what she did on the weekends, when she shut herself off from the rest of the world. She was with him, having a major impact on his development, on how he lived in and viewed the world as an adult.

She was the same at home as she was at work, he told me: super straight, a strong personality. If she told you to do something, you had to do it. Everything had its order. But for Alonso, she did everything with affection. He remembered one day, when he was very young, coming home from school crying. When she asked what was wrong, he told her they had made Mother's Day gifts at school, but he didn't have a mother. She comforted him, but in her stern Regina manner: "Why are you crying? You have your family. And you have me."

"I was attached to her from the time I was very little," he told me. "I knew what she did for a living. I knew she was taking on difficult stuff. But to me she was Mom."

They had a weekly routine: Wednesday or Thursday nights were for shopping. Regina would buy groceries for the week and the things Alonso needed for school, or essentials like T-shirts or underwear. Then she would tell him to pick out something for himself, which was usually a music CD, Guns N' Roses or the Clash.

On Saturdays, he did chores. Regina paid him an allowance to sweep her patio and help her organize her personal library of newspapers and magazines. There were towers of them in her living room—seven, by Alonso's count—and his job was to order them by name and date. Along the way, the young Alonso read the papers he was filing and learned what was going on around him. Regina also taught him about literature, the great Latin American writers like García Márquez, Borges, and Xavier Villaurrutia, and about music.

"She taught me how to really *read* a text," he told me. He meant critically.

Alonso also ran errands to help Regina prepare the afternoon meal. He would buy tortillas, avocados, onion, and *chile seco* for her homemade salsa, which varied in temperature depending on Regina's mood. If she was angry about something, the salsa was particularly hot. The grocery list always included two glass bottles of Coca-Cola and two quart bottles of beer, Victoria and Corona, that would last her all week. She would put one of each in the refrigerator and the rest on the floor under the kitchen table—just where forensic investigators found two of them the day she died, unopened, despite the state's story that "she had left the house to buy beer to party with her visitors."

When Alonso returned with the groceries, his job was to chop. Because he was a vegetarian, Regina always prepared the main Saturday meal with lots of vegetables. His favorite was her pasta with mushrooms. She would make a separate portion for herself with bacon. Alonso loved the times they cooked together, when they could be comfortably and unself-consciously themselves. He would daydream as he sliced, and she liked to sing along with whatever song was on the stereo.

At about four or five in the afternoon, they would sit down to eat. This was when they talked. She told him stories about her travels to Chiapas to cover the Zapatista Rebellion, and to the sierra for her in-depth reports. She told him about life, that they were fortunate to live in a house. "There's a lot of suffering out there," she said.

He missed hearing the things she would say, like to be kind to others, but more important, to be okay with yourself. "She always said something that gave me that 'punch' to keep going."

He missed her face. He had studied her hard, stern features as she spoke, and her eyes. More than her words, her eyes had revealed the person she really was, he thought, the person who abandoned many things in life to pursue her career, who went beyond any limitations to get there. But he also saw her as a person who carried a lot of love without too much ego.

At the end of the day, his allowance went into a jar, not his pocket. Regina was also teaching him to save to afford bigger things.

Alonso never stayed at his aunt's past 8 P.M., because that was the time Regina would begin writing. *Pinche escuincle, te quiero mucho* were often her parting words: "I love you, you pesky little brat."

★

WHEN I FIRST started working on Regina's story, I was still at the Associated Press and, as bureau chief, worked a weekend shift every once in a while, to give the other correspondents a break. For that reason, I was in the office on Saturday, August 1, 2015, checking the breaking news, when I came across a report that five people had been found dead in an apartment in a middle-class neighborhood of Mexico City. It was not by any means an area of town prone to violence, just quiet and residential. Early reports indicated that the victims were related, possibly a family. I thought it might be a murder-suicide of some sort, though such crimes were very rare in Mexico. I checked with the desk supervisor, and he told me to just keep an eye on it. If it was a family affair, it would be too local for the Associated Press and would possibly merit only a brief. As I was leaving, there was no new information, so I headed home to get ready to join some friends. We were seeing one of my favorite Mexican TV actors perform at the Microteatro, a series of live productions, fifteen minutes each, staged in various rooms of an old house.

In the time it took me to drive home, I received a bulletin that a journalist from Veracruz had gone missing in Mexico City. This needed my attention. Another one! It had seemed nonstop that year after the killing of Moisés Sánchez in January. In May, the body of radio reporter Armando Saldaña Morales had been found dumped in Oaxaca state after he reported on petroleum theft for his Veracruz station.

Javier Duarte continued with his message that the killings were the fault of the journalists. In a June media event in Poza Rica, an industrial city in northern Veracruz, his message turned more ominous. The event started normally, with Duarte at a round banquet table surrounded by smiling journalists. But then he started to speak.

"Here's my message for all of you," he said. "Some of the workers and collaborators in the media are involved with [criminal] groups. What am I asking? That please, for yourselves and for your families, but also for me and my family . . . behave yourselves. All of us know who has taken the wrong path. We all know who has ties and who is involved with the Mafia. Behave yourselves, please."

A wave of murmurs of protest rolled through the room.

"Some difficult times are coming . . ." Duarte continued. "We're going to shake the tree, and a lot of rotten apples are going to fall. I honestly expect, and I say this from my heart, that no worker in the media will see themselves affected by this situation."

The talk made headlines as a governor making a direct threat.

Two days later, Juan Mendoza Delgado, another local journalist like Moisés Sánchez from Medellín, was found dead by a highway. He had been a reporter for major newspapers, but of late, he had been driving a taxi and running his own online news website named Writing the Truth. Mendoza wrote about politicians and organized crime in a column called "Why Be Quiet?" Authorities said his death was an accident, that he had been run over by a car. Photographs of the body, however, showed that he had been found with a bloody bandage around his head, indicating that he may have been tortured. He was far from his route, and his taxi was nowhere to be found.

And now the bulletin about the latest missing Veracruz journalist. About two hours after I received the initial alert, there was a second: The missing journalist was one of the five dead people in the Mexico City apartment.

His name was Rubén Espinosa, the photographer I had seen at Regina's memorial, Eddie Romo's neighbor. It turned out that Espinosa was being followed and harassed in Xalapa and had decided recently to seek refuge in Mexico City, where he was from.

I called my friends and canceled the Uber that was already en route to take me to the theater. I had to go back to work.

According to the prosecutor's office, the five dead had been bound and tortured, some had been shot execution style with a 9 mm pistol, and two bodies had signs of asphyxiation. The women showed signs of sexual assault. Some reports said one of the women was Espinosa's girl-friend, the reason he was in the apartment.

But the thing that caught everyone's attention was the fact that Espinosa had fled Veracruz to Mexico City, normally considered a sanc-tuary for journalists, and had still ended up getting killed in a very brutal manner. On Sunday, I returned to work to keep reporting the story. Editors from New York called to ask me if we were safe, if we needed to revisit our safety protocols. I told them we could talk after I was off deadline. But the concern for everyone was that Mexico City had lost its place as a haven from the violence.

Rubén Espinosa had a long history of harassment by officials in Xalapa, including being followed on the street and roughed up while covering events. Eddie Romo, his neighbor, had noticed strange things happening around their apartment building. At one point, a *puesto*, an informal food stand, suddenly appeared outside the door to their complex, selling fresh-squeezed juices. It was an odd place and a strange business. For one thing, although these juice stands could be found all over Mexican cities, the sidewalk in front of their complex was narrow and not the kind of space where you would generate a lot of business. There were few customers. The neighbors assumed the strange juice stand had been set up to monitor something. When Espinosa left for Mexico City, the stand disappeared as quickly as it came.

There was another disturbing development in the case. Among the victims was an activist from Veracruz who also had fled to Mexico City. I called Lev to see if he could track information on her for us. He didn't have to go far. Her name was Nadia Vera, Lev told me, and she had worked as the manager at his bar El Conspirador. Not only did he know her well, but he had trusted her with his business. He said they called her La Ardilla, "the Squirrel," because of her large front teeth, a sign that they knew each other well. Yet he talked about her with no emotion in his voice, as if discussing a stranger.

"I'm so sorry," I said. "This must very hard for you."

He said nothing. This was strike three or four for him, I thought, depending on how you count what had happened to him in the last several years. His reaction to Vera's death seemed like a shutdown.

For Eddie Romo, it was three friends assassinated in the span of a few years. He, too, had worked with Nadia Vera, on a local film festival. The night before he learned that she and Rubén Espinosa were dead, he had a vivid dream in which he was crying violently and couldn't be consoled. The person who came up and wrapped him in a tight hug was Lev García. Frightened, Eddie and another neighbor in the building who had known Rubén Espinosa moved out the next week.

A video of Nadia Vera emerged on YouTube: an interview she gave in 2014 for the Internet TV channel Rompeviento while she was still living in Xalapa. She was a petite woman with dark wavy hair, a beauty mark above her upper lip, and a piercing in the lower. She was bubbly and spoke rapidly, eloquently, the daughter of a poet.

In the video, made in an office at the University of Veracruz, the computer screen behind Vera reflected a poster of Che Guevara on the opposite wall. Vera talked about the repression and violence in Xalapa, especially against the students. She said it was common knowledge that young people were being picked up by the police, never to be heard from again. Families that complained or who tried to look for missing loved ones became the targets of threats themselves. Vera said they had to organize to protest the violence. "We're caught between two fronts of repression, the narcos and the government of Javier Duarte," she said. "Javier Duarte and his cabinet are responsible for anything that happens to us . . . The state is completely responsible for our security, because it's the state that is sending people to repress us."

It was an accusation from the grave: Javier Duarte was responsible for her death.

What I noticed almost immediately in the Rubén Espinosa case was how much it resembled the aftermath of Regina's killing, even though it had occurred in Mexico City, not Veracruz. From the beginning, Rodolfo Ríos Garza, the Mexico City prosecutor, never mentioned Espinosa's work as a journalist as being a possible motive for his killing. He never acknowledged that Espinosa had fled Veracruz, instead saying in an early press conference that the photographer had come to Mexico City for "professional opportunities." When the press corps objected, the prosecutor said that every possible lead would be followed.

The similarities extended to the details of the case. The first stories in Mexican media reported that Espinosa and the women had been partying all night with their killers and that neighbors had reported smelling pot smoke and hearing *banda*, the accordion-style music of Mexican campesinos. (Espinosa's friends laughed at this stereotypic Mexican detail: he had listened to punk rock, *never* Mexican folk music.) The information was leaked to a government-friendly media outlet to build the official narrative.

None of it turned out to be true.

Meanwhile, the Veracruz media followed the official story line as well. In the murders of Espinosa and Vera, they printed nothing about the inconsistencies in the cases, but rather, that autopsies of the two had revealed the presence of cocaine and marijuana. "The crime of being a victim"—the two had brought their misfortune upon themselves.

After his experience with Regina, Jenaro Villamil, the senior writer at *Proceso*, suspected Veracruz authorities might be behind the Espinosa case as well. He went to Patricia Mercado, the number two under Mexico City mayor Miguel Ángel Mancera (not the newspaper editor from Zacatecas) and told her that Mexico City authorities should look into one person in particular in Veracruz: Arturo Bermúdez Zurita, Duarte's secretary of public safety. Villamil gave Mercado some off-the-record information on the feared police chief, who hated reporters and protesters. There were a lot of other accusations surrounding Bermúdez, including that he ran organized crime cells out of the state police.

Shortly after Villamil passed on this information, his parents and a friend received strange phone calls saying that he had been kidnapped. His parents were able to call him and confirm immediately that their son was okay. The friend, a fellow reporter, said the anonymous caller had told him, "You're going to end up like your friend, that journalist." This harassment was the only result of Villamil's tip to authorities— that and the fact that he had to leave the country, spending a month and half in Argentina as a precaution.

At one point in my coverage, I went to talk to the lawyers representing Nadia Vera's family. They told me that Nadia, too, had suffered high levels of harassment in Veracruz. She was detained while filming police arresting protesters, punched, and taken to the police station by people in civilian clothing who didn't identify themselves. There was also a break-in at her apartment that she considered a warning, one of the lawyers said.

"Break-in?" I asked.

Yes, the lawyers told me. In 2013, Nadia went home one afternoon to find that her apartment had been cleaned up. She thought it was her boyfriend or her roommate, but neither said they had done any cleaning.

Someone she didn't know had gotten into the apartment without breaking any locks or leaving other traces. Nadia joked that if it had been a burglar, they would have gone through drawers and made a mess, as intruders do. But because the apartment was already a mess, they had instead tidied up, to show her that her personal space had been breached.

Oh, one lawyer said, as if sharing an afterthought: The bathroom was steamed up, as if someone had taken a shower.

My hand immediately went to my mouth. "Omigod" was all I said. I didn't share with them that the same thing had happened to Regina.

I called Lev later and asked him if he knew about the break-in at Nadia Vera's apartment.

"Yes," he said. "That's when I knew she was a marked woman."

CHAPTER 17

Paranoia

2015

THE MURDERS OF Rubén Espinosa, Nadia Vera, and the three other women were never solved. The men arrested said they had been tortured into confessing. AP New York and I never had that conversation about our safety or whether Espinosa's murder was a game changer for us. I didn't think it translated into a threat for the international press, and they didn't ask again. But it did impact our photo contributor, who lived and worked in Veracruz. Félix Márquez was a good friend of Espinosa's and had been harassed himself on various stories. In 2013, Márquez and Rodrigo Soberanes did a story on bands of vigilantes forming in the hills of Veracruz to patrol their cities against corrupt police. State Public Security Director Arturo Bermúdez accused Márquez of staging the photos and paying people to dress as vigilantes, adding, "The person who needs to be jailed is the one who took the photos." Márquez left the state for a while then. Now that Rúben Espinosa was dead, the AP helped Márquez leave the country.

The Rubén Espinosa killing also started to make me feel paranoid. After my coverage of Espinosa's case for the AP, it became apparent to anyone who cared to pay attention that I had been in Xalapa. I started thinking my phone was tapped and put it in the refrigerator (an Edward Snowden tip to block eavesdropping) whenever I discussed Regina's or the other cases. Some of my online documents on the Regina case went missing, but I could not say for sure whether it was a hack or if I hadn't stored them in the cloud properly.

On August 13, 2015, I got up early after a sleepless night to drive to Veracruz for a trip I had already planned. I received an unexpected message at 6:30 A.M.: Yet another journalist had been murdered there overnight. Shortly after midnight that same day, five gunmen walked into a bar in the industrial city of Orizaba and opened fire, killing six of eight people sitting at a table. Among the dead was Juan Santos Carrera, a journalist who had just left his job with the network giant Televisa to start his own publication. Sitting next to him was the local leader of the Zetas, a man known as El Chichi. Two other journalists in the group survived at the mercy of the gunmen and, as witnesses to the ordeal, were placed in protective custody. They were also fired that same morning by their newspaper, *El Buen Tono*, for cavorting with narcos. Authorities said the killings were a settling of scores between two cells of Zetas. The attack on reporters had nothing to do with freedom of expression, José Abella, owner of *El Buen Tono*, told the media. "They're going to have to explain what they were doing at that table with a crime boss and his assistant," said Abella, a colorful character in his own right, who established the newspaper as a vanity press and who himself was accused of associating with narcos.

This case was the easiest of all for the Veracruz government to dismiss, because when it labeled Santos Carrera a narco journalist, no one protested. The Committee to Protect Journalists didn't investigate, and it doesn't list him among the journalists killed in Mexico under Duarte. Open and shut. No one bothered to find out if he was actually a narco. The circumstantial evidence was too overwhelming.

But the unnerving incidents continued. Lev García and Alonso Martínez came to Mexico City one weekend, and we all got together at my house late one night. Alonso told Lev and me that he felt he was being watched. A strange SUV without plates was parked in front of his house in Xalapa. He had been staying on friends' couches the last few weeks because he didn't feel safe at home. This was the first time I realized that "home" for him was Regina's house. I was shocked to think he could live in the same place where the woman he considered his mother had been brutally murdered. Still, that may have been the only option he could afford.

Lev and I talked to Alonso about safety protocols, about letting people know when he was coming and going. We asked if he could get a throwaway "burner" cell phone to communicate with just Lev and me, so it couldn't be tapped. He said he would try, but he didn't have the money right then to buy one. We told him to let us know in real time anything that was going on, especially Lev, given that the two lived in the same town. By the time we finished talking, it was 3 A.M. In a few hours, I had to head to the airport for an assignment in Guatemala. I called them an Uber so I could monitor on my phone that they had made it safely to Lev's relative's house, in the southern part of the city.

A few weeks later, I returned to Xalapa by bus. As I got closer to the city, my cell phone started ringing, registering a Mexican phone number. I answered, thinking it was Lev calling me from a different number. He was supposed to meet me once I arrived at the bus terminal. There was a flurry of calls. I was in the mountains, so the line kept dropping. Whenever I could answer, there was no one there. When I tried to return the call, I got a recording saying the number didn't exist. The same thing happened again once I arrived at the terminal. I tried calling back again. I got the same message saying the number didn't exist. I took a taxi to the town center and arranged to meet Lev in a coffee shop. When he arrived, I showed him the numbers in my phone.

"That wasn't me," he said. "And those calls aren't from Xalapa."

He googled the area code. "The calls came from Coahuila," he said, a Mexican state on the border with Texas that was also racked by drug violence in 2015. I didn't know anyone there. We both thought it was strange. Perhaps someone was trying to track me, and I had foolishly answered them. I didn't know if answering the calls had put malware on my phone. Or were they just Mexican spam calls? These were the mind games I started playing with myself.

My goals for the trip included obtaining the court file for Regina's case and to interview El Silva's sister, Rosario, who was also kidnapped and had been threatened into declaring to investigators the government's version of Regina's death, according to documents I had seen in Mexico City. I obviously wanted her to tell me firsthand what had happened. Lev helped me file a public information request for the court file—in Mexico, court documents are sealed until the case is resolved—and arranged an interview with the state prosecutor, Luis Ángel Bravo.

I met again with Lupita López, still trying to find out what Regina had been working on just before her murder. Lupita didn't know, but she gave me some other sources who might. I was supposed to meet up again with Lev, but by the time Lupita and I finished, it was after 11 P.M., and he didn't answer his phone. I figured he had fallen asleep. We had talked earlier about trying to find El Silva's sister. I knew from El Silva's lawyer that she ran a candy and cigarette stand in the city center at night, in a place known as Pasaje Enríquez, by day a mini-mall on the main street anchored by an Aldo Conti menswear store. Lev had pointed out the exact location for me. At night, when the stores closed, it made for a wide walkway for placing a stand. I was staying at the Holiday Inn Express, just a block away. It was midnight, and I was wide wake. So, I decided to give it a try on my own.

I spotted the stand immediately, on Calle Enríquez, by day an ever-congested main drag that cut through downtown. At night, it was well-lit but empty, save for a passing taxi or two or a lone pedestrian, in this case, me. The quiet cobblestone was bathed in a yellow-green glow from the street lamps and the avocado color of the massive stucco statehouse across the street. I spotted a fold-out cart on wheels with a large white cooler to one side for the Coca-Colas and waters on ice. A woman sat on the cooler. I guessed she was Rosario, but my attention went to something else: three young men standing around her who were looking at me. I got that gut feeling that tells you something isn't right, even in a situation you've never seen before. I could feel something sinister about the men. They weren't tattooed or in saggy pants or anything else considered stereotypically "gangster." The way they looked, they could have been any college kids on the street. Still, something didn't feel safe.

Instead of approaching the candy stand, I kept walking, as if I were headed to another destination, turned the corner of the block, and headed briskly back to the hotel. They watched me the whole time I walked by and changed course. They were *halcones*, a word that translates to "falcons" in English but that in Mexican slang means "hired lookouts," particularly for drug traffickers. I imagined they were selling something besides candy and Cokes from that stand. I must have seemed suspicious to them as well: a tall, very American-looking woman walking on a deserted street at that hour. It was their job to notice and report anything unusual. I decided I would try again the next day with Lev, earlier, when there were a lot more cars and people on the street.

The next morning, I told Lev about my midnight walk, and he scolded me for trying to do something like that by myself. We had an afternoon interview with the attorney general, at the state justice building, a massive, hulking concrete block built on a hill in the outer part of Xalapa. We climbed the wide stairs, past the guard shack and the metal gate surrounding the entrance, to an open courtyard and a compound of buildings. Eddie Romo was waiting in lobby. With the Veracruz photographer Félix Márquez in exile, I had hired Eddie to take photographs of the interview for the story I was working on for the AP.

After a customarily long wait, Luis Ángel Bravo greeted us in his modern office in a three-piece suit and with every hair gelled into place. It was late afternoon, almost dusk. It was customary in Mexico for bureaucrats to return from lunch at four and then work until seven or eight o'clock. I took a seat opposite his desk. Lev, as usual, sat quietly in a corner; Eddie's camera whirred, but I hardly noticed he was there, either. Bravo, who was Mexican über-polite, said he was "enchanted" to meet me. He thanked me for giving him the opportunity to answer questions with "hard facts," as opposed to all the rumors and speculation around the cases of dead journalists. His was a false congeniality that doesn't exist between reporter and bureaucrat in the United States—and one that American journalists in Mexico liked to mock.

I started by asking how he could explain the assassination of fourteen journalists in one state under one governor. He read from the same script I had heard from other state officials: His office was responsible for only three of those cases, and all had been resolved. Regina's case had nothing to do with her journalism. El Silva had run out of appeals and was going to stay incarcerated.

"And what physical evidence do you have that El Silva was in her place at that time?" I asked.

"All that has already been weighed by the judges. I repeat, this case is concluded. There is no doubt. What happened there has been proven by the courts."

"Yes, but there are many people who still have doubts."

"Of course, and with all due respect," he said, leaning across the desk to make his point, "that comes with living in a democratic society, doesn't it?"

"But this is a case built entirely on a confession," I countered.

"Not necessarily. From that confession, we were able to confirm elements, such as locating Regina's belongings in certain places, belongings that her family identified. That came from El Silva's statement."

There were so many holes in that statement, but I could see he would just keep me running in circles. I was more interested in getting the court file.

"You say the case is closed, right? Then is it possible to look at the file?"

"Yes, we have your open records request . . . and I am delighted to grant you everything that's appropriate. We are making a public version."

"Great, then the rest of my questions will be answered by the court file." I switched subjects. "What are you doing to find El Jarocho?"

"We are looking for him with all the objectives we normally use for locating a fugitive," Bravo said. "I meet at least twice a month with the police chief to go over our progress in apprehending all fugitives. If you know anything about this case, you've heard that perhaps [Jarocho's] no longer in Mexico. Others say he's no longer alive. But we have no indications whether he is dead or alive, so we're still looking for him. There's an active arrest warrant."

"El Silva's lawyer says Jarocho is in Xalapa."

That was just a tactic by the defense lawyer to cloud the case, Bravo said. "I was hoping they were going to tell me where," he quipped. "We're looking, we're looking hard."

"Have you located El Jarocho's partner and their son?" I asked.

"There is someone here that has relations to him, but I ask you to understand that I can't share any details, so as not to interfere with our surveillance of the areas where he might show up."

"Where is she, and the son?"

"That information is part of our intelligence work in order to be able to execute the arrest warrant."

"She also testified that she had been detained for about five days in a safe house and, under torture and threats to her son, had to learn the official version that El Jarocho confessed the crime to her before he disappeared," I continued. "El Silva said his confession was given under pressure and torture, so they both have declared almost the same thing."

"I repeat, Kathy," the prosecutor said, with a calm face and a smooth delivery, "in many, many cases, this is the strategy of the defense lawyers." He told us how to retrieve the court documents when they were ready.

We thanked him profusely and said our overly polite goodbyes.

Eddie decided to hitch a ride with us back to the town center, so we all piled into Lev's pickup, whose cabin had a backseat. It was past 8 P.M. I asked Lev if we could drive by and see if Rosario's candy stand was out, so we could try to interview the woman at the center of the two "killers." I mentioned that Regina's nephew Alonso wanted to meet up afterward, so we could swing by the stand and then pick him up. As we were approaching the main street downtown, Alonso called and said he was waiting for us outside a convenience store. Before I could say anything, Lev pulled a U-turn to go get him.

My gut spoke again. *We should not be seen with Alonso in the center of town*, I thought. *No one should know that I'm even acquainted with Alonso.* But I didn't say anything; I deferred to Lev. I figured he would know better than I if being seen with us in town presented any danger to Alonso.

It was a mistake on my part.

We picked Alonso up across the street from the apartment where he was staying. When we returned to the city center, we saw that, indeed, Rosario's stand was out. Lev left the truck standing in a No Parking zone, because we planned to be only a few minutes. Eddie and Alonso stayed in the backseat and waited.

As we approached the candy cart, we saw a young dark-haired boy of about six or seven years old sitting on the cooler. I assumed he was Jarocho's son. He told us his mother was down the street talking to someone and that she would be right back. As we waited, a kind-looking middle-aged woman came up and waited with us. I assumed she was another customer. She said something to us that I didn't understand. Later, Lev translated for me: "She asked if we were looking for the 'other' kind of cigarettes."

When the proprietor returned to her stand, I asked if she was María del Rosario Morales Zárate.

"Yes," she said hesitantly. "What do you want?"

This woman was the sister of a street criminal, had had a child with a male prostitute, and ran a cigarette and candy stand until four in the morning, with her young son hanging with her the entire time. However I expected a woman who spent her nights on the street to support her child, the son of a fugitive murder suspect, to look, it wasn't like this. Rosario was young, late twenties or thirties, I would guess, casually dressed in jeans and a flowered blouse, well groomed, with a bob of dark hair to her shoulders. She could have been any clerk in any shop or behind a desk in any bureaucracy.

"We're reporters working on a story about your brother being unjustly imprisoned, and we wanted to talk to you."

She seemed confused and asked if she was required to talk to us. Were we police?

"No," I said. "We're journalists."

She looked afraid. "I don't know," she said. "It's very sensitive. I'd have to discuss it with my attorney."

"You're El Silva's sister, correct?"

She said no, but rather that her mother had taken care of him while he was living on the streets, giving him food and clothing. So, he *became* like a brother to her. That seemed to explain why she didn't look like a street person.

"Everyone says your brother is innocent," I continued. "They say he's not capable of doing something like that."

"I can't say he didn't do it," she said. "Off drugs, yes, he's a nice person. But on drugs, he is capable of doing anything."

I told her that I had read her testimony that she, too, had been kidnapped and held in a safe house and threatened into memorizing the state's version of what had happened. She denied it. "They brought me in to declare again and again," she said, "but no, they didn't kidnap me."

This was strange, because I had read her testimony with my own eyes. I decided to let it go. She clearly wasn't comfortable speaking where we were, and I thought it better to give her some time so we could arrange a more discreet conversation. I told her I'd let her talk to her lawyer and then get back to her in a few days.

I was leaving Xalapa that night and Mexico the next day. Lev said he could check in with her for me. We hopped back in the pickup and ended up at Los Álamos, Lev's favorite cantina, where he had his last conversation with Regina. We reviewed the day's work over beers—except for Alonso, who ordered juice. We drank until it was time for me to head to the bus terminal. Lev agreed to drop me off.

Two days later, I was sitting at my mother's house in the United States, where I had gone to do some family business, when I got a frantic text from Alonso: "Help me, Kathy, I'm scared!" He said Rosario, from the candy stand, was outside with two men, talking and looking at his house. He was inside and didn't know what to do.

I felt a tightening in my throat. I was far away and couldn't help. But I used my AP training to stay calm. I knew Rosario lived somewhere near Regina's house.

"She lives nearby," I texted. "Is she just in the neighborhood?"

"No. They're right outside, looking straight at the house." He said he wanted to flee.

"Stay put," I told him, "and let me get in contact with Lev."

He continued to message me: "What do I do?"

"Just sit tight and let me call Lev."

I got Lev on the phone and told him what was happening. He said he would talk to Alonso and see what was going on. "I've heard from Lev," Alonso later wrote. I decided to let Lev take over, because I couldn't do anything from where I was. After a bit, Alonso messaged me that Rosario and the men were gone.

I felt terrible. Clearly their appearance was related to our having spoken to Rosario. They had seen Alonso with us! No one was ever supposed to see him with me.

Lev told me he wasn't so sure. He said the windows in his truck were tinted, it was nighttime, and the men couldn't have seen anything. That's when he told me that there had been *halcones* watching us while we were speaking to Rosario.

"Why didn't you tell me then?" I was a bit upset. This was information we should have acted on in the moment. We should have left immediately.

"You were talking, and I couldn't interrupt you."

"I need you to tell me things in real time!" I said. "And I need to tell my editors about this."

"Let me check it out first," Lev said. "Alonso can exaggerate things."

The next day, Lev told me he had checked things out and that everything seemed to be okay for Alonso. I didn't need to alert my editors about a source getting harassed, so I didn't. Alonso continued to spend the night on friends' couches. What Lev didn't tell me was that he asked two police officers he trusted to go by Regina's house twice a day for about a week. They didn't see anything. Everything seemed calm. But as soon as they stopped their clandestine patrol, Rosario showed up again, this time with a man who stood outside and took pictures, Alonso told me.

About the same time, Alonso said he was jumped by two men while cutting through a wooded park on his way home.

"Do you have the time?" one asked.

"No," Alonso said and kept walking. One of the men pulled out a knife and stuck it in Alonso's face. Alonso grabbed him, and all three fell to the ground, struggling in a ball. The knife dropped, and so did Alonso's cell phone, causing a spiderweb crack in its face. He kicked one guy in the knee while they were on the ground and then got up and fled. He said he ran to two policemen to report the assault, but they said, "As far as we saw, you were hitting them. So, you'd better get out of here before we arrest you."

He didn't think it was a random attack, and his father didn't, either. Alonso started to feel like he needed to get out of Xalapa. But where, and how? He was working a lot, filming that took him out of the city. For the time being, that would have to do.

Meanwhile, Lev didn't think the fight in the park had anything to do with anything. He said Alonso was on edge and making bad decisions. I didn't know what to think. Alonso had showed me his bruised knuckles and cracked phone. But I had no way to verify what either of them was telling me. I couldn't interview Lev's police sources, and none of us wanted to go back to Rosario again. I had approached her as a friendly witness, not knowing she had withdrawn her testimony about being kidnapped. She obviously had been turned. One of my editors at the AP said we shouldn't go back to her: "She's obviously a dangerous person."

I felt like the whole thing was my fault.

When I returned to Mexico, I went back to Xalapa to pick up the court file. Lev and I appeared once again at the state prosecutor's complex and were handed twenty-five pounds of documents. (I tried to transport the file in a duffel bag, and whenever someone lifted it, they, of course, asked if I was carrying a dead body.) The state had offered me a digital version of Regina's court file, but that would have taken weeks to produce. I didn't want to give them time to change their minds about letting me see it.

Lev and I sifted through documents in the ghostly fluorescent light of my hotel room, a boutique colonial establishment with dormitory-style rooms surrounding a stone courtyard. It was my new location, more discreet than the Holiday Inn. The front door always remained padlocked. Even guests had to ring to get in.

Lev was less than enthusiastic about our trove of documents: "There's nothing in there," he said after we had been through some of the bound documents. "It's all fiction." But to me, it was interesting fiction. I didn't read them as I did most court records, which in the United States are considered protected fact. I read them as documents constructed to manipulate a conclusion. I rotated the odd details around in my head, searching for clues in the anecdotes that would lead me to the people who knew something about the real story. For example, Diego Hernández, the street drunk who had said he saw Jarocho on the night of the murder, also testified that, one night about two months before, he saw two men get out of taxi with Regina near her house. One of the men met the description of Regina's former boyfriend Alberto "El Gato" Morales, who was conspicuously large and burly, with a camera always around his neck. Why was this El Gato figure appearing in the narrative at that point? He was never investigated; nor had he played any role publicly in the case. Was that detail thrown in as a warning to him to keep quiet about something he knew, lest he be implicated in Regina's murder?

As I read the testimonies of people, especially the neighbors, I thought they must have been paid off to go along with the official story. What did Diego Hernández receive? Drugs? Isabel Nuñez, the neighbor next door who called the police, had changed her testimony between the federal deposition and the state one, telling federal investigators that it looked like Regina was expecting someone that night, and telling the state investigators that she saw nothing and went to bed. Nuñez expanded her house after Regina died. Was that paid for with money given in exchange for her convenient testimony? I asked Lev at one point if he could get the property records on Nuñez's house, to check the timing and financing of the improvements. He was never able to come up with anything.

I wanted to show the case documents to Alonso, to see if he could identify some of the people referred to in the file. The names had been blacked out for the "public" version. But he was away working, and not in Xalapa, when I received the file. I decided it was safer if he came to Mexico City to look at it, anyway.

That same trip, I continued to track down people who may have known what Regina was working on just before she was killed. I got nothing. No one knew. And I was not getting any material to support

my theory that Regina knew the United States was about to break up
a Zeta horse-racing ring with ties to Fidel Herrera.

After one such interview, in a Denny's-style restaurant in the city
center, a white-haired man approached me just after I bid the source
goodbye. He was elderly but tall and stately, neatly dressed in a jacket
and tie. He said he had heard me talking about politics and asked if I was
an academic. I said yes, that I was researching a book on Mexican politics because he was a stranger and didn't need to know what I was doing.
He offered to help, telling me he had spent many years in government
and as a diplomat and could explain a lot from an insider's perspective.
I was wary for all the reasons I needed to be—government spies eavesdropping in public places, people wanting to know what I was doing
there. But he was polite, and so was I. I also couldn't kick my reporter
habit that perhaps this man could really help me. He gave me his name
and phone number on a slip of paper. And I—yes, foolishly—gave him
mine. I never ended up calling him.

★

WHEN ALONSO FINISHED filming and returned to Xalapa, I invited
him to Mexico City for a few days to get out of the inferno and whatever was happening around the surveillance of Regina's house. I wanted
him to look at the court file and see what he could add for me. It was
also Thanksgiving, and I was hosting a big group, so I invited him for
an American turkey dinner. I said he could stay at my house. I had plenty
of guest space and already had an American student about Alonso's age
staying there while he worked on a justice project. I figured the two
could hang out together, and they did.

I was extremely paranoid by this point, so much so that when Alonso
came to the AP office to look at the court file, I became concerned that
one of my coworkers was paying a little too much attention to him.
Every time Alonso went to use the elevator or the restroom, this man
was there, asking him questions about where he was from and what he
was doing at the AP. Alonso, too, was unnerved by the way the man
kept showing up wherever he went. In fact, he pointed it out to me.
Do we have a newsroom plant, I wondered? It would not have been unheard

of for the Mexican government, which we assumed bugged our phones, also to have a spy planted inside an American newsroom. It was very common for Mexican newsrooms. They were the classic *orejas*, or "ears." But with every paranoid impulse, I had to pull myself together to evaluate the situation rationally. My worries in this case made no sense. This man wasn't Mexican, and he had been in many countries for the AP over many years. And even if we had spies, they would have been working for the federal government, not Veracruz, and they would have been on the lookout for anything critical we were writing about the president. They wouldn't have known or cared about Alonso Martínez. I had to let it go.

Alonso and I sat in the cramped AP conference room to go over the heavy volumes of testimony. I showed him the ones I thought would be most relevant: his father's deposition and those of the neighbors and the people who had done odd jobs at Regina's house. I made sure to steer him away from the very graphic pages of the report, the photographs and information regarding her body.

Alonso devoured the pages. He read much faster in Spanish than I could and even made out some of the words that had been covered by black Sharpie. First, I showed him the testimony of the handyman who said he had worked in Regina's house and that he had bought her ten quart bottles of beer every week for her drinking parties. The handyman claimed he was last in her house the week before she died. As part of his testimony, he described what was in the house, including a "21-inch" television screen and a desktop computer with a "kinescope monitor." He also mentioned a bicycle.

Alonso seized on this testimony as clearly fabricated. He knew the man and said he hadn't worked for Regina for about two years before she died. The man was very humble and lived in the apartments on the hill in back. Alonso said he would never have come close to owning a computer or television, let alone being able to identify the size of a TV screen or a kinescope monitor. What's more, the bicycle the man mentioned had been stolen about two years earlier, around the time the handyman worked there, and therefore wouldn't have been in Regina's house the week before she died.

"If he was working in the house the week before she died, where are his fingerprints?" Alonso asked rhetorically. There was none in the evidence. "I'm not an imbecile."

Then I asked him to look at the testimony of the witness Diego Hernández, who said he had seen Jarocho and El Silva heading to Regina's house the night of her murder. I wondered if Alonso could identify the other people Diego mentioned, La Bola and Paleta Payaso, so I could go to the neighborhood and interview them. As I was flipping through the documents to find his testimony, a piece of evidence on one of the pages caught his eye. It was a grocery slip from Comercial Mexicana dated April 27, 2012, the day before she died.

"What is this? A grocery receipt?"

"Yes, but I don't understand why it's in there."

Alonso knew exactly why it would be part of the evidence: "Because it's the last thing they found, her last purchase," he told me. It would indicate a point at which she was still alive. The file mentioned that investigators went to review the security cameras at Comercial Mexicana to confirm that Regina had actually made the purchases, but the cameras weren't working.

Alonso reviewed the receipt. "Let me see: bacon, white rice, toilet paper, soup, pasta, *milanesa* . . . T-shirts." He stopped reading at the two T-shirts listed on the ticket. "Whoa. I think she bought those for me." He was rattled, knowing that on her last day, she had been shopping for him as she always did.

His mood grew worse as he reviewed the testimony of Diego Hernández. Alonso thought he recognized the man with the bicycle who said he was dating a reporter. At this point, Alonso became agitated. He reached across the conference table, took my notebook and my pen, and started making notes about the testimony:

150 centimeters tall
Straight hair
Lives in a shack on Brazil Street
Supposedly works as a carpenter.
"Polo"

Shoeshine
Investigate "Don Gonzalo"

"These motherfuckers," Alonso said with a bitter laugh. "Did you read what they're saying here?" He read aloud from the court file about the man with the reporter girlfriend, a carpenter and a shoeshine who knew how to sing. That was Don Gonzalo, he said, who was always around the neighborhood looking for work. Whenever he saw Alonso, he talked about how much he loved Regina, his *chula*, because she always gave him work. "And those *cabrones* killed her," Don Gonzalo lamented one day. Alonso dismissed him as speaking in the abstract. Now he saw something different in the man's testimony.

"This guy knows who did it!" he exclaimed to me. "Of course he knows, because that's his circle. It wasn't him, but it was people he knows, like this guy who is testifying, who clearly knows Jarocho."

He continued reading aloud from the testimony, where Diego Hernández described a burly man getting out of taxi a few weeks earlier who fit the description of Regina's old boyfriend Alberto "El Gato" Morales. "El Gato came in a taxi!" Alonso drew back in his chair, shook his head, and closed his eyes, sitting silent for a minute. "Fucking hell."

I was concerned. I had only wanted him to help me identify people. I hadn't thought about how much it would upset him—naïve of me, perhaps.

"It's clear. The declaration is complete. The only thing lacking is naming exactly 'him and him.' But he's describing these assholes," Alonso said of Hernández.

The testimony is credible, he added, because Hernández tells it in the slang that street people would speak, not like an impoverished handyman identifying a kinescope monitor. And the description of El Gato having been near Regina's house some weeks earlier triggered something else: When Regina's house was broken into months before her murder, she told Alonso's dad that she had been betrayed by someone who knew her well, who knew how to enter the house without breaking a lock and go straight for her valuables without having to search. "I know who this could have been," she said, "and I'm going to give him hell where he knows it will hurt."

Alonso shifted in his plastic chair, then covered his face and sighed. I was afraid of what I had unleashed. He was going to try to track down the people in the depositions himself and confront them.

"You're not going to do anything with this information right?" I asked.

"Why would you ask me that?"

"Because I'm concerned about what could happen to you."

"My blood is boiling after seeing this," he said. "Don't you see? These are the people I see every day, the people who say good morning to me. I feel their hypocrisy every day that I walk around there. I can feel how they look at me, some with contempt, some like 'poor guy.' Some with pity. Everyone knows a little bit of something, and no one says anything—some for the fact that they've been bought or sold to keep quiet. These are my neighbors!"

"You can't say or do anything to put yourself at risk," I said.

There was one more thing I wanted him to read: the declaration of El Gato.

"So, they investigated him?" Alonso asked.

"They brought him in to give a deposition."

I located El Gato's testimony in the documents, and Alonso tried to read it but couldn't. Instead, he stared down the edge of the table in disbelief. "Can I take a break?" he asked.

"Yes, yes. Please."

He looked so sad, I wanted to give him a hug. I needed him to be a source, but I felt I needed to protect him at the same time. I felt bad for upsetting him. I was letting emotions rule a relationship with a source. I had always been so clear in my career about keeping those lines distinct, uncrossable. In the United States, you never let your sources get close. In Mexico, you have to somewhat, because information is based on friendship and trust. In this case, I felt it was necessary. Everything was so delicate, I had to get in close to see what was really going on.

"Do not do anything," I pleaded with him again. "For now. Do you want to leave? What do you need?"

"Air."

"You don't drink coffee, right?"

"No, but a tea would help. Or some juice."

"Okay, let's get some juice."

Alonso never read El Gato's testimony, and I never brought up the court documents with him again.

The next day, Alonso stayed for hours on the futon in the TV room where he was camped out, posting his melancholy on Facebook. "Many things fell into place, the truth" he posted.

I texted him to make sure he was okay. He sent me links to stories about Veracruz, one about Javier Duarte gifting watches and soccer tickets to journalists. The other was about a journalist jailed for protesting in another state. From what I could tell, he spent the entire day either on the phone or perusing the protest news: teachers protesting the new national evaluations, police beating protesters and journalists at the demonstrations.

When I returned from work at night, he talked more about Regina. "In the first year after she died, I would wake up in a cold sweat," he told me. "In terror. I would see her as she was being tortured. Those who were doing it were in the shadows, but I could see her eyes. And they would turn into my eyes."

I told him that telling Regina's story could lead to some good. "But it's not going to bring her back. She's not here, and she's not coming back, and it's not worth it to put even one more life at risk, not one. You talk about justice. Yeah, that's nice. But in this country, in the time we're in right now, justice is a television soap opera. Justice is fiction."

I was really concerned for his well-being.

The next day, he stayed in again, posting a poem he wrote, called "Hymn for My Latina":

Crazy/open.
Lover/irreverent.
With people, who feel, love and listen.

Who fight, unite
For one and a thousand causes.
Without pause, moving forward, walking and extending the hand of a
    brother
Latin America
beautiful Latin America.
It will break the chains.
And from the ashes, and from the fields.
And from the bellies.
It will resurge like the phoenix.
The people, the mothers. Mother Earth will give fruit and light to her children.
    That we stay in the fight. That we never break or compromise
We will not give up and we will not betray
Our principles of freedom and justice, which make of our souls an
    independent and united nation. That we never cease to govern the
    humanity and generosity that we give ourselves
with love, respect and courage. For existence.
Give a life of dignity and future
to our firm hearts, now!
Amen./Love.

He dedicated the poem to Regina, Rubén Espinosa, and Nadia Vera. At one point, he said he wanted to leave the house to go the Cineteca, Mexico City's preeminent cinema venue, which screened arthouse and independent films from around the world. We had a brief text chain about how he might pick up the keys to my house so if he left, he could get back in. Later, he told me he had decided to stay home after all.

"I feel very sad, Kathy," he texted me. He messaged me a passage from the philosopher Rudolph Steiner that began:

I refuse to submit to the fear that drives away the joy of my
freedom, that does not let me risk anything, that makes me small
and mean, that ties me, that does not let me be direct and frank,
that persecutes me, that negatively occupies my imagination,
which always paints bleak visions.

Yes, Regina had taught him to read the great minds.

When I returned home that night, I needed to shop for Thanksgiving dinner. I was expecting fifteen people and had hired my friend, a caterer, to provide the turkey. But I had to prepare the rest. Alonso decided to go with me. He offered to make his special recipe of *aguas frescas*, Mexican flavored water, for the dinner, a concoction of cucumber, lime, and chia seeds. At the checkout, I took the receipt and casually stuffed it away.

"Aren't you going to go over the receipt, make sure you weren't overcharged?"

I glanced at it. "It looks okay."

He took charge of the receipt and said we would go over it in detail when we returned to the house. He said he had learned that from his mom. He meant Regina.

In the taxi home, I thanked him for his help shopping.

"It's nothing," he said. "I enjoyed it. It's what I miss about my mom, shopping and cooking."

The next day, I started to set the table, but Alonso took over. He redid the place settings, removing the cloth napkins I had placed under the forks and folding them in neat triangles, which he placed in the middle of the plates, as if to say "This is the proper way." Again, I thought about the person who had coached him to do this, the woman with the strict and proper code. Later, I introduced him to my guests as a student friend of mine who I had met through working in Veracruz. He charmed them. And his pitcher of *aguas frescas* was drained completely. He disappeared into his room early, shortly after dinner was done, but so did my student guest. We were mostly a group of old people, like their parents.

The next day, Alonso had to return to Xalapa for work. I was worried about him going back and asked when he could come back to Mexico City. I felt he was safer there.

"It's just that I'm tight on money," he said.

"Don't worry. I'll send you a bus ticket." We agreed that he would return the following week.

That Monday, I stayed up late binge-watching Netflix and left my cell phone in the TV room when I went to bed. I wasn't too concerned about having it with me, because I was no longer bureau chief, and it was someone else's job now to get woken up in the middle of the night if there was a big story.

On Tuesday, I woke up thinking about my phone for some reason. Finally, I got up to go look for it. I had two messages in Wickr, an encrypted application I used to communicate with people in Veracruz. I opened them immediately. They were both from Alonso: "Help!!" he wrote in English. "Kathy!!"

The texts had been sent at 1:36 A.M. If I had had my phone next to me on the nightstand, the ping would have woken me. But it had been in another room. Now, six hours later, I tried to reach Alonso immediately. Again, my training told me not to panic.

I tried calling, and the call went directly to voice mail, as if his phone had died or been turned off.

"What happened?" I texted matter-of-factly. The message couldn't be delivered.

A lot of times, if I was worried about him, I would check his social media for recent posts, or his WhatsApp, which indicated the last time he was online.

After 1:36 A.M., there was nothing.

CHAPTER 18

The New Organized Crime

2016

A T ABOUT THE same time I decided to look into Regina's story, a tip came from Veracruz to Daniel Moreno, director of a new online Mexico City newspaper, *Animal Político*. Moreno had a long career at various Mexican media giants, including *Reforma* and WRadio, before he decided to take the helm at this totally new exercise in independent and investigative journalism. The tip was a stack of documents about companies in Veracruz that, the tipster said, proved irregularities in state contracting. Daniel, looking over the documents, saw a list of companies and payments on official government stationery, which could have been forged. And nothing else.

This doesn't tell us anything, he thought. Still, he decided to ask one of his reporters, Arturo Ángel, to try to dig a little deeper. Ángel, a young reporter who had studied journalism at Universidad del Valle in Mexico City and spent time covering news in Chile, had a bit of experience in researching companies. As a cub reporter at *24 Horas*, he was assigned to find out about a company set up by a former governor of Tamaulipas state, who faced charges of drug trafficking and money laundering in the United States. From this he learned that if you want to know something about a company, you can seek the articles of incorporation, which tell who owns the company and who the principals are. This information is public in Mexico.

Ángel went to work on the list of companies. A quick Google search brought up nothing about any of them, no official websites or even addresses. "We were starting from zero," he later recalled.

He set out to get the incorporation papers, which required *trabajo en campo*, "fieldwork," what Mexicans call gumshoe reporting. In Veracruz, unlike Mexico City, the documents were not in a central location. You had to guess in what area the company resided and then look up the documents locally. Luckily, he found many of them in the Port of Veracruz, the state's largest city.

Things immediately started to jump out. The principals listed for these companies were often the same names and included the same legal representatives. The addresses were close together, No. 13 for one company and No. 14 for another on the same street. The companies also shared e-mail addresses with Hotmail or Yahoo domains, not the company names, which would have been more customary.

Ángel then went to look up whether the companies received state contracts. Again, the information was public, including details of the bidding process and the competing companies. The records showed that, indeed, the companies had state contracts. But none of the contracts had been awarded through open competitive bids, as state law required. Rather, the state had employed a legal vehicle called closed bidding, in which it could invite just three companies to compete if the contract was under 5,811,000 pesos (about $407,000 at the time). Not only did Ángel notice a coincidence of the same companies involved in the closed biddings, but also many contracts for 5.8 million pesos, just under the legal limit for closed bidding, issued to buy the same thing—for example, five different contracts of 5.8 million pesos all for cement.

Other contracts were granted under another provision of the law that said no bidding was required for emergency materials—that is, items needed to respond to natural disasters or security situations. He found that the no-bid contracts included items such as school materials and educational games, clearly not emergency supplies.

The state contracts in question had been issued by the department of civil defense, intended for victims of natural disasters; and the departments of education, social services, and integral family development, all intended for children, the elderly, and the poor. The alleged contractors provided everything from diapers to publicity to building materials.

When Ángel requested the receipts showing who had received services or materials from the contracts, also public information, he discovered that they listed either general recipients, such as "various schools," or none whatsoever. In one case, he found an invoice for blankets purchased for distribution at *tiendas comunitarias*, stores in marginal areas that sold subsidized goods at a discount. When he went to verify the destination of the blankets, the state social services department told him that such stores didn't exist.

Finally, Ángel went to knock on the doors of these companies at the addresses provided. He found empty lots, abandoned houses, some little more than huts, some on unpaved roads. In one case, he went to look for the offices of Carrirey S.A. de C.V., a company listed at 410 Michoacán Street, No. 13, in the Port of Veracruz. It sold various products and services, including publicity advertising, and it had bid on three state contracts, winning one from the department of education for about $1.4 million. When he arrived at 410 Michoacán Street, he encountered a house with peeling paint, corroded window bars, and a front door of faded, weathered wood. The house, with its spare furniture and battered concrete floor, didn't have so much as a television or a radio, much less office equipment. The owner, José Adrián Álvarez Molina, in white shorts and a lime-green reflector vest, confirmed the address with a utility bill and told Ángel the house had been built by his mother as an inheritance for her children. He had heard of Carrirey only because of strange documents he had received in the mail, which he gave to his nephew, an accountant. But there was no corporation there, he told Ángel.

The address for two other contractors, Abastecedora Romcru and Publicidad Akkira S.A. de C.V., was the modest home of Concepción Escobar. She remembered officials coming to ask her to sign some paperwork in exchange for "help," though they didn't specify what kind of help. The sixty-five-year-old woman couldn't read what she was signing because of her cataracts. Yet she was listed in documents filed with the state as the director of one company, and her son was listed as the director of the other. According to state records, Abastecedora Romcru received eight contracts for 5.8 million pesos each, adding up to about $3.2 million. Publicidad Akkira S.A. received six contracts worth more than $4 million.

Concepción Escobar assured Arturo Ángel that she had no companies and no money. Not even the "help" promised by the officials with their paperwork had ever shown up. Her husband, meanwhile, had to save for three years to pay for her cataract surgery.

In total, the original contracts Ángel reviewed added up to about $45 million. All the companies receiving the contracts appeared to be fake, with no records of how the money had been spent.

The first of the companies was Logistica Estratégica ASISMEX, S.A. de C.V., the one set up right before Duarte took office in December 2010. In June 2011, Regina wrote a piece for *Proceso* entitled DUARTE, ADMINISTRATOR OF DISASTER. She was already reporting irregularities in the spending of the new administration, which had inherited a large deficit and opaque accounting from the administration of Fidel Herrera. Herrera got congress to approve an eight-hundred-million-dollar loan as he was going out the door. He said it was to pay for damage after the state had been socked that fall back-to-back by a hurricane and a tropical storm. At least one million people were affected. The spending of that loan money was never accounted for. Regina only needed to visit the communities hard hit by the storms to see that. Eight months after the natural disasters, she reported that virtually no money had been spent on recovery or reconstruction. One mayor said only 10 percent of his community had been rebuilt, while 180 families still slept in the open, just as the rainy season was about to start again. Four years before the tip came to *Animal Político*, Regina knew that government spending wasn't adding up. But she would be dead by the following spring.

★

I CALLED LEV immediately, my heart beating in my throat, to tell him about the frantic message from Alonso. According to our plan, Alonso was supposed to have returned to Mexico City the day I received his message. Lev said that was his understanding, too: that Alonso was headed to Mexico City. But now he was nowhere to be found.

"We have to reach his dad," I said.

"I'm working on it," Lev responded. "But it's going to take me a minute."

Then Lev told me something disturbing. Back in October, when Rosario from the cigarette and candy stand showed up in front of Alonso's house, the unmarked taxis appeared outside his relative's home in Mexico City, just as they had after *his* attempted kidnapping.

"Why didn't you tell me in October?" I asked. This was even worse than I thought.

"They didn't mention it until recently," he responded. I found this hard to believe, but I wasn't in a position to argue with him. Now wasn't the time to get into a confrontation. I needed him on my side. I wondered who the men in the taxis were looking for, because Alonso was with Lev in Mexico City in October. Either way, it wasn't good.

Because I had been working on a story about Regina for the Associated Press, I had to alert my editors that her nephew was missing. They knew he had come to the office the previous week to look at the court files. I wrote an e-mail to my editors with the subject line "Read this immediately":

> The chico sent me a help message in the middle of the night that
> I didn't see until now and Lev and I can't locate him. I need
> you . . . to talk to me on the US phone in your office. I'll call you
> on my encrypted line.

I called and told them that Alonso had been harassed, with people outside his home, and now he was missing. It went badly. The regional editor, my boss, immediately lit into me, saying I was crossing lines, getting too close to my sources and ignoring my personal security. He said he was no longer comfortable with me on the story and did not want me to do another bit of reporting. "We can't call the police now," he said. "Just sit tight and see if the kid shows up. Maybe he's on his way to Mexico City. Try him every hour."

A higher-ranking editor called me from New York to ask why there had been a breach. What happened? How did the source get exposed? I had screwed up.

It was a low point in my career.

I lay back on my unmade bed in my bathrobe, closed my eyes, and put my palms to my forehead. Was this for real? Was he really in trouble, or was he just being a nervous kid? Was he in self-exile to throw the bad guys off? Was this the opening of a nightmare I would live for the rest of my life?

At 10:45, more than three hours after I first saw Alonso's message, Lev texted me: "He's been in contact with one of his friends." It turned out Lev had put out an all-points bulletin to his and Alonso's friends, including Polo Hernández, who had called Rodrigo Soberanes all the way in Chile, asking if he knew how to reach Regina's family. He didn't. Finally, one of Alonso's friends responded, saying she was in contact with him and he was okay. He was with his dad. Lev said he would reach out later and talk to him about security and sending messages like the one he sent me. I just let it go, instead of trying myself. I didn't want whoever was watching Alonso to see a bunch of calls from me on his phone.

The world had just lifted off my shoulders, and I got ready and headed to work. When I arrived, I learned that three senior editors and my direct boss had had a conference call—without me—and had summarily decided to kill my story on Regina. They told me it was for security reasons. By that time, I thought it was the best decision. I felt relieved. Then they had me call Lev on a regular office line, which we were sure was being tapped, so anyone listening would know:

"We're not going to continue with the story," I said.

"I think that's a good idea," Lev responded.

Now I knew what I would do in the shoes of Patricia Mercado, the newspaper editor who told me she printed news given to her by the narcos because "If it's a question of life or death, I have no trouble making a decision. The lives of my reporters are most important." The story was shut down, and I didn't care. All I could think was that if anything happened to Alonso on my account, I couldn't live with it.

Eventually, I learned that Alonso had left me that frantic message because when he returned home the night before, he found that someone had tried to break in. They made it through the iron gate but didn't get inside the house. The presumed burglar had dropped a voting ID on the patio. Alonso didn't know if it was by accident, or if it had been left as a message. I asked him to send me a copy of the ID, so I could investigate the person's background. I never saw it. Lev, too, asked for a copy and never saw it.

Lev wondered aloud if the incident had actually happened. He thought Alonso might just be getting dramatic. Meanwhile, I was doubting Lev for not telling me about the lookouts and the taxis until months later. Why was he withholding information from me? We all started to doubt one another. It was the power of paranoia. If these events had been orchestrated and were not just coincidence, they were working.

After we announced the end of the story on a presumably tapped phone line, I stopped communicating with Lev and Alonso. I wanted anyone watching to believe that the whole endeavor had been dropped. This was how the pattern went in Mexico. First, you got a warning or a scare, and if it didn't deter you, things would get worse. We wanted everyone to believe we had gotten the message and just let the atmosphere settle down a bit. The AP story was no more. But I wasn't dropping my own investigation. I was just going to lie low for a while until they forgot about me. That worked in Mexico, too. Still, I couldn't stop worrying about Lev and Alonso. And not speaking with them only made worse the scenarios I conjured in my head.

By then, we were upon the holidays. Things got quiet. Even bad guys took time off. I returned to the United States to be with my family. On Christmas Day, my cell phone rang with a number I knew was from Xalapa, but it had no name attached. I answered it. It was the strange professor/diplomat who had approached me in the restaurant in Xalapa and asked what I was doing.

"Hello," I said, surprised.

"I'm just calling to wish you a Merry Christmas," he said.

"Thank you," I said. "Same to you."

And that was it. He hung up.

A man I met briefly and never spoke to again called me on the most intimate of family holidays to offer his greetings like a relative or close friend. It was weird. But how weird? Was it someone-breaking-in-and-taking-a-shower-in-your-bathroom weird? Or just quirky-old-man weird? That's how messages went in Xalapa. Subtly. A Christmas greeting. A box of chocolates in your hotel dresser. Kind gesture or threat? You were left to figure that out.

★

BY 2016, JORGE Carrasco had lost the armed guards and his professional life had nearly returned to normal. He was working on a multinational journalism investigation that would become known as the Panama Papers, a leak of millions of documents that exposed the offshore financing system used by world leaders, celebrities, and criminals to hide wealth, launder money, and evade taxes. During his work on the project, he got a text from an unknown number sending him the link to a story the person thought he might be interested in reading and sharing. He texted back: "Who is this?" The person didn't answer. Jorge didn't click on the link.

He later learned he had been a target in a widespread effort to spy on key people in Mexico, including top journalists, activists, anticorruption groups, and opposition politicians to the PRI government of Enrique Peña Nieto. The link, had he clicked on it, would have installed the spyware Pegasus, which would have taken all the data in his phone and allowed the phone to be used remotely as a camera and microphone. The spyware, made by an Israeli company, was intended only for governments to use against criminals and terrorists. The Mexican government appeared to be using it against its enemies in a high-tech version of the old PRI, though the Peña Nieto government denied it. At about the same time, a source told Jorge that the Mexican intelligence agency CISEN had been reviewing his bank accounts.

They could look all they wanted, he thought. They would find nothing strange, no corruption or deals he had with anyone. He had nothing to hide. He was done living his life paralyzed by fear and ruled by security.

★

ARTURO ÁNGEL'S THREE-PART series on the fake companies of Veracruz stealing state money was getting ready to run in the weeks running up to the 2016 gubernatorial election, in which voters would choose Duarte's successor. The polls showed a tight race, but many people predicted that between the violence and the bankruptcy of the state under Duarte's term, the PRI would be kicked out of Veracruz for the first time since the party was founded more than eighty years earlier.

When Arturo Ángel was in Veracruz conducting his final interviews, he got a call from a fellow journalist who said he was the editor of the newspaper *A-Z Veracruz*, a publication known to be sympathetic to the government. His name was Victor Ochoa. He wouldn't tell Ángel how he got his phone number, but he said he understood that Ángel was working on a story about some companies and that he had information that might interest him. Ángel told Ochoa he was working and would call him back later in the day. Quick research told him that Ochoa had worked for the public security secretary Arturo Bermúdez. Colleagues told Ángel to be careful with Ochoa.

Ángel texted his editors: "They've found us out. They know what we're working on." His editors told him to return to Mexico City immediately. He called Ochoa as promised and made an appointment to see him, so as not to arouse suspicion. Then he left Veracruz as soon as he finished his work, telling Ochoa that something had come up at the last minute and he would have to cancel their meeting.

"No problem," Ochoa responded. "I'll come to Mexico City."

Ángel was concerned, but agreed to meet him at a café across the street from the newsroom. He secretly recorded the conversation, which in Mexico is legal as long as one person on the call knows the conversation is being recorded.

Ochoa cut right to the point. "I've come to see if there's any possibility, and I ask in good faith, that you don't publish anything about the companies operating out there," he said. "We know from your public records requests that you have been looking at this since last year." He told Ángel that the government was willing to negotiate, on whatever terms he dictated. "Whatever you require," Ochoa said, "What would be ideal, according to some highly placed people, is that story not run because of the election. Whether the story is true or not, it's going to impact us in the election." He also asked if Ángel was working at the behest of the opposition gubernatorial candidate, Miguel Ángel Yunes Linares.

Ángel said no, the project was being done out of journalistic interest. And there was nothing to negotiate. The stories would run whenever they were ready, not according to any schedule involving the election or the desires of the Duarte government. Ochoa thanked him and got up to catch his plane back to Veracruz. In parting, he offered Ángel free accommodation anytime he decided to vacation in Veracruz. Ochoa denies this happened, but told me he didn't want to comment further.

Finally, the stories appeared just a week before the vote. *Animal Político* said there was no way to measure the impact, but the PRI was soundly defeated, and Miguel Ángel Yunes Linares realized his dream since the 1990s: to be governor of his state.

The fake companies Arturo Ángel discovered turned out to be just a calving of the iceberg. The nonprofit group Mexicans Against Corruption and Impunity, which gave financial support to *Animal Político* for the initial series, continued digging with its own team of investigative reporters, alongside Ángel and *Animal Político*. Their investigations led to Gina Domínguez, Duarte's spokeswoman at the time of Regina's murder and through the worst years of reporter killings. She, too, appeared to be using fake companies to divert public funds. They discovered, among other things, that receipts to justify the diversion of $38 million in state money to fake companies had been issued by her office. The subsequent investigation by the Yunes government's attorney general speculated that the money from Domínguez's office either had been stolen outright or was used to pay off journalists and media companies to publish government-friendly stories. In another investigation, Mexicans Against Corruption and Impunity found that Domínguez and her successor had moved $1.8 million in less than a month to a fake general construction company called Cordocons S.A. de C.V., without a single bid. On her last day on the job in February 2014, Domínguez paid seven bills from the company, within minutes, totaling $100,000.

Another *Animal Político* story detailed that Domínguez, while government spokeswoman, awarded contracts and publicity agreements to three radio stations and a media company called Servicios de Comunicación e Imagen S.A. de C.V. A year after her departure as spokeswoman, she emerged as the owner of Servicios de Comunicación e Imagen and as the person who editorially controlled the three radio stations. The Xalapa newspaper *Crónica* tried to publish an article describing the luxury compound Domínguez bought in 2013 in the picturesque village of Coatepec, which included three residences and a quarry stone pool. Domínguez herself succeeded in convincing them not to run the story.

The exposure of the Duarte regime didn't stop there. Another Mexico City media outlet, Aristegui Noticias, launched an investigation into Veracruz public security chief Arturo Bermúdez, who resigned after the news organization reported in August 2016 that he had purchased five homes in suburban Houston worth $2.4 million on a salary of $3,200 a month. According to his résumé, Bermúdez had worked solely in the public domain since 1996. The newspaper *Reforma* also found that Bermúdez was the owner of much more than properties in Texas, listing nine properties in Mexico City, five in Xalapa, one in the Port of Veracruz, and two in Quintana Roo, the home state of the resort city of Cancún. He was also an associate or owner of twenty-four companies providing various services.

It became clear that during the time Duarte and his forces silenced the independent press and paid off the traditional media, they had built a kleptocracy of record proportions, even for Mexico. The crime wave was equally unprecedented. People, especially young people, continued to disappear, some at the hands of police. There seemed to be no limits for the stealing or the disappearances: a popular young deejay who did all the "it" parties was kidnapped and is still missing; a former contestant on *La Voz* (Mexico's *The Voice*), kidnapped from his home by men dressed as police and found dead three weeks later; five young people returning from a birthday celebration disappeared after a traffic stop.

But in the end, Duarte was vanquished by the very forces he had tried to control. The Mexico City media reports about Duarte's fake companies led to federal investigations and a wave of criticism from his own party. The PRI suspended his membership that September. The following month, October 2016, he resigned with less than two months left in his term. He said it was to focus on clearing his name of the corruption charges, but two days later, he disappeared. The acting governor, Flavino Ríos, authorized the use of a state helicopter to help Duarte escape with his family.

CHAPTER 19

Mass Graves

2016

IN 2011, SHORTLY after Duarte took office, the Rev. Alejandro Solalinde, a Roman Catholic priest and activist on behalf of migrants crossing Mexico to the United States, made a startling pronouncement. It was the year that authorities discovered nearly two hundred bodies in forty-seven clandestine graves in the border state of Tamaulipas, which was controlled by the Zetas. The victims were presumed migrants from Central America trying to reach the United States who the cartel had kidnapped and tried to recruit as mules or extort for money. It was the first time the notion of mass graves emerged in Mexico. The level of brutality was astonishing for the time. Solalinde, who ran a shelter in Oaxaca along the migrant route, said that Veracruz had even larger mass graves filled with migrants, the largest in all of Mexico. "You have to open up the earth in Veracruz," he said publicly to groups of reporters, "because I think there has to be a swarm of skeletons."

Solalinde turned out to be prescient, though it would be several years before the extent of the mass graves of Veracruz, or who was in them, would be known. Still, in the first year of Duarte's administration, the disappearances started to escalate. Just as Nadia Vera had said in her video statement, many of the people who went missing had been seen carted off by police officers. Families who reported their missing relatives to authorities received threats or extortion calls, which were traced to local police stations.

Fifty young women, many professional escorts, disappeared over five months, starting in 2011, never to be seen. Roberto Casso, the owner of some sporting goods stores, disappeared with his girlfriend on their way to have Christmas dinner with his mother, Rosalía Castro.

In 2011, twenty-nine-year-old Gemma Mávil also disappeared on her way to a job interview. Her father, Pedro, received a call from the kidnappers demanding a million pesos. Not a wealthy man, Pedro knocked on the doors of family and friends and collected forty thousand to take to the designated spot. When the kidnappers showed up, there was no Gemma. Unlike with most kidnapping cases, police arrested three people in the disappearance of Gemma Mávil, but they tortured one of them to death in the interrogation, thus keeping anyone from getting information on her whereabouts.

Clandestine graves, dug by narcos and filled with anonymous drug war victims, became the biggest news story nationwide in Mexico by 2014 and continues to be an enormous human rights crisis in the country. The number of the missing continues to climb, up to one hundred thousand officially as of early 2022, according to the government's own statistics. This is far more than under any of the right-wing dictatorships in Argentina, Chile, or other South American countries during the Cold War, and given the underreporting of crime in Mexico, many think the actual number is much higher. With the missing came the discovery of mass graves in states around Mexico. As was predicted by Father Solalinde, Veracruz continues to rank as one of the states with the largest number of clandestine graves.

The state police were suspected in many cases, including the 2016 disappearance of the five young people returning from a birthday celebration. Known as the case of the Tierra Blanca, the incident became notorious. Seven police officers were arrested in the killing of the *Voice* contestant. That same year, bodies were found in a canyon near the Veracruz state police academy, leading to charges against Duarte's secretary of public security, Arturo Bermúdez, for the forced disappearance of at least fifteen people.

Given the incompetence or presumed involvement of the state, various collectives started to form, organizations of citizens searching for their loved ones. Pedro Mávil, Gemma's father, was an original member. The collectives grew in 2014, when frustrated families of the missing met with Javier Duarte, who promised various changes that never came to pass. In that year, the Colectivo Solecito de Veracruz was born, led in part by Rosalía Castro, mother of the sporting goods store owner who disappeared on Christmas Eve 2011, and Lucia Díaz, mother of the young "DJ Patas," Luis Guillermo Lagunes Díaz, who disappeared in 2013.

In 2016, the Colectivo Solecito, made up of hundreds of mothers of the missing, was holding its annual Mother's Day March when two men in a pickup drove up, handed flyers to some of the leaders, and disappeared as quickly as they had come. When they had time later to review the handout, the mothers realized they were looking at a map of an enormous clandestine grave site in an area known as Colinas de Santa Fe, on the edge of the Port of Veracruz. Colinas de Santa Fe turned out to be the largest clandestine grave in the country, where the collective and, later, authorities found at least three hundred bodies.

Meanwhile, another mass grave story in 2016 caught my attention. In September of that year, the Colectivo Solecito complained that there were bodies hidden by the state in the mass grave at Palo Verde, Xalapa's municipal cemetery. The discovery came from attempts to locate the body of Gemma Mávil. Her father, Pedro, had quit his job as an accountant to mount a five-year investigation into her whereabouts. Through his own detective work, he discovered in court documents and police reports that a body with Gemma's characteristics had been found back in 2011, just four months after his daughter disappeared, in a refrigerator abandoned in a vacant lot. Everything about the body matched his daughter, including the dark hair that had been died bright red. He discovered that the state forensics lab tested the body's DNA but didn't attempt to match it in the state database, which would have revealed immediately who she was. Instead, the body sat in the morgue for ninety days and then was shipped off to the mass grave in Palo Verde, even though the law said the body had to remain in storage for a year in case the family came to claim it. A DNA match wasn't made until 2016, long after Gemma had been buried. Pedro wanted his daughter back.

Records pinpointed her approximate location in the Palo Verde mass grave, and authorities started to dig for her. Two attempts produced nothing. Gemma wasn't where the cemetery records said she was. But the gravediggers found other, unidentified bodies in her place.

Pedro Mávil, along with other members of the collectives and Volga de Pina, an attorney with the Mexican Institute of Human Rights, demanded another dig. The day before it was scheduled, de Pina called state prosecutor Luis Ángel Bravo to say she wanted to know what to expect. She didn't want to take Gemma's father through an exercise that would just be another disappointment. So, if there were going to be problems, she would call off the dig.

"Look, this is a complicated case," Brava told her. "She may be there; she may not be there."

"But I'm worried that we'll find more bodies that aren't identified," de Pina said. That would be particularly upsetting to Don Pedro.

"Don't worry," Bravo said. The prosecutor assured her that everything was in order, that the problem had been corrected and that all remains in the mass grave had been DNA-sampled and properly recorded. He had personally ordered that all unidentified bodies be exhumed, that a DNA sample be taken, and that each body be given an identification tag and reburied.

"Okay, then," de Pina responded. They would go ahead with their plans.

The next day, Pedro, other families of the missing, and independent forensic experts—about twenty people in all—showed up at Palo Verde.

Unlike the ordered, manicured official graveyard where Regina Martínez was buried, or U.S. cemeteries, where the atmosphere is as dead as the inhabitants, Palo Verde was the people's cemetery, as varied, colorful, and messy as life itself. In American cemeteries, a gray tombstone or a white cross clearly announces that a life has passed. Mexican graves in places like Palo Verde resemble little houses for the dead, some brightly painted pink, yellow, or blue, a symbol of how the departed in Mexican culture remain very much a part of the living.

Palo Verde was among the best examples of the span of memorial clutter that is a Mexican pantheon. It is enormous—anywhere from thirty to fifty acres of rolling green, according to various descriptions, housing tens of thousands of dead. Some sources say the cemetery was inaugurated in 1913; others say it's more than two hundred years old. Inside the grounds are oxidized, moss-covered tombstones upended in overgrown brush like something straight out of a Halloween film, chipped markers of the long-forgotten dead and cheerful mausoleums along freshly swept walkways. Some tombstones are so close together they resemble a grave marker sales yard rather than burial plots.

By all accounts, this teeming valley of the dead was close to full. This made the search for Gemma particularly complicated, because anonymous graves had become mixed in with the official ones. In this case, the dig would overlap with the grave of one family's grandmother, and Volga de Pina had to get permission from them to do the dig. The family agreed and showed up for the exhumation. According to the records, only the family's grandmother and one other body were buried there. And officials believed that body was Gemma's.

Volga de Pina stood at the edge of the neatly rectangular dirt hole at one of Palo Verde's more modest graves, marked by a stone cross, as the workers pulled out the bodies. Grandma was in her place, as expected. Then the gravediggers pulled out another body. It had no tag. Then a third. No tag.

De Pina called the prosecutor on her cell phone. "Get over here!" she demanded. "The press is coming. We've taken out five bodies, and not a single one has been recorded. You've made a huge mess of this mass grave."

"I'm two minutes away," Luis Ángel Bravo said. In the short time it took him to get there, he had already called the mayor of Xalapa, who had jurisdiction over the cemetery. When Bravo arrived, his face was blanched.

"Look, for every grave that we've entered, we've found five where there was supposed to be one," de Pina told him. "And there's no record for any of them. This fucking mass grave is full of the disappeared."

The coroner's office, either by omission or deceit, had lost track of untold numbers of dead, the vast majority of whom had died violently. All told, de Pina said, there could be thousands hidden in the mass graves of the Veracruz municipal cemeteries.

Suddenly, the story that Julio Argumedo, aka Don Jules, had told me, which I had earlier dismissed, made sense. These were the very places where Regina Martínez was trudging around asking questions right before she died. She could have been the first to stumble onto the fact that the Duarte government was disappearing people.

This could surely have gotten her killed.

CHAPTER 20

What Was She Working On?
Part II

2020

IN APRIL 2017, JAVIER Duarte was arrested in a hotel lobby in Sololá, a resort city on Lake Atitlán in Guatemala, in an international operation involving Interpol, Guatemalan police, the DEA, and other law enforcement trying to locate his whereabouts. He was extradited that July and later sentenced to nine years in prison, after pleading guilty to charges of criminal association and money laundering.

Arturo Bermúdez was arrested the same year for illicit enrichment (the forced disappearance charges came later), as was Duarte's ex-spokeswoman Gina Domínguez, on charges of abuse of authority and breach of duty in the diversion of public funds.

The Duarte administration had morphed into its own organized crime group, using intimidation and violence to stage a villainous free-for-all. Officials could do whatever they wanted with impunity. In one particularly blatant case, Duarte's director of prisons, Oscar Sánchez Tirado, was accused of ordering his bodyguards to kidnap and kill Carlos David Bautista López, his girlfriend's ex-partner, because Bautista had tried to contact her. Bautista's remains were found in a mass grave four years after his disappearance. His mother has worked tirelessly to get justice.

The ultimate casualties of Duarte's war on the press were not only the press, but the citizens of Veracruz.

★

ON SEPTEMBER 19, 2017, Mexico City shook from a 7.1-magnitude earthquake on the exact anniversary of the 1985 temblor that killed as many as ten thousand people. It was the worst shaking in the intervening thirty-two years. Hundreds were killed, and many buildings fell or were damage beyond repair, especially in the fashionable Roma district, which sits on the gelatinous soil of the city's drained lake bed. Jorge Carrasco was at work at the *Proceso* offices when the tremors started. His two children were in school. But Peniley was home and waited out the trembling in their Roma apartment. As soon as she could, she ran out to do her own reporting for her employer, Univision.

Jorge immediately ran home to make sure his family was okay. He checked on his apartment building: It was still standing, but it was uninhabitable and would have to be taken down. Losing everything in this manner after all they had lived through was too much for the couple to bear. Their home had been their fortress. Now it was destroyed, and with it their marriage.

In late 2017, with all the stress, Jorge developed a hernia and had to be hospitalized. When he went to pay the bill, he discovered that *Proceso*, after so many years of providing health care to employees, had reduced coverage in a cost-cutting measure. Jorge owed thousands to the hospital that he didn't anticipate. His entire Christmas bonus went toward paying the medical bill.

Jorge had had enough. He had given everything to this magazine, including practically his life, and this was the treatment he was getting in a time of need, a health crisis on top of being homeless after the quake. He continued to report and write stories, but he would no longer fill in as editor, something that had become a tradition and for which he was never paid extra. He and I had coffee around this time, and he seemed to be looking for an escape. I recommended a sabbatical and gave him contacts for several fellowships. Perhaps his time with *Proceso* had come to an end.

★

WITH THE NEW accusations about the disappeared in the municipal mass grave in Palo Verde, I wanted to retrace Regina's footsteps on her last story. I asked Don Jules if he would take me to the cemeteries they had visited and show me what they saw. We started at the municipal cemetery in the Port of Veracruz, where he said Regina did a lot of her work. It was late October. The workers were painting curbs and leveling dirt to spruce up the graveyard for Día de los Muertos, when the pantheons in Mexico turn into fairgrounds. One worker was splashing water on a dusty tombstone for a señora and her husband as they prepared to decorate the tomb for the occasion.

We walked to where Don Jules remembered the mass grave to be, but it seemed to have been moved. There was a giant trench, one gravestone mostly buried, and two bunches of flowers stuck in the dirt. We decided to ask at the office for the location of the mass grave. On the way, Don Jules chatted up a gravedigger pushing a wheelbarrow full of water. He told the man he was a journalist from Veracruz Online, the website where Don Jules worked.

"How many people come for Día de los Muertos?" Don Jules asked the man.

"A lot. I don't know how many, but it's hard to pass on the walkways."

"What do they do for the anonymous people buried in the mass grave?"

"The local councilwoman makes an altar for those who have no family."

"How many are there?"

"Thousands," the gravedigger said. "Of all kinds. Accidents. Natural causes. Illness."

Don Jules asked him discreetly about the "other" victims, the ones who died violently. The gravedigger said they had been overwhelmed with those kinds of victims in the last few years.

"One hundred, a hundred fifty a day," he said. "It's almost full right now. It's been capped off."

We made it to the office to ask questions, but the man who looked like the administrator said the administrator wasn't available. With the current controversy over the disappeared, no one was authorized to speak. The man referred us to the local city councilwoman who was handling the issue.

We returned to Xalapa to walk around Palo Verde, but didn't have the same luck. The only people we encountered weren't cemetery employees, but random workers looking to be hired to clean graves for the holiday.

★

BY 2020, LEV had started a new business that had nothing to do with journalism. I made a trip to see him to do some fact-checking after all the conversations we had had over so many years. We hadn't seen each other in a long while, but had stayed in touch. As usual, he arranged everything for me, a comfortable Airbnb, and he picked me up at the airport. My first night, we went out to a restaurant. There, just like in the old days, we ordered burgers and beers and talked. When we got to the fact-checking, I knew I had one big question that had yet to be answered.

Who had Regina been seeing before she was killed?

On my second day there, we were sitting on the balcony of my Airbnb in the muggy afternoon when I started my campaign again. This time, Lev said he couldn't remember the name Regina had mentioned so many years ago in that bar.

"How can you not remember? It's a key piece of information when a person turns up dead!"

He swore he couldn't remember the name. It was someone he didn't know, so it hadn't registered.

"But didn't you want to find him after?"

"Kathy, everything was so foggy then. And *Reforma* pulled me out of there, and, yes, if I think about it now, of course I think it's key information. I wasn't thinking that way at the time."

Again, I felt he was holding out on me. I was staring into his eyes and face for any sign, a twitch or tic that would tell me that he really did know. He just smirked at me. *Pinche Kathy.*

"I swear, Kathy. I swear I don't remember."

"Do you pinkie swear?" I asked.

In that moment, sitting across from him at a small wooden patio table, I leaned over and made him lock pinkies with me, to promise he was telling the truth.

"Pinkie swear," he said, lifting our interlocked fingers until we both had our hands in the air.

It's hard for me to say that I didn't believe him. He had done so much for me, and we had become good friends. But I wasn't satisfied. There was a piece of information that I still needed to pry from him. For whatever reason, it was being held hostage in his brain.

★

JUST AS I was wrapping up my research, a group of international journalists based in Paris decided to investigate the Regina Martínez murder. Known as Forbidden Stories, the group was dedicated to continuing the work of slain journalists around the world. They had already taken on the 2017 assassinations of Daphne Caruana Galizia in a car bomb attack in Malta, and of Miroslava Breach, a Mexican journalist gunned down point-blank in her car as she was taking her son to school. Caruana wrote about corruption and shady financial networks, while Breach reported a link between the local cartel and two municipal political candidates.

Forbidden Stories approached *Proceso*, and Jorge Carrasco agreed to be part of the project. Of course, as a journalist, I didn't want them trampling all over my territory. I had worked slowly over the years to build sources and didn't want my work to be confused with theirs, nor for them to scare off any of my connections. The group did a blitzkrieg of sorts, with an international camera crew and a group of reporters, including one from *Proceso*. In one instance, they stood outside Regina's house yelling Alonso's name until he had to come out to ask them to be quiet. "Don't you know a drug cartel controls this area and there are lookouts everywhere?" He agreed to speak to them at a coffee shop.

I hadn't really thought much about this foreign crew finding Don Jules Argumedo. But their report, which appeared in December 2020 in publications in twenty countries and at least seven languages, declared that Regina "had been preparing to publish an explosive report about thousands of individuals who had mysteriously disappeared . . . She believed that she had determined where some of the disappeared had been buried. This time, however, it wasn't the cartels that made them disappear, she believed, but the authorities themselves," the story said. The sources for this information were Don Jules and an anonymous friend.

Forbidden Stories also published the photographs from Regina's reporting trip to the municipal cemeteries I had asked Don Jules for—and that he had said he didn't have. I started to doubt him. It seemed he had changed his story, telling Forbidden Stories that Regina's investigation went beyond the municipal graves. I texted Don Jules to try clear up the discrepancies. He was rattled because he was getting phone calls from media around the world.

He refused to do more interviews. "Kathy, I don't want to talk anymore about this topic," he texted back.

What? I thought. "But we've been talking for years," I wrote. "You know me."

He didn't answer. I decided to give it some time.

Ironically, the Forbidden Stories project helped me disprove my own theory that Regina had been killed for investigating the municipal mass graves. In fact, they uncovered something I hadn't known: The reporting that Regina gathered in the cemeteries *had* been published, in *Proceso*, a full nine months before she was killed. I had reviewed her *Proceso* stories dozens of times and had read nearly every edition of *Política* she appeared in, but I had missed this story because it didn't appear under her byline.

In July 2011, *Proceso* ran a cover story entitled IN THE WAR ON DRUGS THE DEAD WITHOUT NAMES, about bodies piling up in morgues around the country that were simply dumped into municipal mass graves without being identified or processed. *Proceso* had sent reporters to eleven states to gather statistics, including Regina in Veracruz. The story showed that there was neither a specific nor an approximate record of how many bodies were being dumped in municipal mass graves across the country. Based on media reports, the National Human Rights Commission estimated that at least ten thousand unidentified bodies had been mishandled by state forensic agencies, the vast majority of them victims of organized crime. The story carried Regina's name at the end as a contributor.

When I finally tracked him down months later, Don Jules said he told me Regina was still working on the story when she died because he, too, never saw it in print. He didn't get paid for his photos, so he assumed the piece wasn't published. And he was telling me the truth when he said he didn't have the photographs: Forbidden Stories had found them in the *Proceso* archive.

Forbidden Stories also acknowledged that Regina's mass graves reporting had been published, but said that she continued to investigate the disappeared and mass graves and, in early 2012, was about to publish something explosive.

I asked him if this was true.

"No," he said.

"After you turned in your photos in July 2011, did you know she was working on anything else?" I asked him.

"No." His story had not changed from what he originally told me.

Were Forbidden Stories and I both wrong about what Regina was working on?

Jorge Carrasco had doubted Don Jules's information from the start. I thought that his information had been misconstrued. Either way, she had published what she reported on the municipal graves. And she wouldn't have been the sole target for that article because multiple reporters from around the country were named as contributors. Though *Proceso* published the Forbidden Stories series, when it came to the reporting about the disappeared in mass graves, Jorge insisted that it wasn't what got Regina killed. "The correspondent had no assignment or instructions to cover this theme from *Proceso*. Nor did she ever comment that she was working on such an investigation or reporting on it," *Proceso's* article for Forbidden Stories said.

My final hypothesis was shot. After all this time, I was back at square one.

What had gotten her killed?

CHAPTER 21

Who Killed Regina Martínez?

2021

SHORTLY AFTER I knocked on Isabel Nuñez's door that rainy afternoon, I stopped by the corner store a few doors away, at the bridge over the open sewage canal. It was 8 A.M. on a work holiday. The streets were quiet, and I figured it would be a good time not to call too much attention to myself. I heard that the store owner was there early.

The state had tried to say in its case that Regina had gone to that store the night she died, to buy beer when El Silva and El Jarocho, her alleged love interest, came by to party.

"She never came here to buy beer," the owner testified in the court documents. "We didn't sell the brand she liked." She had contradicted the state's story. I wanted to know what that cost her. Was she pressured? Did they try to offer her something to support the official version?

The store was a typical Mexican *tienda*, set up in the front room of a house and crammed with racks of cellophane-wrapped snacks and a menagerie of refrigerators cooling soft drinks, milk, and beer. There was a giant basket of Mexican *pan dulce* on the counter, and early-morning shoppers came in for bread and yogurt.

When I arrived, a thirty-something woman was standing behind the counter. I asked for Rosamaría.

"How did you get my name?" was her first question. I told her another store employee had given it to me when I had dropped by the day before.

She was pleasant, but wary after I told her my purpose. She said she hadn't known Regina well and that she very rarely came in to buy things. I told her I read the documents saying that Regina had bought beer at their store the night of her murder. Rosamaría said yes, the report said that, but it wasn't true.

"Did they pressure you to say she did?" I asked.

"No. They just asked. There are a lot of stores around here, and they were trying to find the one where she bought beer," Rosamaría said. "It wasn't here. I hardly think she drank."

She was clearly reluctant to talk and just kept repeating that she didn't know Regina or anything about what happened. I asked her if there was anyone in the neighborhood who did, but she didn't want to name names.

"Just knock on doors."

Then I asked her where I could find Diego Hernández Villa, the local drunk who put El Jarocho and El Silva near the crime scene the night of the murder.

"Oh, he's dead," Rosamaría said.

I was startled. Did it have something to do with the Regina case? "When did he die?"

"About a year ago."

"How?" I asked.

"Well, Diego drank a lot," she said. "One night, he was drinking with friends, and they got in an argument and beat him badly. He never recovered from that."

The key witness was no longer alive. (I later checked Hernández's death certificate. He died from internal bleeding and complications from diabetes and alcohol. No one seemed to think it was anything but a bar fight).

Perhaps his family could help me. "Do you know where he lived?" I asked.

"Up the hill," Rosamaría said, pointing out a humble white house along the concrete stairway into the neighborhood. I returned later the same afternoon to knock at Diego Hernández's former home and ran across two women on a bench outside another corner store. I approached them and told them what I was working on. Yes, they knew Regina, they said, but not very well. She really kept to herself. One of the women almost immediately excused herself and said it was time to cook lunch, disappearing into a house across the way.

I later learned that this woman was Señora Lucia, Diego Hernández's mother-in-law. It turned out that Rosamaría's store was the neighborhood lookout and had sent word to everyone that I had been there looking for Hernández. Señora Lucia was the woman Hernández claimed in his testimony to have visited the night of Regina's murder.

She and others wouldn't speak to me. Then, in 2020, she died. But I discovered a few things about the government's version of events. I can't say how, for the protection of sources. But I now know that the men watching Rosario, El Jarocho's partner, the ones I saw at the candy stand who ended up harassing Regina's nephew Alonso, were state police assigned to keep an eye on her. For a long time after Regina's killing, there was a squad car parked at the foot of the street where Rosario lived.

I know that Jarocho didn't confess to Rosario, contrary to the court documents. Nor did he have any of Regina's possessions, as the documents claimed. He likely had nothing to do with her murder, but he may have known something about it. He hasn't been heard from since a week after her killing, and many speculate that he, too, may have been disappeared.

I also know that the government's star witness, Diego Hernández Villa, wasn't at his mother-in-law's house the night of the murder, contrary to *his* testimony. He and his family didn't arrive to visit Señora Lucia until the following afternoon, when they saw the yellow caution tape and the neighborhood blanketed in squad cars.

A little more than a week after Regina's death, Diego Hernández was sitting on the hillside steps drinking when he was grabbed by men in balaclavas. He couldn't say how many men, because they came up from behind him. They took him to a room at the state prosecutor's building, where he was beaten and tortured. They zapped his testicles with electric shocks and shoved a broomstick up his rectum. First, they tried to get him to admit that he had killed Regina. Instead, when he was set free a couple of days later, he left a signed testimony that he saw El Jarocho and El Silva walking toward Regina's house hours before she died. He didn't see any of that; he was on the other side of town.

★

I WANTED TO save for last the interviews with people who I suspected knew the most about this case. If they had known my mission earlier, I may not have been able to roam freely around Veracruz. Or their knowledge could have shut down other sources. I had to have all my information in hand by the time I contacted Javier Duarte, or Arturo Bermúdez, Reynaldo Escobar, or Alejandro Montano, in the event I would be chased out with no possibility to return.

I didn't expect anyone to speak to me, but as a reporter, you always ask. You can't imagine how many times we've gotten lucky just by asking. I sent Javier Duarte, who was tweeting from jail, a tweet saying I wanted to talk with him. He didn't answer. His lawyer was even more elusive; no one I knew even had a contact number for him. When I reached out to a Veracruz journalist who had interviewed Duarte in jail and asked for his help, he lit into me. Sure, I wanted his help. But where was I for the Veracruz journalists living in an inferno? Where was my help? I told him I understood his anger and politely left him alone.

Amadeo Flores, the state attorney general overseeing Regina's case, said through another person that he didn't discuss the case and was now retired. César Villa, who was head of forensics, the ones so poorly collected, agreed to meet me and then canceled. He wouldn't reschedule, even when I knocked on his door. "Where did you get this address?" was all he said.

I tracked the ex-secretary of public security Arturo Bermúdez, also out of public life, to the upscale hotel he owns in Chachalacas, a Gulf Coast beach town about an hour and a half from Xalapa. He was hanging out in the lobby in a turquoise shirt and orange swim trunks, casually chatting with some other men, looking very happy and relaxed. When I approached him to ask for an interview, he said he couldn't talk because of the forced disappearance charges pending against him; there were four in all. He said he had already beat three of them. He was going to beat the final one, too, he said, and then he would speak to me *con mucho gusto*.

No one had a number for Gina Domínguez, and I tried everyone. No one had an address for her, either, but by description, I was able to find the three-home compound she had in Coatepec, scene of locally farmed restaurants and fenced-in estates hidden in the hilly coffee-growing terrain. The compound was at the end of a small street and joined together by a high wall of cyclone fencing topped with coiled barbed wire. This and the guard shacks for each house gave her bucolic mountain getaway the look of a penitentiary.

When I rang the bell at one of the residences, the giant iron gate rolled open onto the yard of a white stucco house with wood-trimmed windows and a large tile patio. No one asked who I was before opening the door, giving me my first clue that this wasn't Domínguez's house. There were people in the back around a grill who apparently assumed I was a guest for their party.

I asked for Domínguez. A man stepped forward as the owner of the house and said he had bought it from her a few months back. He said he was only in touch with her son. I asked how to reach the son, but he wouldn't give any more information, though he said he believed she still owned the house two doors down. The second house had also been sold recently, according to a relative of the new owner there. At the third house, with a solid wall along the front and security cameras, no one answered.

I also had a list of lower-level players who I was sure knew something about what had actually happened. The first name on it was Walter Ramírez, the man who was spreading the official story from day one that Regina had been killed by a boyfriend. Ramírez was the person who had tried to commandeer Regina's family at the morgue and the one who, Regina said, had asked her for a loan. He clearly was in need of money. I wondered if he had been paid to spread the fake story. People told me to be careful with him.

★

WALTER RAMÍREZ SEEMED more than happy to talk. We met in the same restaurant where the strange man had approached me years earlier. I hadn't been back since. There was a new administration in Veracruz, and though the killings and violence continued, the state government didn't seem to be spying on journalists like Duarte had. I felt a little bit more at ease moving around.

Ramírez was surprised that I had contacted him. No one else wanted anything to do with him. He said he was persecuted by all of Regina's friends for speaking his mind on the murder, for saying that he believed she was killed by a boyfriend. He accused them of making her into a martyr, a victim of the government, for their own gain, recognition, prizes, and, in the case of Andrés Timoteo, asylum. He made fun of their theories.

"It was the fucking government, the oppressor, the harasser who killed her. But not one of them can tell us today one single bit of evidence they have to identify anyone directly responsible." *He* was the one who knew her well, Ramírez insisted, since their days as reporters for *Política*. They even dated for a short time, around 1996 or '97. He said his wife, Marisa Sánchez, remained a close friend and that she and Regina often had dinner or drank together. He said a lot things inconsistent with what I had heard elsewhere.

On the night Regina was found dead, Ramírez said, he got a call from a federal government official in Xalapa saying something had happened at her house. When Ramírez went and saw the scene, he returned home to tell his wife. She started to cry and said she wanted to go the coroner's office so she could pray over Regina's body. They arrived at about 8:30 P.M. and waited until 2 A.M., when the body finally arrived.

The investigators wouldn't let them enter. Ramírez said he asked them what happened. The investigators wanted to know who they were. "I said we were friends. 'Are you willing to help us?' 'Yes, but I want you to tell me what you suspect. What evidence do you have? What causes? What motive?'" he said he asked. "'Well, I think we might be dealing with a crime of passion.' That's what they told me."

That was the conclusion, just hours after finding her body and before a real investigation had started. The investigators gravitated toward Ramírez, he said, because he knew Regina. He could describe her house and her routine.

The information he said he gave them sounded suspiciously like El Silva's account of Regina's evening with Jarocho, which, like Diego Hernández's testimony, was also invented. Walter Ramírez said Regina had parties on Friday nights and that, when they were dating, he and Regina would get drunk and dance salsa in the living room. Then he offered another curious factoid: "Regina didn't trust banks," he told me. "She kept all her money and put it in the mattress." (El Silva said, in his trumped-up testimony, that when Jarocho was hitting Regina and demanding to know where her money was, she said it was in the mattress.) I told him there was no evidence that the two men were ever inside the house.

Still, Ramírez said he had no trouble believing the state's story.

"What makes you think they were there?" I asked.

"I knew her routines. I was her boyfriend. I was with her. I know a lot of things because I spent time with her."

"But that was a lot of years ago," I said.

"Yeah, ten years," he said. "More than ten years. But she was a person of habits."

The investigators showed him things in the following days. They showed him empty beer bottles of the brand that Regina drank, Corona. They said she bought perfume. They said she bought cosmetics, and they showed him some receipts.

"Why would that mean she was dating someone?" I asked.

"Because Regina never wore makeup! Regina never wore perfume!"

He had no problem believing that the "someone" was Jarocho, a street criminal. "Because Regina was an older woman, single, and she had her needs, like all women," he said. "Jarocho was from the neighborhood. El Jarocho and Regina had known each other for years. They coexisted as neighbors."

"How do you know that?" I asked.

From the investigation, he said. "All these things that I am telling you today, they were putting them together and were commenting and saying based on how they were investigating."

"But why is there no evidence that the killers were ever in her house?" I asked him. "No fingerprints. No DNA. They said they were drinking beer, but she had no alcohol in her system."

"According to whom? Who said that?"

"It's in the court file."

"I didn't know that." He said they wouldn't let him see the court file.

I told Ramírez that, according to what I read in the court documents, *he* was the one who testified that she had a boyfriend, not the other way around. It was *he* who told investigators that she was killed by someone she knew well and that it didn't have to do with her work. And it was *he* who said everyone knew she was dating Polo.

"Polo. What Polo?" Ramírez said.

"Leopoldo Hernández, the reporter from Notimex."

"I don't even know him." At this point, he became agitated and said the court documents were lying. "I didn't say that, ever."

"Then why is it in your declaration? You signed it."

"Because they're assholes. It's what they wrote."

"Well, there are a lot of lies in the court documents, so that's why I'm asking."

"Will you allow me to call the Doctora Consuelo?" He was referring to Consuelo Lagunas, the head of the investigation, who never spoke publicly after it ended. I had tried to interview her, but the attorney general's office denied my request. She answered the call on his second try.

"Good afternoon, Doctora," he said.

"Hello, Walter. What's up?" He put the call on speakerphone.

"Doctora, I'm scared. I'm talking to the reporter Kathy. She tells me she had access to my file, the investigation file, and she's telling me there are things written in my statement that I declared to you, Doctora. She's giving me the name of a character, Leopoldo Hernández, a reporter for Notimex who I don't even know, and that I said I knew he was going out with Regina Martínez. She's telling me things that, yes, I said, but they got changed.

"The reporter Kathy wants to talk to you. When can the three of us get together and talk?"

We made arrangements to meet Lagunas, who said she wasn't in Xalapa. I said we would travel to see her. Ramírez told me he couldn't afford to, so I said I would pay for his bus ticket. Then we waited for Lagunas to confirm the appointment.

She never did. She stopped answering Ramírez's phone calls.

I continued to ask him about the inconsistencies in the state's story. Why weren't they looking for El Jarocho? He was a fugitive.

"I asked Javier Duarte that several times," Ramírez said. "And several times, Javier told me that, well, there was a suspicion that he was dead, because he sold drugs and he was an addict. And he abandoned his wife and his child."

"Did anyone in the government offer you money to disseminate their official story of what happened to Regina?" I asked him.

"Naw, naw, nobody. The only thing was that Javier Duarte de Ochoa told me that he was very appreciative that I supported the government's truth." Then he contradicted himself.

A couple of years after Regina's murder, Ramírez told me, Duarte called him out at a press conference at the state police academy. "'Walter, I've been looking for you,' he told me. 'Don't leave. You're going with me afterward,'" Ramírez recalled. He returned to the Casa Veracruz with Duarte, government secretary Erick Lagos, spokesman Alberto Silva, and Duarte's chauffeur. "We've treated you badly," Ramírez said Duarte told him. "'I'm indebted to you, Walter, because your questions and positions legitimize me.' In the case of Regina, he was very specific. He told me, 'You've helped me a lot. I know your version [of what happened] has made it very difficult for you. It cost you a lot of things. But you've helped me a lot, and I really appreciate it.'"

Then one of Duarte's secretaries handed Ramírez a gift bag. Inside were 300,000 pesos (about $23,000 at the time) in cash. That was a generous two years of a reporter's salary for Xalapa at the time.

My suspicion was right. Walter Ramírez had been paid, but after the fact. He said it was for supporting the Regina story, but for other things as well.

Later, I sent Ramírez the pages of his testimony that he denied saying and called him to follow up. He had completely changed his demeanor.

"Yes, I stand by it," he said. "I don't remember some aspects of it, but I have no reason to suppose I didn't say what was written here. I accept it, and I have nothing more to say about it."

I wondered who had gotten to him in the meantime.

Then he told me something else: After I had pointed out the discrepancies in the story that Regina was killed by a boyfriend, Ramírez said he no longer thought that. But it occurred to him that there was one person who might have been capable of her murder: Alejandro Montano, the subject of the *Proceso* story about his wealth, published just before Regina was killed.

I asked Ramírez why he changed his mind.

"I just got to thinking."

Then I asked him if he had asked Regina for money just before she was killed because he needed help for his mother's cancer treatments.

He became infuriated. "Whoever said that, can I say, can go fuck themselves!" He said his mother paid for her own cancer treatment. "This is stupidity. Why are you asking me this? It has nothing to with what happened to Regina. It's just to ruin my life and bother me. And if you ask me, if that's the theme of your book, what an embarrassment. You're not looking for the truth. You're looking for gossip and to ruin people's lives."

Then he hung up on me.

But there I was, back with Montano, Escobar, and the original theory that I had dismissed.

★

MARIELA SAN MARTÍN, Regina's seamstress and alleged government spy, was a harder sell. I had heard that she had quit the informant job. Everyone I spoke to knew her, but no one had a contact for her. They told me that she was very smart and ambitious, that she carried a pistol, and that I should be very careful. I first went to Facebook to see what I could find out and to see what San Martín looked like. Then I asked a lawyer friend if he knew her.

"I'm not sure," he said. "Is it this person?" He sent me a photo of the same person I saw on Facebook that carried both her last names.

My lawyer contact asked San Martín if he could give me her number, and she refused. She told him not to text her, because her phone was tapped, and that she could not meet with me because she was being watched. She said any talking to strangers could affect her job. I hadn't even told her my subject.

But I now had her full name. In Mexico, the Spanish-origin names are so common that you need both last names to identify a person. Once I had this, I had a stroke of luck. Mariela San Martín was in the phone directory, address and all, and within walking distance of my hotel. My colleagues in Xalapa told me that making a cold visit to her home would startle her and likely not turn out well. I also thought about the rumored pistol. So, I hired a local journalist as a fixer, someone who knew her, someone who could get me an interview and vouch for my trustworthiness and discretion. I didn't give the fixer the subject, either, because I didn't want anyone to know what I was after. That way, if San Martín did decide to talk to me, no one would know she was my source.

The fixer was a disaster. San Martín told her she was too afraid to talk and to not give me anything. The fixer stopped answering my phone calls. Apparently, the person I had hired to work for me was working for *her*. When I asked the fixer to confirm San Martín's address, which I had from the phone directory, she said, "I don't know the address. I just know how to get there." I fired her.

Finally, I decided that Mariela San Martín had plenty of warning that I was looking for her and that I could show up at her door. I also decided to say I was looking for a seamstress as a cover for her, in case she really was under surveillance. I wrote a note explaining who I was, the book, and how, as a courtesy, I wanted her to know that her name would appear in it. I also needed to confirm the information I had about her. After two tries, she answered the door.

She looked much younger than her years, with a round face and straight black hair in a bowl cut. She was dressed professionally, in a yellow blouse, flowered skirt, and low heels.

"Señora Mariela?"

"Yes, what?"

"I'm looking for a seamstress to make a dress with these measurements," I said and handed her my note.

"I don't make clothes anymore," she began, then read my note. "So, what do you want to know?"

I figured I had time for two questions.

Was she a government informant, an *oreja*?

"I worked in official information."

Was she with Regina when Regina demonstrated to Fidel Herrera's wife's secretary that she had a telephone with Herrera's number and was therefore receiving his phone calls?

"Never. That didn't happen."

Did she testify that Regina had asked her for miniskirts and bought products to enhance her libido?

"That's not true. I don't know where these people make things up from."

"It's in the court file," I said.

"Well, I've never seen it, and it's not true. I knew Regina for twenty years. Maybe when she was younger, she asked me for miniskirts, but not lately."

"But the court case says she asked you to make her miniskirts just before she was killed."

"No. She asked me for vests and blouses."

It was exactly what Mariela San Martín had testified to investigators. She said she had known Regina for about twenty-three years and that seventeen or eighteen years ago, she started making clothes for her, some vests and some miniskirts, because that was the style back then. Most recently, Regina had asked for vests and blouses. San Martín had sold her Estée Lauder perfume and said Regina asked about buying some face creams from Yves Rocher.

But when the investigators wrote up a profile of Regina, they said she bought fabric for miniskirts just before she died and that they found soaps designed to get rid of cellulite, and ginseng packets designed to enhance libido.

"No way," San Martín said. "I never sold products that would . . . what did you call it?"

"Enhance libido."

The ginseng packets were for her hair, San Martín said.

Then she told me she needed to go to an appointment, but I could walk with her. She explained that she didn't sew anymore, but declined to say what work she did now. I told her my initial question was a pretext, mainly to protect her. The rest of the walk involved a lot of I don't knows.

Did someone change your testimony? Did you ever see any evidence from her house? USBs or notebooks? You were in her house to measure curtains, right?

"No. I never entered her house. Regina took the measurements and gave them to me."

Who wanted to kill her?

"I don't know. I don't know what she was working on."

So, you think it was for something she was working on?

"I don't know."

Were you pressured to give testimony about the miniskirts?

"I didn't."

Can I bring you a copy of the testimony, so you can see what's in there?

"No. I don't want to see it. I don't have time."

Did anyone ask you to describe the inside of Regina's house?

"I never went in her house. Why are you trying to put me in her house?"

Did you ever hear anything in your informant job about officials manipulating the case?

"No."

Who were her enemies?

"I don't know."

I was hitting a wall, so I decided to try to appeal to the affection and esteem she said she had for Regina.

Don't you want to know who did it? Aren't you curious? Don't you want justice for her?

With these questions, San Martín's demeanor softened.

"I can tell you that Regina was an honest, brave, and brilliant person," she said. "The truth is I didn't know much about her. Like I told you, I sewed for her, but nothing that had to do with her work. Do you understand? In fact, I really appreciated that she never put me in a difficult situation, workwise. Never."

San Martín said she was always straightforward about what she did. Regina knew who she was. San Martín wasn't like other people, who pretended to be reporters or someone else while informing for the government. Those were the real *orejas*, the people paid the big money. She was always upfront about the fact that she worked for the government and collected her salary, nothing more.

Then she talked about the last time she saw Regina and the trip to the fabric store. Regina had handed Mariela the cloth as soon as she bought it and said she was in a hurry for her new clothes.

"I'll have these ready for you on Wednesday," San Martín said she told Regina. "Imagine," she said to me, "when I heard she was dead, I had already cut pieces for her vests. I was working on her clothes so I could give them to her by Wednesday." Her eyes moistened and a tear slipped out. We had arrived at her appointment.

"I really appreciate you talking to me," I said. "If you happen to remember anything that might be relevant, you have my phone number."

When I got back to my hotel, I realized that the note I had written her was in my pocket. She didn't have my phone number. She *was* very clever. She read the note and handed it back to me without my even noticing. She had no evidence that we had ever talked.

The next morning, I woke up to a text from my lawyer friend: "Mariela will meet you at 6 P.M. at her dress shop. She says you know where that is."

I was a little confused. Dress shop? I figured it was her cover and that I should just show up at her home. I tried not to get my hopes up about why she had summoned me. This story had had so many ups and downs.

When I knocked on her front door that night, she opened a separate door that I hadn't noticed the first time and nodded me inside. I was in her dress shop. She did sew. It was spare, like a garage, with a corrugated roof, but spacious, with a cutting table, ironing board, patterns stacked everywhere, and at least four sewing machines, one a sixty-year-old Singer that was her mother's and still worked, another an industrial-looking high-tech machine she told me she bought the year before with her Christmas bonus.

Hanging on one wall was a lavender dress covered in netting and flowers. She had made it for her granddaughter, but she didn't like it. I said some "wows" and "what beautiful work" as she showed me around the shop. I asked her more questions about the case and still got nothing. Then I thought about everyone saying how smart Mariela San Martín was. Had she called me there to find out what I knew?

Finally, she turned secretive, indicating that I was about to hear the reason she summoned me. "Come here," she said, and pulled three kinds of folded fabric out of a large pile and stacked them on a table. Then she laid out pieces of cloth still pinned to their patterns with "Regina" written on the patterns. These were the pieces San Martín had cut for Regina's vests, the gray material with the silver stripes, just as they were when Mariela found out Regina was dead. She had saved the pieces for nearly ten years. Then she showed me the three types of cloth that Regina had bought for her blouses.

"I never finished, of course," she said. "I didn't know what to do with these." Then she explained: "I wanted you to see her taste, what she picked out. I want you to write about the real person, not the gossip or invented stories." She flipped the pieces of patterned cloth. "Look. Look how tiny she was."

I got nothing more out of her.

Maybe she did a number on me. But after our second meeting, and the fact that her story checked out with those of others, I walked away thinking she had nothing to do with it.

★

ANOTHER NAME ON the list was Alberto "El Gato" Morales, Regina's ex-boyfriend. According to Diego Hernández, the government's star witness, El Gato appeared with Regina near her house just weeks before her murder. Now that I knew for sure that Hernández's testimony was invented, I wondered why whoever wrote the cover-up had stuck El

Gato in the script? A lot of people told me he hung out with some dark characters. And Regina had accused him of informing on her. Maybe he knew something, and they wanted to keep him quiet.

El Gato was a photographer and cartoonist who accompanied Regina on many stories and filled the pages of *Política* with his Robert Crumb/1980s-style alt comic strips. He was one of very few people who had spent a lot of time in Regina's house.

I wrote him on Twitter, and he answered me immediately, very kindly so. He told me to meet him at La Parroquia, the famous coffee/cafeteria chain based in the port, but with restaurants all over. The one he chose was a sad, quiet version of the cathedral of coffee. It sat behind the Veracruz statehouse and was almost always empty, with a faded orange color scheme and diner décor that clearly hadn't been touched since the 1970s: linoleum floor, graying white tablecloths, and banquet chairs. The famous Veracruz *café lecheros*, strong coffee with foaming milk, were terrible there, just regular coffees with too much milk and no fanfare in the pour.

When I arrived, El Gato was already seated at a deuce against the wall with another man, who got up and moved to a nearby table when he saw me.

"Get him something," El Gato ordered the waiter.

It was clearly his domain. The waiter acted like his personal attendant, and several men passed by offering him a subtle nod during our conversation, or a *¿Todo bien?* "Everything okay?" I wondered if they were his *halcones*.

I sat down into a broken chair cushion, but made do.

I can't say El Gato was a villain, only that he looked like a cartoonist's version of one: a large man with a flat, corpulent face and a salt-and-pepper goatee that he stroked often as he spoke. His dark, almond-shaped eyes were set very close together under wide, perfectly shaped black eyebrows. Other than his neat eyebrows, everything about him was weathered and frayed: his driver's cap with side flaps, his khaki photographer's utility vest, his iPad cover.

When presented with the rumors about him, he had a practiced way of spreading his thin lips and wide cheeks into a smile, as if he thought everyone else in the world a fool, or of throwing himself back in his chair and letting out an exaggerated guffaw. And there were several rumors. The biggest one was that he knew who had it out for Regina and what really happened that night.

What followed was not a conversation or an interview, but a performance. El Gato, the thespian, spoke in riddles, as if he thought he could beguile you or, more important, distract you with tangents and circles. "I want to tell you many things," he said early in the conversation, as if to win me over.

He did tell me a lot, but as I listened, very little of it seemed useful. I thought of giving up at times and ending the interview, but I pushed ahead in blind hope.

¿Me explico? he asked me at one point after one particularly long rant. "Am I making myself clear?"

"No," I said honestly. "I'm completely lost."

He would not let me record him. I wondered if he was recording me.

His antics started when I told him I was working on a book about Regina's murder. Coincidentally, two media groups had been through Xalapa just before me to ask about the Regina Martínez case. When he heard I was working on the same, he warned me about listening to the "activists," meaning the journalists who were still demanding justice. Like Walter Ramírez did, El Gato told me they were all opportunists who didn't know Regina at all.

"We are all Regina!" he cried, leaning back in his chair, waving his arms, and pretending to tear at his shirt in an act of expiation.

"Of course, I reached out because you knew her well," I said. "You were a couple, right?"

"No." He shook his head. This was the first trip down the rabbit hole with him.

"We lived together as family," he said. "We grew up together, and our paths converged for a while. But we were not a couple."

Then he went on a tangent about the newspaper *Política* and the presidential candidate Cuauhtémoc Cárdenas and the political *parteaguas* (watershed) occurring in Mexico at the time he and Regina met.

I stopped him.

"Yes, yes. I know all that. I've read all the issues of *Política*, including the one where you were called to find an anonymous envelope with a tip in La Parroquia's men's bathroom."

He laughed and said he went looking in both restaurants, this one and the one across from Parque Juárez, little more than a block away.

He returned to the politics of the state, the PRD breakaway party from the PRI, the former governor Miguel Alemán.

I interrupted him again and tried to get back to Regina.

"When they killed Regina," he began.

"Who?" I asked. "Was it Jarocho?"

He shook his head no. "Have you heard of Harvey Oswald," he said, forgetting the "Lee."

I nodded.

"Clearly you know Kennedy and Jack Ruby." He started down a tangent about JFK.

I pulled him back. "Yes, I know." I tried more direct questions: "You don't think she was killed for her work?" I asked, based on his mockery of the people demanding justice.

He stopped, looked off into the distance with a small catbird smile, and stroked his goatee for a moment. "They killed Regina because she trusted. She got careless."

"Who?"

A ver, he said. "Let's see. How many journalists were killed in Mexico during that time? Do you know?" He liked to answer questions with questions.

"A lot. Eighteen," I said, the number I remembered for Duarte's term.

"And were they all killed for their work?"

"No."

"Exactly," he said. "It was a very violent time."

"Then, what was it?"

He opened his electronic pad, which he was drawing on when I arrived, and took out the pencil as if to illustrate something. Instead, he scrolled through his photos and showed me a picture of himself at age twenty-five: clean-shaven, still corpulent, but handsome. I could see how Regina would think he was attractive in a pudgy, mischievous-kid way. He showed me a shot of Regina standing at a desk next to a lanky man with a longish 1970s haircut. That was Raciel Martínez, her editor for many years, who nicknamed her "Macha."

El Gato kept scrolling, stopping at various black-and-whites of Regina. She was young, in her twenties, with thick, wavy shoulder-length hair, pretty, which wasn't a word people normally used to describe her. I could see her close resemblance to her nephew Alonso. She stared at the camera without smiling, confident, as if the world were hers to explore. Another photo of the two of them, El Gato with an impish look and Regina with that same straight-faced confidence.

"Where was that?" I asked.

"Right over there." El Gato pointed to another of the tables in the café.

More scrolling. Another photo of young Regina, this time with a dark-haired man sitting casually in jeans. I think El Gato chose this photo for shock factor. Regina was interviewing a young Andrés Manuel López Obrador, the president of Mexico at the time of my interview with El Gato. He showed me more photos of Regina and the young AMLO, as the president is known.

I decided to try for some simple biographical details. "You have a webpage, right?"

"And a magazine," El Gato said.

"And you also work for the government?" It was a sincere question. Someone had told me he worked in some department, maybe communications.

He gave his exaggerated, full-toothed laugh, as if to say, *Me? Working for authorities? What a joke.*

Another tangent: He told an involved story about how he was the first journalist to have a cell phone, big old boxes that they were, and he mimed speaking on a giant one. You had to have a bank account to get one. You had to give your Mexican social security number. It was a huge ordeal, he explained in detail. But he always had the best radios. He monitored the fire department and the marines on them.

Then he leaned to one side of the table and cupped his hand against his mouth, imitating someone telling a secret. *"That guy with all the radios, he must work for the government. He's with the FBI,"* he whispered. "People always thought that about me. I just had the best equipment."

"I mean now," I said. "You have a salaried position, in a ministry or something?"

Another overdone laugh. "No." At one point, he volunteered that Regina's brother Ángel had accused him of informing on her. He said he would see Ángel from time to time when Ángel came to the newspaper to visit Regina, but El Gato would just say hi. "He knew nothing about me," he protested.

"Yes," I responded. "Regina told a lot of people that. She called you a *pinche coludido*." A damned snitch.

He laughed again in his dramatic manner. "What information would I have that the government would care about? The location of Osama bin Laden? The cure for Covid? What could I have possibly been passing on that would destabilize the political system? What could I be telling them that they didn't already know?"

For the first time, he admitted that he and Regina had been a couple. I asked for the specific dates for their relationship. He said they "hung out" together from 1988 to 1992, then spent just four months of 1992 as a couple. He said she was angry with him not because he was informing on her, but because she wanted something serious, up to and including children. But that wasn't his style. Yet, a short time later, he met another photographer who he described as the love of his life, and married her. He and Regina never spoke again. He said it was jealousy, not corruption, that led her to treat him so coldly.

He was getting into the tough questions I had planned to ask without my having to ask them. So, I kept going to another sensitive point: He was mentioned in the case file. A witness described someone just like him, a distinctive figure of large stature with long hair and a camera, getting out of a taxi near Regina's house just a couple weeks before she died. Regina was with him.

El Gato gave me a calm, wry smile. "I am? This is the first I've heard of that."

I didn't share that I knew the testimony was false and that the witness was now dead. "Why do you think you're in there?" I asked.

"Because they were gunning for everyone."

"I think it was a message: 'Behave, or we're coming for you.' Like you knew something."

"Nah." He shook his head.

"Did you have keys to Regina's house?" I asked.

"Never.

"Why did the police conduct a campaign of terror afterward?"

"Because they had nothing, no details to go on." When Regina was killed, he said, the commander of the AVI, the Veracruz Investigations Agency, showed up outside El Gato's house, lurking in an intimidating way. El Gato went for help to the son of Don Yayo, who worked for the prosecutor's office, and then showed up at the AVI. "If you want to talk, ask me. Don't just stand outside my house," he said.

They took a DNA sample and a mold of his teeth, as they had with other reporters who knew Regina. But he said they told him they wanted his help in making a profile of Regina, even though he hadn't spoken to her in twenty years.

I asked him again why he thought Regina had been killed. He said he had three hypotheses, which he wouldn't share with me because he, too, was working on his own treatment of the case. But he answered: "I knew Regina. I knew her house. I knew her routines. She got careless."

"She let her guard down," he repeated. "She had something, and someone found out."

"But what? What did they find out?"

"Well, ask Villamil what they were up to!" he said, waving his arms in the air.

Again, the *Proceso* story.

CHAPTER 22

The Gray Zone

2022

I HAD DISMISSED THE *Proceso* article about Alejandro Montano and Reynaldo Escobar as too small, hardly an exposé, and old news. But in talking with people like Walter Ramírez and El Gato, I did feel I was much closer to the flame than I had been in five years of interviewing. And both of them mentioned the article.

In my final reporting days, a source who had spoken to me earlier on the record, explained why that article would have been received differently in that particular moment by two longtime dark figures of politics. The source had been in the pig swill of Veracruz politics for some time, and on this subject, he didn't want to be named.

We were sitting in a café in Xalapa when he ripped a page from my notebook and started to draw (something I found Mexicans I interviewed did fairly often):

He drew a time line and marked the late 1980s, early 1990s, when Regina was ramping up her career covering social issues. Here was 2002, when a leader of the Gulf Cartel was arrested while living quietly as a neighbor of the governor of Veracruz, Miguel Alemán. Slash mark. And here is where it comes to light that people are flying contraband into

Veracruz via clandestine airstrips. Slash mark. Even though Regina wrote allegations about corrupt officials in this context, my source said (drawing a circle around Regina and social issues in this primitive schema), nothing happened. The officials denied involvement, and everything continued as normal.

Here was 2004, when Fidel Herrera was elected governor and everything changed. Slash mark. Herrera was accepting narco money for his campaigns, according to testimony in the United States. Here is the big point that marks the before and after, my source said. Huge slash mark.

According to my source's homemade graphic, the "before and after" regarding organized crime in Veracruz split at around 2005. Fidel Herrera (one circle) marked the "after," the new world of political exploitation. The man who ran Herrera's government was Reynaldo Escobar, (arrow to the "after"), who later had to resign as Duarte's attorney general because violence in the state was out of control.

Montano (another circle) had distanced himself from former governor Miguel Alemán Velasco ("before") and became closer politically with Herrera (a line from Montano to the "after"). Montano ("before") was also related by marriage to public security director Arturo Bermúdez, who was accused and later exonerated of illegal enrichment, but still faced charges of forced disappearances (a line to the "after").

Then my source put Regina on the time line, covering land conflicts, labor disputes, and government misspending ("before") and covering public corruption, violence, and misspending ("after"). She had been a local reporter ("before"), but now every Veracruz scandal she wrote about was published in a national magazine ("after").

My source's crude graphic made absolute sense. It was the morphing from standard public corruption ("before") to criminal governance ("after"), when organized crime and elected officials became indistinguishable, Guillermo Trejo's so-called gray zone.

I asked my source if I could have the drawing to refer to. He said no, folded it into his pocket, and left.

★

AFTER THAT, I took every name I could find in the court documents and tried to track people down, knocking on doors in and around Xalapa and the port. Most people turned me away or said the person I was seeking had moved. I tried to reach Fidel Herrera through his son, Javier Herrera Borunda, who didn't respond. But he told Forbidden Stories that his father wasn't available for interviews because of his health. But I did find one person who let me inside to talk. The conversation was on the record but useless, with the person only reinforcing all the fiction in the case and denying that the state had ever smeared Regina's reputation. If nothing else, it gave me a window into how public officials in places like Veracruz operated. As long as they didn't see something with their own eyes, they could deny it happened, and maintain some semblance of professional integrity while pushing a false government narrative. It's a systemic way of thinking among officials, a means of self-protection that I found impossible to break. But after so many years in Mexico, whenever I encountered it I would just call them on how ridiculous the logic was.

"You *know* the details of this case were made up," I told this source point-blank. "You *know* that, in Mexico, torture is not used to extract the truth. It's used to memorize the official story."

The official's eyes eyes danced at that point, in a kind of humorous recognition. But I didn't know if the look meant I had caught them or if they were just amused at how hard I was trying.

"What do you think of the theory of the article that was published just before, about Escobar and Montano? A lot of people say it was that," I said.

"The one in *Proceso?*"

"Yes, did they investigate that? How did they discard that?"

"Off the record?"

I agreed to go off the record.

"I don't believe it, because Reynaldo [Escobar] is a person who wouldn't be interested in what that article was saying. Reynaldo worked his bars and cantinas. That was his interest, nothing else. And [Alejandro] Montano is a politician. More than anything, he's a person who rose politically because of his ties to Miguel Alemán [Velasco] . . ."

"But it said Reynaldo had ties to the Zetas," I said of the article.

"Reynaldo had cantinas and bars."

"But those are the businesses of the Zetas."

"Probably. But Regina wasn't investigating that. That wasn't in the [*Proceso*] article. The article wasn't the motive. But if you come to me and say she was investigating the bars—well, now, that's new. That would be a new line of investigation. That's the subject that would have affected that guy," the source said, referring to Reynaldo Escobar, "and that was not in the article."

I had come to the end of years of investigation, of tiptoeing around, disappearing for periods to protect my sources; of registering with false names, paying cash, changing hotels, and giving all my vital information to colleagues back in Mexico City, who had an action plan ready in case anything terrible happened.

After all that, I had nothing.

I too was in despair.

★

THEN ONE NIGHT, I was reviewing old interviews, searching for a way to end this story, when I came upon a startling piece of information that had been sitting in my notebook for five years.

In 2016, I interviewed Veracruz journalist Miguel Díaz, director of an independent online magazine called *Plumas Libres*. Díaz, Regina, Andrés Timoteo, and Jorge Morales, who later went to the state Commission for the Attention and Protection of Journalists, had founded *Plumas Libres* together as an investigative magazine around 2010. All had strong reputations as journalists who couldn't be bought, and all had dreamed of having their own outlet.

But the group fell apart, the story goes, over egos. Regina didn't like the fact that Jorge Morales was put in charge and was making all the editorial decisions, when she personally had put up the money to create and host the website. Miguel Díaz told me in the 2016 interview that her departure was over "professional differences."

She and Díaz remained friends and confidants, however. In our interview, he called her the journalist with the most credibility in all of Veracruz.

"What was she working on?" I asked in that 2016 interview, as I had asked everyone.

For whatever reason, I didn't catch his answer in that moment: "The last report she did was about the ties of two politicians with the sale of drugs. She linked two politicians with drug trafficking."

"Montano and Reynaldo Escobar," I interjected.

"Yes, [Alejandro] Montano and Reynaldo Escobar. Reynaldo was an owner of a bar," he said. Regina was investigating a tip that they were selling drugs there.

I thought he was referring to the Jenaro Villamil article that implicated the two politicians just before Regina was killed. But it said nothing about drugs or bars. And I pointed out that Regina didn't write it, and I took the conversation on another track.

When I reviewed his words so many years later, I couldn't believe what I was seeing. Díaz said Regina *was* investigating a tie between Reynaldo Escobar, drugs, and bars. "She told me she had informants, police, and they gave her information that she was putting together regarding links between drug trafficking and politicians," he said at the time. I wrote Díaz immediately for clarification. We had stayed in touch over the years, and he answered. I shared what was in my notes, what he told me so many years before when I asked what Regina was working on.

"Yes," he wrote back.

"I never found the article," I said. "Was that for *Plumas Libres*?"

"She never finished reporting it," Díaz said. "They were going to publish it in *Proceso*. They published something else about those politicians, but not this topic specifically."

"How do you know she was investigating drugs and the [bars]?"

"She told me she was working on that and some other stories."

"How long before she died did she tell you that?"

"Reynaldo was attorney general at the time and very powerful in the Duarte administration."

"So, it was 2011?"

"About that time," Díaz confirmed. "At the end of that year."

"Did she have anything, or it was just speculation?"

"She had heavyweight sources who were ex-police and ex-officials. She never revealed her sources. They told her this, and she was investigating."

"Did you ever see anything from her, any do ments?" I asked.

"No. I think when she told me that, it was out of a moment of carelessness."

Díaz's information crossed with El Gato's: Regina knew something, and she let her guard down. I thought of that official who spoke to me off the record: The only thing that would have concerned Reynaldo Escobar was if someone was investigating the bars.

I wrote Escobar two e-mails requesting an interview. I also called his office thirteen times over a three-month period to follow up. He never responded. At the time that Jenaro Villamil's original *Proceso* article came out, before Regina's murder, Escobar said in a media interview that he represented various bar owners as an attorney but was never an owner himself, and that he had absolutely no links to organized crime.

"They've always said that, but no one could prove it, simply because there are no facts to back it up," Escobar told the reporter. "I have no link or tie to any criminal group. I've always acted in a way that conforms to the law, stuck to the law, and if there were anything out there, they would have jailed me."

Most of the rest of the people on my list didn't want to talk. But earlier, before this revelation, I was able to get Alejandro Montano on the phone twice. He wouldn't meet with me in person, he said, because of the Covid-19 pandemic. In the first call, I told him what I was working on, that he would be appearing in the book, and that I wanted to do some fact-checking with him. (I had hoped to see how he would react to my questions in person, but I had to do the best I could over the phone.) I wanted to talk to him because of the *Proceso* article and said that I didn't think he was behind Regina's murder—because I didn't—but I was sure he knew who was. I told him many thought the *Proceso* article about him and Escobar had led to her killing.

"What article?" he said. "Why are you bringing all this to me now?"

I told him that I knew that he was also a victim of the journalist killings because, as director of the news website Milenio in Veracruz, he had lost one of his own reporters, Victor Manuel Báez Chino. (Báez, who covered crime news, was found beheaded in a garbage bag less than two months after Regina's death. The federal attorney general at the time said they were looking into possible involvement of state officials, among other lines of investigation. In the end, the Veracruz attorney general said the men responsible for Báez's death were killed in a shootout.)

So, maybe Alejandro Montano could tell me what he knew about the Regina Martínez case.

He said he knew Regina only marginally. Then he told me he was nothing more than a retired public servant, now in his senior years, who loved God and worked to help children with cancer.

He also made a veiled threat: "If you can prove it, print it. If you can't, don't print it," he said. "People can file lawsuits, and you can get yourself into some trouble."

In the second phone call (he always called me back, and noted that if he had anything to hide, he wouldn't be so transparent), I asked about protecting Jesus Albino Quintero Meraz. He said that whole testimony had been debunked by *Proceso*, though I wasn't able to locate the story. Then I asked if he ever told Regina that he wanted to invite her for a *pan de muerto*. I didn't even have to explain that she took it as a threat. He already knew what it meant.

"No, no, never," he said.

Whoever said that should be investigated, because they clearly had no proof, he added. "People say these things because they want to do damage," he said. "They're jealous." Then he gave the same explanation as Escobar did for his innocence: "If I had done anything, I wouldn't be walking around here freely."

But the road kept leading me back to the article. One of the other groups investigating the Regina Martínez murder got a telephone interview from prison with El Silva in the fall of 2020, while I was waiting for the pandemic to pass and for my request for an in-person interview to be approved. In that call, El Silva said he was drinking with Jarocho a week after Regina's murder. Jarocho told him he was recruited to do the job but said no. After that, Jarocho disappeared.

El Silva, too, said it had to do with a "political matter," and mentioned the magazines disappearing from the newsstands.

Montano won his election to Congress two months after Regina's death, despite the *Proceso* article. After that, he was named the head of security for the 2012 inauguration of the new president, Enrique Peña Nieto. Reynaldo Escobar lost his election. But in my time on this project, no one would ever talk to me about Escobar on the record. They said he still wielded a lot of power behind the scenes.

The problem was that the people closest to Regina had a hard time believing she was investigating anything when she died. She was scared. She told *Proceso* no more and Lev that she wanted to dial back.

But *somebody* was investigating Reynaldo Escobar. According to the state and federal archives of public information requests, there are at least a half dozen requests in the databank seeking information about Escobar—three of which were filed in the weeks leading up to Regina's death. I wrote a third email to Reynaldo Escobar asking if he knew about these inquiries in 2012 and who was behind them. No answer.

One request for information was to the Mexican attorney general's office asking if there were any criminal complaints against Escobar with regards to drug trafficking, kidnapping, organized crime, or any other crime. It also asked if the Organized Crime Unit had investigations against Escobar. The request acknowledges that details are confidential; it just asks if any cases exist. The response on March 13, 2012, was that the office was prohibited by law from saying yes or no. A second request sought any investigations or criminal cases from the assistant attorney general for legal and international affairs, including any involving electoral fraud or crimes against journalists. The response, dated April 30, 2012, two days after Regina's death, again was no comment. There was no indication who filed either request.

A third information request went to the Veracruz state attorney general's office, which on March 6, 2012, acknowledged that there were two state criminal investigations involving Escobar but that it was prohibited by law from providing any details.

That request was made by a Juan Salvador Gaviota.

I googled the name. It turns out that it's the Spanish title for the 1970s New Age mega-bestseller *Jonathan Livingston Seagull*, a fable about a special bird who eschews the flock to find a higher purpose in life.

EPILOGUE

In the years since Regina's murder, nothing has changed. Seven journalists were killed in Mexico in the early months of 2022. The killing of Regina Martínez ran a lot of good people out of journalism. Lupita López stopped writing about organized crime and politicians. Polo Hernández could never return to Xalapa. Finally, he gave up doing journalism in Mexico City and went to Canada to pick fruit, learn English, and get away from the pressure. Eddie Romo turned to experimental cinema and decided to earn a PhD.

When I shared with Lev García my surprise at how easily he left journalism after all those years, he said, "I told you. Kathy, one of the first times we met, that I would leave when I was ready. Not when anyone else told me to."

But there was good news for journalism over the years as well.

In February 2020, just before the lockdown for Covid-19, Jorge Carrasco was named the top editor of *Proceso*, the position held originally by Julio Scherer, with the mission of taking the magazine into the future. Both Rafael Rodríguez and Salvador Corro had retired. It was a circuitous route from disillusioned employee in 2018 to being named to one of the top journalistic posts in all of Mexico. But that's his story to tell.

In all their discussions, Julio Scherer never gave Jorge any indication that he wanted him to be the future director of his magazine, apart from one small exchange. Jorge was filling in as editor for the vacationing Salvador Corro one time, working to put out that week's edition, when Don Julio walked into the newsroom.

"I like seeing you in that role" was all he ever said to Jorge.

Jorge's appointment was a personal and professional victory. Despite all he had been through, he had survived as an independent journalist in Mexico, remaining a hard-hitting reporter beyond reproach whose mission now was to save Mexico's most storied news magazine. Under Jorge, the magazine is as aggressive and rigorous as ever.

Others continued in the profession as well:

Rodrigo Soberanes maintained his crusade as a journalist, focusing on migration and the environment. He started his own online news portal, *La Marea* (*The Tide* in English), for long-form and investigative reporting.

Norma Trujillo kept at it, too, despite receiving various threats, to the point that her teenage children asked her to stop. She founded a group called Voz Alterna, a coalition of journalists who wrote stories and stuck together for protection. She was recognized internationally for her work in defending press freedom in Veracruz. She also kept investigating the case of Ernestina Ascencio, the elderly woman believed to have been raped and killed by soldiers in the mountains of Veracruz. Norma's stories helped push the Inter-American Court of Human Rights and the López Obrador government to reopen the case. But eventually she, too, needed a break, and she went to work for the communications department at the University of Veracruz.

Good investigative reporting in Mexico has grown steadily, nationally and in Veracruz, since the time of Duarte's arrest. The turning point nationally was an investigation in 2014 into President Enrique Peña Nieto's private seven-million-dollar mansion, nicknamed the "Casa Blanca." It was built, financed, and held in the name of a mega-construction company that had gotten hundreds of millions of dollars in public works contracts from the Peña Nieto government, including one for part of a nearly $4 billion high-speed train. After they published the article, radio journalist Carmen Aristegui and her team of investigators were booted off the air, even though Aristegui had the number one early-morning drive-time news show in the country. In a testament to the newfound muscle of the press, Aristegui sued, asserting that her right to free speech had been violated. She won and eventually returned to the air on another station in the same time slot. The high-speed train contract was canceled.

Other investigations revealed a federal shell company scheme under Peña Nieto that made the Duarte kleptocracy appear amateurish.

Journalists for *Animal Política* and Mexicans Against Corruption and Impunity revealed that 128 fake businesses were used to divert nearly 7.7 billion pesos from 11 federal agencies. Rather than make contracts directly with the ghost firms, as Duarte's administration had done, the *Estafa Maestra*, or "Master Scam" as it became known, funneled the money first through public universities, which then made the contracts.

Investigative nonprofit Quinto Elemento Lab created stipends and training for journalists around the country, while doing their own digging. Among other things, Quinto found that Peña Nieto's director of the state oil company, Pemex, Emilio Lozoya, received millions in bribes from the international company Odebrecht, some around the time of Peña Nieto's presidential campaign. Lozoya fled the country, but not without Quinto reporters, working with their European counterparts, tracking the fugitive's whereabouts through Germany and other parts of the continent. Lozoya was eventually extradited from Spain to face charges.

★

THE IRONY OF this project is that more than anything else, it made me think of my own country. In the time I was in Mexico, I watched from afar as the concept and importance of truth deteriorated in the United States. And the first steps in shattering our notion of common standards of truth as a society and a democracy came in the form of attacks on the press.

We, the press, are by definition the bearers of bad news, so we are an easy target. But we are not the ultimate target.

Amid a reign of terror, Veracruz had no reliable counterweight, no trusted public voice. That allowed the government to commit atrocities against its own citizens, the people they had pledged to protect. Billions of dollars were stolen, and thousands of people disappeared. Average citizens took to reporting what they knew via social media, and they were cut off or gunned down as well. After a while, people started pointing fingers at the press for not doing its job.

Veracruz politician Miguel Moreno Brizuela told me that, during one of his campaigns for congress, he had arranged to meet a group of voters, followed by a second event with the press. But the two groups happened to overlap, and people started confronting the reporters. They called them *vendidos*, "sell-outs."

"My son was murdered, and you said nothing," Moreno Brizuela recalled hearing from the crowd.

"We were afraid," the journalists answered.

"It was really, really interesting," Moreno Brizuela said. "The press afraid. The municipal governments afraid. A terrible era. That has generated a decomposition in the social fabric. And now I say our society is rotten. Today it's rotten."

In his book about Mexico's seminal newspaper *Excélsior*, professor of Mexican history Arno Burkholder put it this way: "A democratic press can only emerge if it has readers willing to defend it before a state that wants to impose itself at all costs. Engaged journalists also need the support of their readers so that together they can contribute to the betterment of their country."

In exchange, he wrote, the media needs to be transparent about its income, political leanings, and special interests.

This trust and alliance, once a given, at least in the United States, is receding all over the world.

★

ONE DAY EARLY in my reporting, Rodrigo Soberanes and I were sitting in a café in Mexico City having breakfast. He told me about a vivid dream he recently had. He saw Regina. She was the same as always, brusque, and was seated at a long table outside a large colonial house she had purchased, a house she had always wanted to own. On one side of her at the table was Walter Ramírez. On the other side was a person Rodrigo didn't recognize, but who he understood to be her killer.

In the dream, Regina was calmly looking over some papers through her large aviator glasses. The other two remained silent, except to say they were helping her. She was in the process of pardoning the two men. Then she sent Walter inside the house to retrieve something.

Rodrigo was surprised to see her and wanted to give her a big hug. "You're here!" he cried.

She responded coolly, as if it were any normal day. She told him to sit down between her and the stranger. "I never left," she said.

He didn't remember her exact words after that, but they were something like, "Everything has been as it was meant to be." Then she added: "Would you and everyone please calm down? Please stop suffering."

He had the dream when he was in self-exile in Chile.

ACKNOWLEDGMENTS

A book is always a group effort, and I've had a great community of support over the many years it took to put this together. It started with the generosity and bravery of the "Fab Four": Rodrigo Soberanes, Lev García, Leopoldo "Polo" Hernández, and Pablo "Eddie" Romo. If not for your time, trust, and friendship, this project would not have been possible.

There were those who went far beyond the call of friendship to give me food and shelter. Thank you Carrie Kahn of NPR, Ramón Beristain, Gina Manfredo, José de Córdoba of the *Wall Street Journal*, Elisabeth Sabartés, and Giulio Petrocci. Your support and company took the edge off this often difficult work.

Early on, I sought the advice of several colleagues who became allies in the process, Tracy Wilkinson of the *Los Angeles Times*, Marcela Turati of Quinto Elemento Lab, Alfredo Corchado of the *Dallas Morning News*, documentarian Roberto Hernández, and Associated Press reporter Alberto Arce. Along the way, I received great backup and support from Dudley Althaus, the Hon. Anthony O. Garza, Anne-Marie O'Connor, Deb Donnelly, Jude Joffe-Block, Elisabeth Malkin, Laura Barranco, Olivia Sánchez Correa, and Mark Johnson, executive deputy secretary, U.S. Department of State. Thank you also to my dear friend and colleague, Alejandra Xanic von Bertrab, who indulged me by listening for hours when we should have been doing other work. The late Dolly Mascareñas gave support and security advice. We miss you terribly.

I could never have written my first drafts without the help of expert editor Fran Smith. Luis C. Schmidt of Olivares gave me invaluable feedback. Jorge Carrasco was far too generous with his limited time and the tedious American who kept asking for more of it. Also thanks to *Proceso* editors emeriti Rafael Rodríguez Castañeda and Salvador Corro for your time and use of *Proceso* archives. The General Archive of the State of Veracruz dug out twenty-plus years of editions of *Política*, and was eminently helpful with my requests.

Steve Fisher helped me wade through the world of government transparency laws and document requests, and Jorge Morales was infinitely available and helpful as an expert journalist/lawyer who knows Veracruz inside and out. I have many journalists to thank for reporting help, sources, and support, including Norma Trujillo, Miguel Ángel León Carmona, Noë Zavaleta, Miguel Díaz, Félix Márquez, Julio Argumedo, Arturo Ángel, and Eirinet Gómez. Thank you to Samuel López Amezquita for the long drives, boring waits, and for always being vigilant. Adrián López of Sinaloa's *El Noroeste*, Jan-Albert Hootsen of the Committee to Protect Journalists, and Balbina Flores of Reporters Without Borders were generous with time and interviews.

My colleagues at the Associated Press were also invaluable in this process: Marjorie Miller, John Daniszewski, Paul Haven, Eduardo Castillo, and Dario López. Lars Hansen and Arin Pereira Farrington helped in technical and creative ways.

My work was supported by several fellowships. Thanks to Margaret Engel and the Alicia Patterson Foundation; to the Logan Nonfiction Program, where I did the best work of my writing career while snowed in in Upstate New York. Thank you Josh Friedman, Carly Willsie, Jonathan Logan, Tom Jennings, Rafil Kroll-Zaidi, and the entire Carey Institute staff, as well as the Winter 2019 fellows who helped me sort out so many things. I am also very grateful to the Kellogg Institute for International Studies at the University of Notre Dame. Thank you Paolo Carozza, Steve Reifenberg, Denise Wright, Sharon Schierling, Guillermo Trejo, Juan Albarracín, Reyes Ruiz, Gema Kloppe-Santamaria, Ted Beatty, Notre Dame President the Rev. John Jenkins, Vice President Ann Firth, and special thanks to retired Vice President Paul Browne, who was so supportive of me finishing this project while I worked as associate director for international media relations. I'm happy to share the final project that you all had such a large hand in creating.

Thank you to former dean Christopher Callahan and the Walter Cronkite School of Journalism and Mass Communication for making me a writer in residence.

I am forever indebted to John Diaz, who read many versions of this manuscript with the careful eye of the great journalist that he is. Thank you to Eduardo García and Verónica Bustos, who read it for "gringo-splaining." Vero was also my expert translator and cheerleader throughout. Thanks to my dear friend June Allen, who always encourages me at every turn.

Last but not least, enormous thanks to my agent, Gail Ross, who worked hard and quickly to make this book a reality, as well as Dara Kaye of Ross Yoon Agency. Thank you Anton Mueller, my expert and patient editor, Morgan Jones, Laura Phillips, and the entire team at Bloomsbury Publishing. You "got" this book completely and made it so much better. You are a joy to work with.

And thank you to my friends at my favorite Xalapa hotel who took very good care of me. I won't name you so I can keep going back. And to the Girls of Notre Dame. You know who you are. I hope to have many boxes for you to carry.

NOTES ON SOURCES

This story was reported by me firsthand and is my own account of what I discovered in trying to investigate the Regina Martínez murder case and those of other assassinated journalists in Mexico. It is based on hundreds of interviews and dozens of trips to Veracruz and Mexico City—I lost count—starting in February 2015. All information that I didn't report directly is given a citation here. The parts not footnoted are a result of my original reporting in the field and my firsthand experience.

Conversations are not invented, but rather are either recorded or based on what someone present told me was said. I granted requests for anonymity, considering that one journalist had been killed and her family and others had been threatened for discussing this case. It is not clear today, ten years later, that they are out of danger. I also offered to change names for protection. But of the dozens of people named in this book, only two sources are listed under pseudonyms.

Wherever possible, I tried to cross-reference the information from my interviews against documents, articles, books, or the accounts of other people present during an event. If the versions varied, I went with the one I thought made the most sense. In reporting this book, I was unable, for the most part, to tell anyone outside the Fab Four who I was talking to (though, each of the Fab Four knew I was talking with the other three). This made it difficult to cross-reference information, because I couldn't share the names of any of my sources with the other ones. It was potentially problematic for anyone to be talking to me, and I had to protect them. In the end, I concluded that stories whose facts coincided among several people's versions were the most plausible.

I did my best to share my own experience of Mexico and of this case without the tone of a white foreigner explaining an entire complex country to the rest of the world. This is my story, my experience alone, and I try to be transparent about the fact that I view things through a foreigner's lens.

This book is my personal Valentine to two things I treasure dearly: Mexico and independent journalism.

NOTES

CHAPTER 1: TIME

xiv   By the time we received the threat, fifty-one journalists had been killed: "53 Journalists Killed in Mexico," Committee to Protect Journalists, n.d., https://cpj.org/data/killed/?status=Killed&motiveConfirmed%5B%5D =Confirmed&motiveUnconfirmed%5B%5D=Unconfirmed&type%5B %5D=Journalist&cc_fips%5B%5D=MX&start_year=1992&end_year =2010&group_by=year.

xiv   That Sunday, the paper ran a headline and a front-page editorial: Staff, "¿Qué quieren de nosotros?" *El Diario de Juárez*, Sept. 19, 2010, front page, https://diario.mx/Local/2010-09-19_cfaade06/_que-quieren-de -nosotros/?/.

xv   No one has ever been detained: Luz del Carmen Sosa, "Jose Armando Rodriguez Carreon," and Rocios Gallegos, "Luis Carlos Santiago Orozco," Matar a Nadie, https://mataranadie.com/.

xvi   In the United States, even if polls at times showed that the public hated us: Lydia Saad, "U.S. Ethics Ratings Rise for Medical Workers and Teachers," Gallup, Dec. 22, 2020, https://news.gallup.com/poll/328136 /ethics-ratings-rise-medical-workers-teachers.aspx.

3   "When I get home, I'll give her a call": Isabel Nuñez testimony, Investigación ministerial 019/2012/PC, Procuraduría General de Justica, Estado de Veracruz-Llave, Tomo I, pp. 28–30.

4   The neighborhood had its share of petty crime: Interviews with various neighbors, none of whom wanted to be identified.

7   "We don't talk about it": Chapter 1 is a reconstruction based on Isabel Nuñez's testimony to both state and federal investigators and on interviews with three people who knew Regina Martínez and Isabel Nuñez and who want to remain anonymous. It was put together over several years of reporting.

CHAPTER 2: IF NOT YOU, THEN WHO?

13 "Well," Polo answered, "if not you, then who?": Chapter 2 was reconstructed from interviews with all the people named.

CHAPTER 3: "WE'RE LIVING IN MADNESS"

15 With few exceptions, the media over the decades: Enrique Krauze, *Mexico: Biography of Power—A History of Modern Mexico, 1810–1996*, 1st Harper Perennial ed. (New York: HarperCollins, 1998), p. 579.

17 In the vast Maya territory on the Yucatán Peninsula: Grant D. Jones, *Maya Resistance to Spanish Rule: Time and History on a Colonial Frontier* (Albuquerque: University of New Mexico Press, 1991), pp. 107–108.

18 Mercado had been educated in the United States, was a Knight Fellow: Patricia Mercado Sánchez, Fundadora y Directora General en Conexión Migrante, Mexico City, Mexico, Linkedin profile, https://www.linkedin .com/in/patriciamercado/?locale=es_ES.

18 "If it's a question of life or death, I have no trouble making a decision": Katherine Corcoran, "Mexico Journalists Debate Cartels, Self-censorship," Associated Press, Sept. 23, 2010.

21 The situation has only grown worse over time, with Mexico more recently ranking number one: "32 Journalists Killed in 2020: Motive Confirmed," Committee to Protect Journalists, https://cpj.org/data/killed/2020/?status=Ki lled&motiveConfirmed%5B%5D=Confirmed&type%5B%5D=Journalist &start_year=2020&end_year=2020&group_by=location.

21 Gómez, who was counting out bills for the journalist: Staff, "Periodistas dan su versión sobre reunión y 'media coaching' a 'La Tuta,'" Aristegui Noticias, Sept. 22, 2014, https://aristeguinoticias.com/2209/mexico /periodistas-dan-su-version-sobre-reunion-con-la-tuta/.

22 The station killed the story: Interview, anonymous, Veracruz (city), Veracruz, May 18, 2016.

23 In the Colombian drug war of the 1990s, the media: Tina Rosenberg, "The Long, Hard Road of Investigative Reporting in Latin America," *New York Times*, July 2, 2006, https://www.nytimes.com/2006/07/02 /opinion/the-long-hard-road-of-investigative-reporting-in-latin -america.html.

23 The sculpture depicts a pre-Colombian ceremony: UNESCO, "Browse the Lists of Intangible Cultural Heritage and the Register of Good

Safeguarding Practices," Intangible Cultural Heritage, n.d., https://ich
.unesco.org/en/RL/ritual-ceremony-of-the-voladores-00175.

23 Just as Mexico's state prosecutors were set: Olga R. Rodriguez, "Gunmen
Dump 35 Bodies Under Overpass in Veracruz," Associated Press, Sept.
21, 2011.

26 Most journalists there worked at a minimum: Jorge Morales, "Diag-
nóstico sobre las condiciones laborales para periodistas en Xalapa,"
Comisionado de la Comisión Estatal de Atención y Protección de los
Periodistas de Veracruz, 2015, p. 12.

27 When the story came out, three thousand copies of *Proceso*: Jenaro
Villamil, "La década trágica," *Proceso* 1853 (May 6, 2012): 12.

CHAPTER 4: A HEAVEN INSIDE HELL

28 In the famous mariachi song "Guadalajara," the crooners: Vicente
Fernández, "Guadalajara" [lyrics and audio,] Letras, n.d., https://www
.letras.com/vicente-fernandez/755526/.

28 Hernán Cortés landed near what is now the Port of Veracruz: Martín
Aguilar Sánchez and Juan Ortiz Escamilla, *Historia General de Veracruz*
(Veracruz: Gobierno del Estado de Veracruz, 2011), p. 136.

28 It was also the place where the last Spaniards were kicked out: "Breve
cronología de la lucha por la Independencia de México," *Milenio* website,
Sept. 16, 2020, https://www.milenio.com/cultura/independencia-mexico
-lucha-independentista-paso-paso.

29 People from the port are known as the original *jarochos*: La Asociación
de Academias de la Lengua Española's definition of a *jarocho* is a person
who is abrupt, disordered, and of somewhat insolent manners.

29 One TV comedian added the term *odio jarocho*: "¿Qué significa odiar con
odio jarocho? Aquí te decimos," *El Heraldo de México*, March 13, 2021.

29 It was the first destination for most of the slaves: María Elisa Velázquez and
Gabriela Iturralde Nieto, *Afrodescendientes en México: Una historia de silencio y
discriminación* (Mexico City: Colección Conapred, 2020), pp. 61–75,
https://archivos.juridicas.unam.mx/www/bjv/libros/13/6041/9.pdf.

29 and the site of the first free black colony: Jonathan Custodio, "Afro-
Mexicans Fight for Visibility and Recognition," Pulitzer Center, May 2,
2019, https://pulitzercenter.org/stories/afro-mexicans-fight-visibility-and
-recognition.

29   It is a state where Mesoamerican cultures: Martín Aguilar Sánchez and Juan Ortiz Escamilla, eds., *Historia General de Veracruz* (Veracruz: Secretaría de Educación del Estado de Veracruz, Universidad Veracruzana, 2011), p. 10.

29   where the Totonac, indigenous people whose civilization: Sánchez and Escamilla, eds., *Historia General de Veracruz*, p. 50, https://www.sev.gob .mx/servicios/publicaciones/colec_veracruzsigloXXI/Historia_General _Veracruz.pdf.

29   Americans know "La Bamba," recorded by Ritchie Valens: "La Bamba," Mexico Remixed, University of Indiana Bloomington, website, https:// collections.libraries.indiana.edu/cookmusiclibrary/exhibits/show /sounds_of_mexico/la_bamba.

29   high-pitched jarana-plucking sound known as *son jarocho*: "La Bamba."

30   Others say the killing was ordered by a rival capo: Itzel Loranca, "Una década sin narco/caballos a galope en Villarín," *Expediente* (blog), March 24, 2017, https://noticiasdeveracruz.com/nota/24521/periodico-de -veracruz-portal-de-noticias-veracruz/una-decada-sin-narcocaballos-a -galope-en-villarin.

30   In all, two men were murdered: Jorge Fernández Menendez, "Zetas, Colorado, Villarín: La pista de dinero," *Excélsior*, June 15, 2012, https://www.excelsior.com.mx/opinion/2012/06/15/jorge-fernandez -menendez/841429.

31   It preserves elements of another era, one with organ grinders, cotton candy: Ulysses S. Grant, *Memoirs and Selected Letters: Personal Memoirs of U. S. Grant, Selected Letters, 1839–1865* (New York: Viking Press, 1990), p. 922.

31   From that hillside balcony on a clear day: "Cofre de Perote," Summit Post, https://www.summitpost.org/cofre-de-perote/567645.

32   In Duarte's first year in office, 2011: "41 Journalists Killed in Mexico Between 2004 and 2010: Motive Confirmed or Unconfirmed," Committee to Protect Journalists, search page at https://cpj.org/data /killed/?status=Killed&motiveConfirmed%5B%5D=Confirmed&moti veUnconfirmed%5B%5D=Unconfirmed&type%5B%5D=Journalist&cc _fips%5B%5D=MX&start_year=2004&end_year=2010&group_by=year.

33   The day after she was found, a video appeared on YouTube: "Cártel de Jalisco Nueva Generación 'Mata-Zetas,'" Telenews Noticiero Online via

YouTube, Aug. 20, 2011, https://www.youtube.com/watch?v=sv9 WBSrKhcI.

33 State Attorney General Reynaldo Escobar called a press conference: Staff, "Asesinan a la reportera Yolanda Ordaz, del periódico Notiver," *La Jornada,* July 27, 2011, https://www.jornada.com.mx/2011/07/27/politica /012n1pol.

33 *Notiver,* the newspaper where both Ordaz and Milo Vela worked: Regina Martínez, "Exige 'Notiver' la renuncia del procurador," *Proceso* APRO (July 27, 2011), https://www.proceso.com.mx/nacional/2011/7/27 /exige-notiver-la-renuncia-del-procurador-89987.html.

34 But the tweeters' information happened to be false, and Escobar: "Capturan a tuiteros por difundir rumores de violencia en Veracruz," Associated Press via *Excélsior,* Aug. 25, 2011, https://www.excelsior.com .mx/node/763830.

CHAPTER 5: "MR. GOVERNOR, WE DON'T BELIEVE YOU"

42 The first comment, by "Laura," asked why police arrived so quickly: Photocopy of the comments in my possession.

42 They put their grief into planning a protest march: Staff, "Anuncian creación de comisión especial para investigar muerte de Regina Martínez," *Animal Político,* April 29, 2012, https://www.animalpolitico.com/2012/04 /anuncian-creacion-de-comision-especial-para-investigar-asesinato-de -regina-martinez/.

42 Walter Ramírez, a fellow reporter in the early days: Ramírez gave his version of that night in my conversation with him, March 26, 2021.

45 Julio Scherer's was a riches-to-rags story: Vicente Leñero, *Los periodistas* (Mexico City: Seix Barral México, 2015), Kindle ed.

45 Julio's journalism trajectory started in college: Arno Burkholder, *La red de los espejos: Una historia del diario Excélsior, 1916–1976,* Vol. 1 (Mexico City: Fondo de Cultura Económica, 2016), Kindle ed.

45 It wasn't difficult in many cases: Benjamin T. Smith, *The Mexican Press and Civil Society, 1940–1976: Stories from the Newsroom, Stories from the Street* (Chapel Hill: University of North Carolina Press, 2018), Kindle ed.

45 Scherer set out to shake up the journalistic status quo: Burkholder, *La red de los espejos.*

45 His goals, he said, were to make the journalism: Burkholder, *La red de los espejos.*

46 It was produced by some of the top writers: Burkholder, *La red de los espejos.*

46 Coincidentally, the late 1960s: Smith, *The Mexican Press and Civil Society, 1940–1976.*

46 One study, by the University of London, ranked *Excélsior*: Burkholder, *La red de los espejos.*

46 the newspaper's editors decided to print a manifesto: Leñero, *Los periodistas.*

46 decrying a campaign that had cast them: Leñero, *Los periodistas.*

47 By workday's end, Julio Scherer and his editors were told: Jenaro Villamil, "El golpe a Excélsior: 40 Años del parteaguas del periodismo mexicano," *Proceso* APRO (July 8, 2016), https://www.proceso.com.mx/reportajes/2016 /7/8/el-golpe-excelsior-40-anos-del-parteaguas-del-periodismo-mexicano -167015.html.

47 The international press certainly took this angle: Alan Riding, "Mexican Editor Ousted by Rebels," *New York Times,* July 9, 1976, p. A5; "The Man who Killed Excélsior," *Washington Post,* July 14, 1976, p. A16; Paul Gill- ingham, Michael Lettieri, and Benjamin T. Smith, eds., *Journalism, Satire, and Censorship in Mexico* (Albuquerque: University of New Mexico Press, 2018), p. 248.

47 Don Julio told him as much to his face in a heated standoff: Leñero, *Los periodistas.* (Leñero called his book fiction so he could recreate conversa- tions where he wasn't present, but the book is considered an accurate account of Scherer's ouster.)

47 as the first edition of *Proceso*: "De Excélsior a Proceso: Lucha por la Voz Publica," *Proceso* 1 (Nov. 6, 1976): 14.

47 In the months leading up to the magazine's inauguration: Leñero, *Los periodistas.*

47 A strange "architect" showed up at the rented offices: Leñero, *Los periodistas.*

47 The government agency that controlled the sale of newsprint: "De Excél- sior a Proceso: Lucha por la Voz Publica," p. 15.

48 The man with journalistic *huevos* of steel, who had interviewed: Inter- view with Jorge Carrasco, Nov. 3, 2020.

49   Javier Duarte, a portly man with a nasally tenor voice: "Javier Duarte idolatra a Francisco Franco," YouTube, May 10, 2010, https://www.youtube.com/watch?v=ZNoTp7votic

49   He was dressed in a carefully pressed white guayabera: Jorge Carrasco Araizaga, "Crimen y ¿castigo?" *Proceso* 1853 (May 6, 2012): 7.

50   Julio Scherer found Duarte's words to be "abusively boring": Julio Scherer García, *Vivir*, (Barcelona, Grijalbo: Oct. 1, 2012), Kindle ed.

50   He decided to interrupt. "What we've just heard is nothing . . .": Jorge Carrasco Araizaga, "Crimen y ¿castigo?" *Proceso* 1853 (May 6, 2012): 7.

51   Ángel Martínez knew how the justice system worked: Investigación ministerial 019/2012/PC, Procuraduría General de Justica, Estado de Veracruz-Llave, Tomo I, p. 36. (Ángel told me the expediente was a lie on the part of the state. He never said any of these things and said he didn't want anything to do with this book.)

53   As the overnight homage was getting under way, Julio Scherer was back in Mexico City: Julio Scherer García, *Vivir* (Barcelona: Grijalbo, 2012), Kindle ed.

54   The terrace was the site of many classic: Eduardo García, "World Music Instrument: The Jarana Jarocha," Center for World Music, *Latest News* (blog), March 21, 2016, https://centerforworldmusic.org/2016/03/the-jarana-jarocha/.

57   That same day, Julio Scherer arrived to address: Ibid.

58   The two met in the main justice department headquarters: Staff, "Excélsior en la Historia: La metamorfosis de Paseo de la Reforma," *Excélsior*, July 31, 2013, https://www.excelsior.com.mx/nacional/2013/07/31/911511.

CHAPTER 6: THE FAB FOUR

Chapter 6 is based on my individual and group interviews with the Fab Four over a period of five years.

60   The kids teased young Javier for being fat: Arturo Ángel, *Duarte, el priista perfecto*, (Barcelona: Grijalbo, 2017), Kindle ed.

64   It was the first Mexican newspaper: Mireya Márquez Ramírez, "Professionalism and Journalism Ethics in Post-Authoritarian Mexico: Perceptions of News for Cash, Gifts, and Perks," in *The Ethics of Journalism:*

Individual, Institutional and Cultural Influences, ed. Wendy N. Wyatt (London: I.B. Tauris & Co, 2013), p. 55.

CHAPTER 7: CASE CLOSED

70 Now serving eleven consecutive life terms: Mark Fineman and Liane Hart, "Drug Lord Sentenced to 11 Life Terms, Fined $128 Million," *Los Angeles Times*, February 1, 1997. https://www.latimes.com/archives/la -xpm-1997-02-01-mn-24349-story.html

70 The state representative called it "decomposition of the state . . .": Regina Martinez, "Robles Guadarrama: Debieron Indagar la Protección que CSG y PCH le Daban al Narco," *Política*, Jan. 19, 1996.

71 Investigators had received mounds of training in forensics: Clare Ribando Seelke, "Supporting Criminal Justice System Reform in Mexico: The U.S. Role," Congressional Research Service, March 18, 2013, https://sgp.fas.org/crs/row/R43001.pdf.

71 and judges were now forced to throw out: This information came from my own coverage of the 2008 justice reform.

71 The other main tool for prosecuting a criminal case: Leopoldo Maldonado, "El delito de ser victima," *Horizontal*, Feb. 23, 1016, https://hr .adigital.mx/el-delito-de-ser-victima/.

71 They carefully documented the scene, measuring: Investigación ministerial 019/2012/PC, Procuraduría General de Justica, Estado de Veracruz- Llave, Tomo I, p. 225.

73 The same day she arrived, before any evidence: Staff, "Robo podría ser móvil del asesinato de periodista: Procurador de Veracruz," SDP Noticias, April 30, 2012, https://www.sdpnoticias.com/estados/periodista -asesinato-movil-robo.html.

76 Claribel Guevara became incensed and called a press conference: Staff, "Caso Regina: Limitan investigación a entorno y círculo de amigos," *Proceso* APRO (June 18, 2012). https://www.proceso.com.mx/regina -martinez/2012/6/18/caso-regina-limitan-investigacion-entorno -circulo-de-amigos-104371.html.

77 Walter Ramírez seemed happy to keep reinforcing the state's story: Although Polo Hernández's name is blacked out in the public version of the court documents, it is easy to tell from the description that Ramírez is referring to him. Ramírez denies this. He says he doesn't know who Polo is.

78 A few days before the deposition, authorities leaked to friendly: Staff, "Filtran versión de que el asesinato de Regina Martínez, corresponsal de Proceso, fue "pasional," Sin Embargo, June 23, 2012, https://www .sinembargo.mx/23-06-2012/273476.

79 Carlos Loret de Mola, a high-profile Televisa news anchor: Carlos Loret de Mola, "¿Habrán logrado armar su caso?" El Informador (original de El Universal), June 21, 2012, https://www.informador.mx/Ideas/Habran -logrado-armar-su-caso-20120621-0249.html.

80 Jarocho was with another man of similar build and look: Testimony of Diego Hernández Villa, Investigación ministerial 019/2012/PC, Procuraduría General de Justica, Estado de Veracruz-Llave, Tomo I, pp. 334–36.

81 The two arrived at Regina's house at around 10 P.M.: Events of the night of the murder, Investigación ministerial 019/2012/PC, Procuraduría General de Justica, Estado de Veracruz-Llave, Tomo III, p. 1422.

82 When authorities picked up El Silva six months later: Events of the night of the murder, Investigación ministerial 019/2012/PC, p. 1552.

83 As soon as El Silva got before a judge: Personal notes from federal case AP/34/FEADLE/2012, which I was allowed to view but not copy.

83 He signed his confession with a fingerprint: Investigación ministerial 019/2012/PC, Procuraduría General de Justica, Estado de Veracruz-Llave, Tomo II, p. 1290.

83 María del Rosario Morales Zárate, El Silva's sister: Personal notes from federal case AP/34/FEADLE/2012, which I was allowed to view but not copy.

CHAPTER 8: THE YOUNG RADICALS

87 Rafael Lucio, which dated back to 1586: "Rafael Lucio," entry in Enci-clopedia de los Municipios y Delegaciones de México, online, http://www.inafed.gob.mx/work/enciclopedia/EMM30veracruz /municipios/30136a.html.

89 Diseases like typhus and smallpox were eradicated: Enrique Krauze, Mexico: Biography of Power—A History of Modern Mexico, 1810–1996, 1st Harper Perennial ed. (New York: HarperCollins, 1998), p. 658.

89 Alongside sending the army to bust up strikes, or assassinating activists: Ibid, p. 642.

89   His staff joked that he woke every day asking, *Que hacemos hoy*: Ibid, p. 663

89   He would become the role model for a future PRI president: Andrés Becerril, "El reflejo mexiquense, para Peña Nieto, López Mateos es un ejemplo," *Excélsior*, March 19, 2012, https://www.excelsior.com.mx/2012 /03/19/nacional/819534.

90   Under López Mateos, Mexico saw: Ibid. p. 643.

90   Even on her small salary, she died owning: Investigación ministerial 019/2012PC, Procuraduría General de Justica, Estado de Veracruz-Llave, Tomo II, p. 935.

91   From her father, Regina got her long upper lip: from author comparing photos of the two.

92   "She always wanted to better herself, leave town . . .": Anne Marie Mergier, "Sé que me van a matar," *Proceso* 1904 (April 28, 2013): 6.

92   While some sectors of the country had flourished to: John W. Sherman, "The Mexican 'Miracle' and Its Collapse," *The Oxford Handbook of Mexican History*, ed. William Beezley and Michael C. Meyer (Oxford, UK: Oxford University Press, 2010), p. 537.

CHAPTER 9: THE MOUTH OF THE WOLF

96   In 2011 and 2012, Mexico's national election season: Valeria Durán and Raúl Olmos, "Red Fantasma de Duarte Trianguló Dinero a Campaña Presidencial en 2012," Mexicanos en Contra de la Corrupción, Jan. 11, 2018, https:// contralacorrupcion.mx/red-fantasma-2012/.

96   In early 2012, two Veracruz state officials were stopped: "La PGR decomisa en Toluca 25 mdp del gobierno de Veracruz," *ADN Político*, Jan. 30, 2012.

97   Public enrichment reached "stunning new proportions": John W. Sherman, "The Mexican 'Miracle' and Its Collapse," *Oxford History of Mexico*, ed. William H. Beezley and Michael C. Meyer (Oxford, UK: Oxford University Press, 2010), p. 543.

97   His cronies benefited handsomely as well: Pablo Piccato, "Careful Guys: Pistoleros and the Business of Politics," *A History of Infamy: Crime, Truth, and Justice in Mexico* (Oakland: University of California Press, 2017), p. 173.

98   The U.S. government reported at the time: Smith, *The Mexican Press and Civil Society, 1940–1976.*

98 Among the group was a man named Marcial Montano: Alfonso Diez García, "La Mano Negra," *Crónicas de Tlapacoyan*, Jan. 6, 2013, http://codigodiez.mx/cronicas/lamanonegra.html; Antonio Santoyo, "La Mano Negra en defensa de la propiedad y el orden: Veracruz, 1928–1943," *Secuencia* 28 (Jan.–April 1994): 81–98.

99 Not satisfied with only media control, Alemán: Benjamin T. Smith, "The Year Mexico Stopped Laughing: The Crowd, Satire, and Censorship in Mexico City," in Gillingham, Lettieri, and Smith, *Journalism, Satire, and Censorship in Mexico*, p. 105.

99 Alemán also set in motion the process for the creation of Televisa: Claudia Fernández and Andrew Paxman, *El Tigre: Emilio Azcárraga y su Emperio Televisa*, Edición del 20° Aniversario (Barcelona: Grijalbo, 2021), Kindle ed.

99 His successor, Adolfo Ruiz Cortines, though a fellow Veracruzano: Enrique Krauze, *Mexico: Biography of Power—A History of Modern Mexico, 1810–1996*, 1st Harper Perennial ed. (New York: HarperCollins, 1998), 601.

100 Veracruz was initially controlled by the Gulf Cartel: "Congressional Research Service, Mexico: Organized Crime and Drug Trafficking Organizations," July 28, 2020, p. 21, https://sgp.fas.org/crs/row/R41576.pdf.

100 But with the example of El Padrino: Peter Lupsha, "Transnational Narco-Corruption and Narco-Investment: A Focus in Mexico," *Transnational Organized Crime*, Spring 1995.

100 The home where he was living without disturbance was just a few doors: José Luis Ortega Vidal, "Historia de los Cárteles en Veracruz: Más vieja que el pleito de los Yunes," *Plumas Libres*, May 15, 2016.

101 In late October 2004, *Reforma* published information: Abel Barajas, "Vinculan a priista con narco," *Reforma*, Oct. 31, 2004, p. 1.

101 Herrera had a group of political protégés: Telephone interview with Alberto Olvera, investigador del Instituto de Investigaciones Histórico-Sociales de la Universidad Veracruzana, Aug. 2015.

101 One in particular helped him finance his populist machine: Carlos Caiceros, "Bursatilización: la deuda eterna de Fidel Herrera y Duarte," *e-consulta Veracruz*, July 22, 2019, https://www.e-veracruz.mx/nota/2019-07-22/estado/bursatilizacion-la-deuda-eterna-de-fidel-herrera-y-duarte, and: Decreto Número 255 que Autoriza La Constitución de

un Fideicomiso Bursátil y La Afectación al Mismo de Los Ingresos Municipales del Impuesto Sobre Tenencia o Uso de Vehículos, June 10, 2008, https://www.segobver.gob.mx/juridico/decretos/decretoslegis /Vigente44.pdf.

102 They didn't like Duarte. He was a chubby: Various interviews with journalists and politicos in Veracruz.

103 In 2015, the federal government's own unit for protecting journalists: *Informe Estadístico de la Fiscalía Especial para la Atención de Delitos Cometidos en contra de la Libertad de Expresión*, Sept. 2015.

104 When new parties started winning elections: Guillermo Trejo and Sandra Ley, *Votes, Drugs, and Violence: The Political Logic of Criminal Wars in Mexico* (Cambridge, UK: Cambridge University Press, 2020), Kindle ed.

104 The PRI allowed these security forces: Trejo and Ley, *Votes, Drugs, and Violence*.

104 A tape of the torture and interrogation of DEA agent: Kim Murphy, "Tape of Drug Agent's Torture Is Made Public," *Los Angeles Times*, June 7, 1988, https://www.latimes.com/archives/la-xpm-1988-06-07-mn-3854 -story.html.

104 The final DFS director, José Antonio Zorrilla: William Branigan, "New Corruption Charges Emerge in Mexican Case," *Washington Post*, June 26, 1989, https://www.washingtonpost.com/archive/politics/1989/06/26 /new-corruption-charges-emerge-in-mexican-case/c6d592d1-3988 -43de-aa33-924fcce95b79/.

105 The new governor's closest collaborators were offered bribes: Trejo and Ley, *Votes, Drugs, and Violence*.

105 The old corrupt institutions, the ones created: My interviews with Guillermo Trejo, 2017.

106 The killing of local journalists skyrocketed: "41 Journalists Killed in Mexico," Committee to Protect Journalists, https://cpj.org/data/killed/ ?status=Killed&motiveConfirmed%5B%5D=Confirmed&motiveUnco nfirmed%5B%5D=Unconfirmed&type%5B%5D=Journalist&cc_fips%5 B%5D=MX&start_year=2004&end_year=2010&group_by=year.

106 Between 2004 and 2018, there were 178 current: David P. Esparza and Helden De Paz Mancera, "Mayoral Homicide in Mexico: A Situational Analysis on the Victims, Perpetrators, and Locations of Attacks," James A. Baker III Institute for Public Policy, 2018.

107 Starting in 2007, Veracruz under Fidel Herrera: Ibid, p. 14.

107 As was his style, Herrera's number two, Interior Secretary Reynaldo Escobar: Regina Martínez, "Veracruz: Los alcaldes bajo de la extorsión de los Zetas," *Proceso* 1664 (Sept 21, 2008): 26.

107 Or, as Guillermo Trejo put it, they used targeted killings: Trejo and Ley, *Votes, Drugs, and Violence.*

108 The reality of the new world order was that: Trejo and Ley, *Votes, Drugs, and Violence.*

CHAPTER 10: SIDELINED

109 With *Política*, Regina had stumbled into the perfect job: Chapter 10, the story of *Política* and Don Yayo, was written from interviews with ex-assistant directors Salvador Muñoz and Raciel Martínez and with Don Yayo's daughter Yolanda Gutiérrez Carlín and others who knew Don Yayo but didn't want to be named. Their stories didn't all coincide. Yolanda, Don Yayo's daughter, disputed the fact that Regina had to fight for her severance or that she was let go for stories criticizing the government. But Gutiérrez Carlín was not at the newspaper when Regina left, so I decided to go with the stories of those who were.

109 Despite his Spanish lineage on his father's side, Don Yayo: Los Tuxtlas Biosphere Reserve, Mexico, UNESCO, https://en.unesco.org/biosphere /lac/los-tuxtlas.

109 His village, Tres Zapotes, was where two of the famous colossal heads: "Cabezas colosales Olmecas," Pueblos Originarios, https://pueblos originarios.com/meso/golfo/olmeca/cabezas.html.

109 The area drew tourists from all over Mexico: "La Isla de los monos una experiencia inigualable en Veracruz," *Fotografiando Mexico*, Aug. 11, 2019, https://www.fotografiandomexico.com/veracruz/lugares-de-interes/95 -isla-de-los-monos.

110 Mel Gibson filmed much of his movie: Irineo Pérez Melo, "Mel Gibson en Los Tuxtlas," *Al Calor Politico*, April 8, 2005, https://www .alcalorpolitico.com/informacion/mel-gibson-en-los-tuxtlas-11068.html.

110 When he wasn't running the two newspapers: Interview in 2021 with Yolanda Gutiérrez Carlín, Don Yayo's daughter.

113 One day, assistant editor Raciel Martínez (no relation to Regina) was waiting on deadline: For those who don't remember, photos were once

developed in bins of chemicals in blacked out rooms, "darkrooms," with only red light. If you opened the door at the wrong time and exposed the room to light, you could ruin the photos.

115 In the months leading up to Veracruz's 1992 gubernatorial election: Regina Martínez, "Fuga de PRIistas," *Política*, July 23, 1992, p. 1.

115 The PRD accused the PRI of using premarked ballots and falsified voter credentials: Regina Martínez, "Empezo el Jaleo: PRD: Denuncia Irregularidades; Detectan Boletas Marcadas y Credenciales Falsas," *Política*, July 28, 1992, p. 1.

115 The PRI would not allow a special election: Regina Martínez, "Rumor de 'Zapatazo,'" *Política*, Oct. 5, 1992, p. 1.

116 The expulsion left eleven people missing: Regina Martínez, "A la gente no se le puede desparecer," *Política*, Oct. 7, 1994, p. 1.

116 Yunes denied that the casualties even existed: Martínez, "A la gente no se le puede desparecer," p. 1.

116 Witnesses told the National Human Rights Commission: "Caso de las comunidades indígenas de la Huasteca veracruzana," National Human Rights Commission, Recomendación 019/1997, México, D.F., March 24, 1997, https://www.cndh.org.mx/sites/all/doc/Recomendaciones/1997/Rec_1997_019.pdf.

116 Yunes's crackdowns in the rural communities of Veracruz led to: CNDH/122/95/VER/912, CNDH/122/95/VER/3364, CNDH/122/ 95/VER/3904, CNDH/122/95/VER/4821, CNDH/122/95/ VER/7178, y CNDH/122/95/VER/I230, Comisión Interamericana de Derechos Humanos, INFORME N° 1/98, CASO 11.543, ROLANDO HER NÁNDEZ HERNÁNDEZ, MÉXICO, 5 de mayo de 1998.

120 Dated 2001, the documents outlined a complaint: Regina Martínez, "FBI y SSP: Abrir red de sobornos del narco," *Política*, Jan. 9, 2003, p. 10.

120 Miguel Alemán published a full-page letter in *Política*: *Política*, Jan. 8, 2003, p. 15.

120 Montano called the allegations "political": José Pastor Sánchez, "No se descarta movil politico en la acusación a Romano," *Política*, Jan. 9, 2003, p. 10.

121 She also tied him at one point to Fidel Herrera's questionable finances: Regina Martinez, "El consentido de Veracruz: Rafael Herrerías: si durante el gobierno de Miguel Alemán Velasco el empresario taurino Rafael Herrerías desfalcó al erario por más de 682 millones de pesos,

según cifras registradas en la cuenta de 2003, ahora, con Fidel Herrera Beltrán como gobernador, recibió más de 270 millones de pesos," *Proceso* 1512 (Oct. 23, 2005), 93.

121 In late 2010, when the new governor, Javier Duarte: Regina Martinez, "Duarte, administrador del desastre," *Proceso* 1792 (March 6, 2011), 48.

122 The documents cited a photograph of him: Also known as Juan José Esparragoza-Moreno, according to the FBI Most Wanted list, https://www.fbi.gov/wanted/cei/juan-jose-esparragoza-moreno.

122 In a preelection story for *Proceso*, Regina: José Gil Olmos and Regina Martínez, "Elección sin reglas," *Proceso* 1452 (Aug. 29, 2004): 28.

122 Herrera, when asked about them, called the accusations: Gil Olmos and Martínez, "Elección sin reglas," p. 28.

123 At one point, Miguel Alemán came looking for Regina: Source is Rodrigo Soberanes, who worked with Regina at the time.

123 One was Norma Trujillo, who in the 1990s: Norma Trujillo, "Mas allá de la justicia, el otro Silva," *Pie de Pagina*, Nov. 25, 2015.

124 When her investigation was published in the newspaper: Trujillo, "Mas allá de la justicia, el otro Silva."

124 Arturo Marinero was a young mental health counselor in the mid-1990s: Interview with Arturo Marinero, Sept. 2019.

125 Marinero and his staff put a premium on making Matraca a safe haven: Interview with Arturo Marinero.

127 With the arrival of Governor Fidel Herrera in 2004: Regina Martínez, "Inpugnarán el fallo ante el TEPJF," *Política*, Oct. 6, 2004. p. 4.

128 The newspaper marked the end of Alemán's controversial tenure: "Satisfacción por un deber cumplido," *Política*, Nov. 16, 2004, p. 1.

128 Another time, he was pictured on the front page with: "Una entrega muy cristalina," *Política*, Nov. 29, 2004, p. 1.

128 Journalist Raúl Gibb Guerrero was fatally shot eight times: "Raúl Gibb Guerrero, La Opinión/Killed in Poza Rica, Mexico/April 8, 2005," Committee to Protect Journalists, https://cpj.org/data/people/raul-gibb-guerrero/.

129 *Proceso* in particular was feeling pressure: Interview with Jorge Carrasco, Nov. 17, 2020.

129 According to her scathing retrospective: Regina Martínez and José Gil Olmos, "Veracruz: El desastre alemanista," *Proceso* 1460 (Oct. 10, 2004).

129 The younger Yunes was willing to ignore her disputes: Interview with Miguel Ángel Yunes Márquez, April 29, 2015.

130 At the end of the Fidel Herrera administration: Regina Martínez, "El hurucán 'Fidel,'" *Proceso* 1771 (Oct. 10, 2010): 42.

130 When Regina started on her exclusive report, Kamel Nacif: *La Jornada* (Feb. 14, 2006).

130 A year earlier, in 2005, the investigative reporter Lydia Cacho: *Los Demonios del Eden* (Barcelona/Madrid: Debolsillo, 2005).

130 In the Wild West of impunity that is Mexico, Nacif: Staff, BBC News, "Lydia Cacho: el caso de tortura a la periodista mexicana por el que foe detenido en ex-gobernador," Feb. 4, 2021, www.bbc.com/mundo/noti cias-america-latina-55939444.

131 Regina's favorite part of the whole story was the headline: Regina Martinez, "El otro gober precioso," *Proceso* 1530 (Feb. 26, 2006): 28.

131 Herrera called the story "reckless unfounded": Regina Martínez, "Gobernador se defiende. Caso Nacif: Equivocaron, quienes quieren descreditarlo," *Política*, Feb. 28, 2006, p. 15.

CHAPTER 11: *Reginazos*

133 On a chilly late-February afternoon, seventy-three-year-old Ernestina Ascencio: There are several spellings for Ernestina Ascencio's last name in the articles cited here. I went with Ascencio, the spelling on the reports at the Inter-American Commission on Human Rights, which is now handling the case.

134 Herrera arrived by helicopter the next day: Regina Martínez, "Violación impune," *Proceso* 1583 (March 4, 2007): 72.

134 According to one local mayor, families stopped sending: Blanche Petrich Enviada, "El ataque a Ernestina Ascención, posible 'mensaje de escarmiento': autoridades," *La Jornada*, April 9, 2007, p. 1, https://www.jornada .com.mx/2007/04/09/index.php?section=politica&article=010n1pol.

135 Driving over a winding mountain pass: Regina Martínez and Rodrigo Vera, "Fueron los soldados, m'ija," *Proceso* 1584 (March 11, 2007): 18.

135 In all, it took ten hours to get Ernestina: Informe No. 144/17 Petición 49-12 Informe de admisibilidad Ernestina Ascensio [*sic*] rosario y Otras México, Comisión Interamericana de Derechos Humanos, https://www .oas.org/es/cidh/decisiones/2017/MXAD49-12ES.pdf.

135 The cause of death was a fractured skull: Martínez and Vera, "Fueron los soldados, m'ija," p. 18.

135 Fidel Herrera called it "a horrible, murderous assassination": Regina Martínez, "El gobernador se dobla; investigación de asesinato de la anciana Ernestina Ascencio," *Proceso* 1592 (May 6, 2007): 22.

138 The commission slammed the local medical examiners: Regina Martínez and Rodrigo Vera, "'Mano negra' del gobierno federal; investigación de asesinato de la anciana indígena Ernestina Ascencio," *Proceso* 1585 (March 18, 2007): 28.

138 And no one believed that her daughter Marta had been: Regina Martínez, "¡Tenemos corraje!" *Proceso* 1587 (April 1, 2007): 26.

138 "We don't know if the president gave his opinion": Martínez, "El gobernador se dobla," p. 22.

138 "We Mexicans are very screwed if the [Human Rights Commission] caves": Martínez and Vera, "'Mano negra' del gobierno federal," p. 28.

139 He listed his twenty years of experience and his university training: Regina Martínez, "Me voy a defender: el legista veracruzano; Entrevista," *Proceso* 1588 (April 8, 2007): 11.

139 "Three months after Carmen's daughter was born: Regina Martínez, "Otra vida rota; violaciones perpetradas por miembros del Ejército mexicano en zonas rurales," *Proceso* 1589 (April 15, 2007).

140 Regina's ultimate bombshell in the Ernestina Ascencio case was a photograph: *Proceso* 1588 (March 11, 2007): 19.

140 Regina's final story on the case ran under: Martínez, "El gobernador se dobla," p. 22.

141 Less than a month after the case was closed, the Mexican Congreso: "Gaceta del día Miércoles 04 de julio de 2007 Gaceta: LX/1SPR-25/13027," Senado de la Republica, Gaceta de la Comisión Permanente.

141 Regina was able to negotiate a severance package with Carlín: This is according to several of her friends and sources, some who didn't want to be named.

141 Reporters Without Borders issued a press release demanding action: "El corresponsal en Veracruz del diario La Jornada sufre dos sospechosos atracos," Reporters Without Borders press release, Jan. 22, 2008.

142 Two years before she was killed, a Veracruz newspaper columnist, Carlos Lucio Acosta: Carlos Lucio Acosta, "Periodistas Críticos ¿Bajo Investigación?" *Diario Eyipantla Milenio*, Nov. 26, 2010.

143 At about this time, Lev García wrote a small story about Javier Duarte: Lev García, "Dan a 'Góber' Duarte concierto de abucheos," *Reforma*, July 9, 2011, p. 1.

144 the newspaper published a story, top of the front page: Staff, "Destapa jefe Zeta red en Veracruz," *Reforma*, May 20, 2012, p. 1.

145 As a result of the wave of violence, Reynaldo Escobar stepped down: Staff, "Escobar renuncia a procuraduría de Veracruz 'por motivos personales,'" *Animal Política*, Oct. 7, 2011. https://www.animalpolitico.com /2011/10/escobar-renuncia-a-procuraduria-de-veracruz-por-motivos -personales/.

145 She also agreed to be interviewed by an organization of journalists: Marcela Turati, "Inermes antes las mafias," *Proceso* 1853 (May 6, 2012): 16.

148 Villamil had received leaked documents about two Veracruz PRI politicians: "Dos Regresos Peligrosos," *Proceso* 1849 (April 8, 2012), 18.

151 The following Sunday, alongside his story about the Peña Nieto campaign: Interview with Jenaro Villamil, senior correspondent, *Proceso*, Sept. 2016.

CHAPTER 12: THE COVER-UP

152 He was convinced that Regina was killed because of his story: Interview with Villamil.

153 The story said not a drop of blood or DNA found at the scene: Jorge Carrasco Araizaga, "Una sentencia cubridora," *Proceso* 1902 (April 14, 2013): 22.

154 Borbolla backed it up with her own examples: Interviews with Laura Borbolla, 2015 and 2016.

155 "They," according to the source, was a group of current: My notes from federal complaint filed by *Proceso* after Jorge Carrasco was threatened.

CHAPTER 13: ARRANCANDO MOTORES

164 Besides the three photographers killed within a week: "12 Journalists Missing in Mexico in 2012," Committee to Protect Journalists, n.d., https://cpj.org/data/missing/?status=Missing&cc_fips%5B%5D=MX& start_year=2012&end_year=2012&group_by=location.

164 Meanwhile, the mainstream Xalapa newspapers seemed to be: The headlines for the two newspapers appeared on Feb. 13, 2015.

164 Just two weeks before Jorge was forced to flee the country: Staff, "Premian a Javier Duarte por 'defender periodistas'; es una burla: Artículo 19; 'Veracruz es el más peligroso de AL'" *Sin Embargo*, April 2, 2013, https://www.sinembargo.mx/02-04-2013/577897.

CHAPTER 14: WELCOME TO XALAPA

175 The day he was let out for violation of his human rights, Regina's brother Ángel: PDF of his letter to the public.

175 Another court restored the conviction, and in October 2014: "Recapturan y encarcelan a asesino de la periodista mexicana Regina Martínez," Agencia EFE, Oct. 23, 2014.

CHAPTER 15: WHAT WAS SHE WORKING ON? PART I

177 It wasn't difficult for people to pinpoint Alejandro Montano: Jenaro Villamil, "La Década Tragica," *Proceso* 1853 (May 6, 2012): 12.

184 But the other figure, Francisco "Pancho" Colorado: Patrick Corcoran, "Horse Racing Arrests Kick Off Bad Week for the Zetas," InSight Crime, July 19, 2012, https://insightcrime.org/news/analysis/horse-racing-arrests-kick-off-bad-week-for-the-zetas/.

186 central square, named for Xalapa native Sebastian Lerdo de Tejada: Turismo Xalapa, "La Plaza Lerdo," https://www.xalapaveracruz.mx/la-plaza-lerdo/.

CHAPTER 16: A PATTERN EMERGES

190 Xalapa is a metropolitan area of nearly eight hundred thousand people: Censo de Población y Vivienda, Secretaría de Finanzas y Planeación, Veracruz, http://ceieg.veracruz.gob.mx/wp-content/uploads/sites/21/2019/10/SEFIPLAN-2021-CensoPobbViv202.PobTotalTasasCrec.Veracruz.pdf

CHAPTER 18: THE NEW ORGANIZED CRIME

226 At about the same time I decided to look into Regina's story: The narrative of Arturo Ángel and the fantasy companies was constructed from interviews with reporter Arturo Ángel, *Animal Político* director Daniel

Moreno, articles published in *Animal Político*, and Arturo Ángel's book *Duarte, el priista perfecto* (Barcelona: Grijalbo, 2017), Kindle ed.

227 Not only did Ángel notice a coincidence of the same companies: Arturo Ángel, "Los 73 contratos que entregó el gobierno de Veracruz, a detalle," *Animal Politico*, May 24, 2016 https://www.animalpolitico.com/2016/05 /los-73-contratos-que-entrego-el-gobierno-de-veracruz-a-detalle/.

228 When he arrived at 410 Michoacán Street, he encountered: Arturo Ángel, "Las sedes de la red de empresas de Veracruz son casas, tiendas y lotes baldíos," *Animal Politico*, May 26, 2016.

228 The owner, José Adrián Álvarez Molina, in white shorts and a lime-green reflector vest: Ángel, "Las sedes de la red de empresas de Veracruz."

228 The sixty-five-year-old woman couldn't read what she was signing: Arturo Ángel, "Socios de las empresas fantasma son choferes o vendedores," *Animal Politico*, May 26, 2016.

229 Her husband, meanwhile, had to save for three years: Ángel, "Socios de las empresas fantasma son choferes o vendedores."

229 In June 2011, Regina wrote a piece for *Proceso*: Regina Martínez, "Duarte, administrador el desastre," *Proceso* 1792 (June 2011): 48.

229 Herrera got congress to approve an eight-hundred-million-dollar loan: Regina Martínez, "El Hurican Fidel," *Proceso* 1771 (Oct. 10, 2010): 42.

235 Their investigations led to Gina Domínguez, Duarte's spokeswoman: "Gina y Silva, exvoceros de Duarte, usaron la misma empresa para desviar 24 millones de pesos," Mexicanos en Contra de la Corrupción y Impunidad, May 21, 2017.

236 Another *Animal Político* story detailed that Domínguez, while government spokeswoman: Ángel, *Duarte, el priista perfecto*.

236 Another Mexico City media outlet, Aristegui Noticias: David Ordaz, "Renuncia el titular de la SSP-Veracruz, tras investigaciones sobre sus casas," Aristegui Noticias, Aug. 4, 2016 https://aristeguinoticias.com/0408 /mexico/renuncia-el-titular-de-la-ssp-veracruz-tras-investigaciones -sobre-sus-casas/.

236 There seemed to be no limits for the stealing or the disappearances: Juan Diego Quesada Veracruz, "Un agujero negro en México," *El Pais*, May 22, 2014.

237 a former contestant on *La Voz* (Mexico's *The Voice*): Staff, "Video: Él era Gibrán, cantante de 'La Voz México,' asesinado en Veracruz," Aristegui Noticias, Jan. 20, 2014.

237 five young people returning from a birthday celebration: Staff, "Cronología: la desaparición de los 5 jóvenes en Tierra Blanca," *Milenio*, Jan. 25, 2016, https://www.milenio.com/policia/cronologia-desaparicion -5-jovenes-tierra-blanca.

237 The acting governor, Flavino Ríos, authorized the use of a state heli-copter: "Flavino Ríos es detenido e ingresado a un penal por dar helicóptero a Duarte," *Expansión*, March 12, 2017, https://expansion.mx/politica /2017/03/12/flavino-rios-dice-ser-inocente-tras-ser-detenido-en -veracruz.

CHAPTER 19: MASS GRAVES

238 In 2011, shortly after Duarte took office, the Rev. Alejandro Solalinde, a Roman Catholic priest and activist: Staff, "Veracruz, el cementerio de migrantes más grande de México: Solalinde," *Animal Politico*, May 17, 2011, https://www.animalpolitico.com/2011/05/veracruz-el-cementerio -de-migrantes-mas-grande-de-mexico-solalinde/.

239 Fifty young women, many professional escorts, disappeared: Falko Ernst, "Las desaparecidas de Veracruz," Nexos, Oct. 1, 2014. https://www.nexos .com.mx/?p=33903.

239 Roberto Casso, the owner of some sporting goods stores: Lourdes López, "Ausencias que lastiman: madre rastrea a maestro desaparecido desde 2011," *Excélsior*, Dec. 17, 2014, https://www.excelsior.com.mx/nacional /2014/12/17/998185.

239 Her father, Pedro, received a call from the kidnappers: Verónica Danell, "Mueve el cielo y la tierra para hallar a su hija secuestrada," *Excélsior*, Jan. 2, 2012, https://www.excelsior.com.mx/2012/02/01/nacional/806960.

239 The number of the missing continues to climb: Gobierno de Mexico, Comisión Nacional de Búsqueda, https://versionpublicarnpdno.segob .gob.mx/Dashboard/ContextoGeneral.

239 The state police were suspected in many cases: Lev García, "Mexican Police Allegedly Used Near Death-Squad Tactics," Associated Press, Feb. 28, 2018, https://apnews.com/article/8769d301cbe54c54ac1ea2c71c74a4f9.

240 The collectives grew in 2014, when frustrated families: Colectivo Solecto de Veracruz, https://www.idheas.org.mx/colectivo-solecito-de-veracruz/.

240 In September of that year, the Colectivo Solecito complained: Eirinet Gómez, "La FGE de Veracruz inhumó 192 cuerpos sin cumplir

protocolos," *La Jornada*, Sept. 4, 2016, https://www.jornada.com.mx/2016/09/04/estados/023n1est.

240 Her father, Pedro, had quit his job as an accountant: The details of the Gemma Mávil case and the dig in Palo Verde are from my interviews with Volga de Pina, an attorney with the Mexican Institute of Human Rights, who worked with the Mávil family.

243 "Look, for every grave that we've entered, we've found five": See previous note. I gave the ex-prosecutor, Luis Ángel Bravo, this version of events to comment on or correct. He didn't respond.

CHAPTER 20: WHAT WAS SHE WORKING ON? PART II

244 In April 2017, Javier Duarte was arrested in a hotel lobby in Sololá: Staff, "Detienen a Javier Duarte en Guatemala," *Animal Politico*, April 15, 2017, https://www.animalpolitico.com/las-empresas-fantasma-de-veracruz/entrada.php?slug=detencion-guatemala&id=detencion-guatemala.

244 He was extradited that July and later sentenced to nine years in prison: Staff, "Duarte pacta sentencia; le dan 9 años de cárcel," *El Universal*, Sept. 27, 2018. https://www.eluniversalqueretaro.mx/nacion/27-09-2018/duarte-pacta-sentencia-le-dan-9-anos-de-carcel.

244 Arturo Bermúdez was arrested the same year: "Momento de la detención de Arturo Bermúdez, ex colaborador de Duarte (Video)," Aristegui Noticias, Feb. 3, 2017, https://aristeguinoticias.com/0302/kiosko/momento-de-la-detencion-de-arturo-bermudez-ex-colaborador-de-duarte-video/.

244 as was Duarte's ex-spokeswoman Gina Domínguez: "Gina Domínguez, ex vocera de Duarte, encarcelada en Veracruz," Aristegui Noticias, May 21, 2017, https://aristeguinoticias.com/2105/mexico/gina-dominguez-ex-vocera-de-duarte-encarcelada-en-veracruz/.

244 Officials could do whatever they wanted with impunity: Antonio Osorio, "Vive Sánchez Tirado el mismo infierno a que condonó a miles de reos," *Expediente* (blog), Feb. 13, 2018, https://www.blog.expediente.mx/nota/28455/periodico-de-veracruz-portal-de-noticias-veracruz/vive-sanchez-tirado-el-mismo-infierno-al-que-condeno-a-miles-de-reos.

249 "She believed that she had determined where some of the disappeared had been buried": Paloma Dupont de Dinechin, "Uncovered: The Buried Truth of Assassinated Journalist Regina Martínez," Forbidden Stories, Dec. 6, 2020, https://forbiddenstories.org/the-buried-truth-of-assassinated-journalist-regina-martinez/.

250 *Proceso* had sent reporters to eleven states to gather statistics, including Regina in Veracruz: Patricia Dávila, "Pura estadistica . . ." *Proceso* 1811 (July 17, 2011): 6.

250 Though *Proceso* published the Forbidden Stories series: Verónica Espinosa and Lilia Saúl, "Caso Regina Martínez: las dudas y contradicciones que la 4T debe esclarecer," *Proceso*, Dec. 6, 2020, https://www.proceso.com.mx /reportajes/2020/12/6/caso-regina-martinez-las-dudas-contradicciones -que-la-4t-debe-esclarecer-254005.html

CHAPTER 21: WHO KILLED REGINA MARTÍNEZ?

252 "She never came here to buy beer," the owner: Investigación ministerial 019/2012PC, Procuraduría General de Justica, Estado de Veracruz-Llave, Tomo I, p. 591.

CHAPTER 22: THE GRAY ZONE

278 "They've always said that, but no one could prove it": Ylia Ortiz Lizardi, "Soy honesto y no tengo vínculo con criminales; si así fuera, estaría encarcelado: Reynaldo," *Al Calor Politico*, April 9, 2012, https://www .alcalorpolitico.com/informacion/soy-honesto-y-no-tengo-vinculo -con-criminales-si-asi-fuera-estaria-encarcelado-reynaldo-90512.html.

279 In that call, El Silva said he was drinking with Jarocho: "The Murder of Regina Martínez: An Opportunity for Justice," Safer World for Truth, March 17, 2021, p. 27.

280 Escobar lost his election: Staff, "Hartazgo y voto de castigo contribuyena derrota de exprocurador veracruzano," *Proceso* APRO (July 6, 2012), https://www.proceso.com.mx/nacional/estados/2012/7/6/hartazgo-voto -de-castigo-contribuyen-derrota-de-exprocurador-veracruzano-10534 5.html.

A NOTE ON THE AUTHOR

KATHERINE CORCORAN is a former Associated Press bureau chief for Mexico and Central America and a former codirector of Cronkite Noticias, the bilingual reporting program at Arizona State University's Walter Cronkite School of Journalism and Mass Communication. She has been an Alicia Patterson fellow, the Hewlett Fellow for Public Policy at the Kellogg Institute at the University of Notre Dame, and a Logan Nonfiction Program fellow. At the AP, she led an award-winning team that broke major stories about cartel and state violence and abuse of authority in Mexico and Central America. Her columns about Mexican politics and press freedom have appeared in the *Washington Post*, the *Houston Chronicle*, and Univision Online, among other publications. She is currently codirector of MasterLAB, an investigative editor training program in Mexico City.